Journey of Faith

The incredible true account of a young girl named Faith,
her remarkable journey with cystic fibrosis,
a double-lung transplant, and her inspiring faith in God.

SUSAN BROOKS SHAW

UNITED 》→ HOUSE

Dedicated to:

Danny Quesada
(11/04/2000 - 09/25/2019)

Another courageous warrior who lost
His battle with Cystic Fibrosis
But ultimately won the war

Foreword

On the evening of November 11th, 2019, my wife Ann and I left our Florida home and boarded a plane bound for North Carolina's Raleigh-Durham Airport, where we rented a car and arrived at a Chapel Hill motel around midnight. In the morning, we drove to the University of North Carolina Hospital where we joined a sizable group of family members, friends, clergy, and hospital staff, gathered together to carry out a task of inconceivable difficulty—namely, saying goodbye to Faith Shaw, our beloved eighteen-year-old granddaughter.

Faith's life-long battle with cystic fibrosis had finally reached its end. There were no more options, no more glimmers of hope—if only this or that miracle treatment would somehow materialize. There was no escaping the continuing pain and indignity of too many needles, too many incisions, too many tubes, too many heart-wrenching disappointments. Manifesting the incredible courage that had characterized her entire life and buoyed by her confidence in the promise of a Heavenly home, Faith had simply realized it was time to accept the inevitable and turn off the machines that were keeping her alive.

One by one, each of us in that hospital room spoke briefly and privately with Faith, struggling to find the right words, while trying to keep emotions in check. I promised her that she would live in my heart forever, a promise I will have no trouble keeping. Ann invoked a smile from her by saying, in her mind's eye, Faith would always be dancing. Finally, everyone left the room except for her two sisters and her mother—my daughter Susan—who held her through her last breath.

And with Susan, we arrive at this book. *Journey of Faith* is a remarkable read about a remarkable life, but Susan was a full participant at every step. She too underwent countless rounds of crisis, progress, hope, setback, and ultimate loss. The book chronicles two immensely difficult yet tightly interwoven journeys – both Faith's and Susan's.

Susan and Faith were much more than mother and daughter, although they were certainly that. They were also close friends and partners in an all-consuming eighteen-year struggle. This book, then, is a natural outgrowth of that relationship – and it was important for Susan to write it. Indeed, I think she had no choice in the matter; it was something she had to do.

While all readers will find benefit, I suspect the book will be particularly meaningful for those who knew Faith or at least were tuned in to her life and circumstances. It conveys a strong sense of the kind of person Faith was, the deep love she had for her family and friends, the almost unfathomable difficulties she endured, and the religious faith that helped her triumph over those difficulties. The book also provides the reader with a keen understanding of what it was like to share Faith's journey as a loving parent.

For me, as Susan's dad and Faith's grandpa, reading the book was both difficult and affirming. It reminds me of what the world lost on that incredibly sad fall day in 2019, but it also provides a wonderful memorial to Faith's life. Those who knew and loved her will read the book, as I did, with laughter and tears – and those who did not know her may struggle to escape similar reactions.

Faith was loved by many, and she loved many in return. In the final analysis, in fact, I consider *love* to be this book's central theme. And I am so very proud of Susan, Faith's mother, and my amazing daughter, for writing it.

Michael Brooks
December 2022

Table of Contents

PART ONE

Getting to Know Faith

1

In The Beginning

Her name was Faith. I was as sure of that as I was sure I was pregnant, even though I technically couldn't take a test for another four days. I don't know how, but I knew I was pregnant, that it was a girl, and that her name would be Faith. The test I took four days later was merely a formality as far as I was concerned. I was terrified for a number of reasons. I was a single mother of two very young daughters, broke, and a Christian woman who had lost hold of her own faith out of anger at God over the circumstances that led me to *be* a single mother. I restored my relationship with Christ only three weeks prior to discovering I was pregnant. Many fears and doubts clouded my thoughts over the next several days—Was I being punished? Should I put her up for adoption? Should I move to another city to avoid the shame of my fall from grace becoming public knowledge? How was I going to raise a third child by myself when I was struggling with raising two? What would people think of me? Would my new child be accepted in the church or be looked upon harshly? The only thing I knew for certain was that all life is sacred and ending the pregnancy was NOT an option! But all other thoughts remained in turmoil and disarray.

A few days after confirming my pregnancy, with the secret still held tightly to my chest, I received an irrefutable message from God and knew that everything was going to work out. It would not be easy, by any means, but He made it clear to me that He was still on the throne, this situation had not taken Him by surprise, and He had already prepared the path on which I was about to embark. This message came to me in the form of a song. A gentleman from church had given me a cassette tape to listen to, asking me if I would sing it with him at church. I listened to it on the way to work the next morning and was immediately reduced to tears. The song was titled "God Gave Me Back Tomorrow," by *Ray Boltz* and *Cindy Morgan*, and the words were as follows:

Journey of Faith

There are voices on the road of life
And I have made choices
That I know weren't right
And they brought me to my knees
At the end of a lonely street
And I am standing here today
I want to say

CHORUS:
God gave me back my tomorrow
When I threw tomorrow away
He took this life
Full of sorrow
And suddenly everything changed
The moment it happened
It was the moment I knew
It was like walking in the darkness
When the light comes shining through
I said that God gave me back tomorrow

When you're struggling
With the guilt and shame
You traded your tomorrows
And all you got to show for it
Was heartache and pain
And it's brought you to your knees
At the end of a lonely street
He is standing here today
And He'll help you say

CHORUS (repeat)

The moment it happened
It was the moment I knew
It was like walking in the darkness
When the light comes shining through
I said that God gave me back tomorrow[1]

So, her name was Faith. Not only was I sure God had given me her name, but I knew that it was going to take a whole lot of faith to make this journey as a single parent. I also knew if I ever again felt as though I were losing hold of my faith, all I had to do was wrap her up in my arms, and I could be holding tightly to my faith once more.

Additionally, I knew as long as I held onto this secret (which for obvious reasons would not remain secret for long), Satan had a handhold on the situation. But the moment I brought what was in darkness into the light, it would be wholly God's.

I first confided in my pastor, Pastor Todd, and asked if I could stand before the church to give my testimony and confession. He was extremely gracious, displaying nothing but the love of Christ, as he gently replied, "We *love* babies!" He then prayed with me and agreed with my request.

The day I stood before the congregation, I opened by singing a song titled, "I Know Who Holds Tomorrow," by the *Gaither Vocal Band*, then nervously shared my news. Most of the words I said that day are lost to me now. I do, however, remember saying how awesome it was that God could take our mistakes and turn them into blessings, that no life was a mistake, and that I hoped and prayed they would accept my baby as just as much a part of the church family as my other daughters. When I was done speaking, I was completely blown away by receiving a standing ovation from the congregation. As I tearfully returned to my seat, one of the older ladies in the church gave me a huge hug and whispered into my ear, "Oh, honey . . . we all make mistakes. You just got caught at yours," then she told me she loved me. That's when I knew for certain that my daughters and I would not be making this journey alone!

Faith was born at 9:02 am on Tuesday, May 15th, 2001. She weighed 7lbs 14oz and was 21 inches long. She entered the world with as much "flair" as she would live her life. When it was apparent the time had come, the nurse told me to do a practice push with the next contraction. When I did, she exclaimed, "Aaaaand there's the head! Let me go get the doctor!" That was at 8:55 am.

After Faith was cleaned up and swaddled, the nurse handed her to my dear friend, Cindy, who had stayed the night in the hospital room with me and another dear friend, Terri. As Cindy held Faith in her arms, she remarked at what an intelligent girl she could already tell Faith was because of how she kept looking all around the room with wide eyes as she appeared to soak in her new surroundings.

Faith was without a doubt a beautiful, sweet, largely good-natured, trouble-free baby who very seldom cried or complained during the first few years of her life. Even if she was hungry or needed a diaper change, it was hard to know because she just didn't cry. She was always smiling or laughing or watching the world around her with great interest as she took it all in.

But starting at about three months, she developed a bad cough, and nothing seemed to help. The doctor we saw kept assuring me it was just a cold and to wait it out. After multiple trips back and forth to the doctor, and my insistence that it had to be something more than "just a cold," I finally demanded a different doctor. It was then discovered her white blood cell count was extremely high, and she had pneumonia. She was immediately admitted to Northeast Medical Center in Concord, North Carolina, for intravenous (IV) antibiotics. She responded beautifully to the treatment and was discharged after only three days.

Over the next six weeks, Faith seemed to be getting steadily better, but then she took a sudden turn for the worse. She had pneumonia again—and was admitted again into the hospital for IV antibiotic treatments. The doctor on call, Doctor Greg, was the first one to say her symptoms seemed consistent with something called "cystic fibrosis" and wanted to have a specific physician in Charlotte, Doctor B, examine her. This would require her being transported to Carolinas Medical Center (CMC Main), just south of downtown Charlotte. The only thing I knew about cystic fibrosis was that I had recently made a small donation to their "65 Roses" campaign because I was so touched by the story.

In summary, "the '65 Roses' story dates back to 1965 when an observant 4-year-old, hearing the name of his disease for the first time, pronounced cystic fibrosis as '65 Roses.' Today, '65 Roses' is a term often used by young children with cystic fibrosis to pronounce the name of their disease."[2]

Doctor Greg made me promise not to go home and look up "cystic fibrosis" on the internet, due to there being a lot of scary and inaccurate information out there, and he first wanted to have a confirmation before we delved into the details.

Faith was transported by ambulance that evening from the local hospital in Concord to CMC Main in Charlotte, where she would end up spending the next three weeks as they tried to knock out the infection. The day after her transfer, they performed what is called a sweat test, which measures the amount of salt in the sweat; and on Christmas Eve 2001, at the tender age of seven months, it was confirmed that Faith had this life-shortening disease, cystic fibrosis (CF). We were now about to embark on a journey that would teach me more than I ever wanted to know about the medical world, and it would be only the first of many Christmas Eves and Christmases Faith would spend in the hospital.

2

The Early Years

Nearly 40,000 children and adults in the United States live with CF, and there is presently no cure. "Cystic fibrosis is a progressive, genetic disease that affects the lungs, pancreas, and other organs. . . . In people with CF, mutations in the cystic fibrosis transmembrane conductance regulator (CFTR) gene cause the CFTR protein to become dysfunctional. When the protein is not working correctly, it's unable to help move chloride—a component of salt—to the cell surface. Without the chloride to attract water to the cell surface, the mucus in various organs becomes thick and sticky.

"In the lungs, the mucus clogs the airways and traps germs, like bacteria, leading to infections, inflammation, respiratory failure, and other complications. For this reason, avoiding germs is a top concern for people with CF.

"In the pancreas, the buildup of mucus prevents the release of digestive enzymes that help the body absorb food and key nutrients, resulting in malnutrition and poor growth. In the liver, the thick mucus can block the bile duct, causing liver disease. In men, CF can affect their ability to have children."[3]

Some people are affected only in the lungs, some only in the pancreas, and some are saddled with complications in both. Faith happened to be one of those dealing with both.

After receiving the devastating diagnosis, life changed drastically for all of us. There were multiple treatments each day with a nebulizer; chest physical therapy (chest PT) in which I would pound Faith's back, sides, and front for fifteen to twenty minutes twice a day to help break up the mucus in her lungs; a supply of daily medications; and constant doctor appointments. In the early years, Faith grew quite accustomed to the routine, would typically fall asleep while I pounded on her back, and even learned to administer some of her own medications when she was barely old enough to really talk. Thankfully, Faith didn't end up in the hospital again until after she turned three years old at which point it became a once-or-twice-a-year occurrence, each stay being a minimum of two weeks for administering the IV antibiotics.

When she did end up in the hospital, Faith was always beloved by the nursing staff and doctors and ate up all the attention she could get. Unfortunately, as a single parent, I had to keep working during the day. The nursing staff would many times have Faith sit with them at the nurses' station so they could play with her and keep her company (this was prior to the contact precautions which later became the norm for CF patients). The medical team was always very sad to see Faith leave. They were always quite happy to see me leave, however, as "mama bear" would often emerge any time I did not feel like things were being done as they were supposed to be done or exactly according to the doctor's instructions.

For instance, while in the hospital, her chest PT was supposed to be done three times a day for twenty minutes each time. I was furious to learn one day that they were doing it for only about five minutes. As my daughter's advocate, I became quite angry and complained—rather loudly—to the manager of the respiratory department. I exclaimed that she was there for *increased* treatments, and if all she needed was mediocre care, I could certainly manage that by myself at home without having to deal with all the troubles, expenses, and challenges of having to be at the hospital. They said something about being very busy and having lots of patients, to which I replied that each *one* of those patients was there because they needed *extra* care, and that was a horrible and unacceptable excuse. Her treatment regimen was handled correctly moving forward.

There was another time in which the PICC line in her arm (peripherally inserted central catheter, an IV line that could be kept in for extended periods of time) did not appear to be working, but they had already taken out the temporary IV line from her hand. Rather than wait for the IV team or interventional radiology to be available the next day to try and unblock the line, multiple staff seemed to think that they would be the ones who could fix the problem in the PICC line. So, with each shift all through the day and night, this poor baby was messed with and kept awake while someone thought they would be the "hero." Meanwhile, she was not getting any sleep and was not receiving her IV antibiotics. I kept asking them to just put a new temporary line in her hand, get her medicines started, and let this small child get some rest! Finally, at approximately 1:30 in the morning, they determined the PICC line was just not going to work, and they would have to put in another temporary line. It then took four of us to hold down this now exhausted, irritable, and scared little baby while they put in the new line. All I wanted to do was reach across her and strangle somebody. It was not until after the new line was put in, everyone had left the room, and Faith had finally fallen asleep that I allowed myself to break down in quiet sobs. The next day when the IV team was able to get her on their schedule, they rather quickly got the PICC line working properly.

And through it all, Faith continued to be the sweetest baby. She handled everything with such an amazing grace. She never really went through the terrible twos, but when the threes hit, she made up for lost time! She would have such terrible meltdowns that all I could do was wrap my arms around her and hold her tightly until she eventually calmed down. Only then could I talk with her. She became very strong-willed and stubborn and remember telling my mom that I dared not break her strong will since she would undoubtedly need it later in life as she dealt with this disease—but boy, was it hard to parent!

When Faith reached four years old, Doctor B switched her from the manual chest PT to a percussion vest earlier than the usual five years old, due to my wrist beginning to show signs of carpal tunnel syndrome. A percussion vest looks similar to a life vest, plugs into an outlet, and vibrates, shaking up the mucus in one's lungs. Faith loved to sing songs or make noises while doing the vest because of how the rapid vibrations made her voice sound.

When she reached the age of five, Doctor B determined we would be able to do any IV antibiotic treatments from home, rather than require her to be in the hospital for two or more weeks at a time. This proved to be a mixed blessing. While it was a relief to have Faith out of the hospital after only the few days it took to make sure the PICC line was working properly, the medication and treatment schedule was *brutal*, mainly for me, as Faith slept through a lot of it. Following is a detailed sample of one such daily schedule, keeping in mind that I still had to work full time, Faith still had to attend daycare or school, and I had my other two daughters to take care of and spend time with as well:

Zenpep pancreatic enzymes	4 with meals / 3 with snacks
Daily Calorie Goal	2500-4500
Hydration	Drink as much water as possible throughout the day

5:00 AM
- Pull ANTIBIOTIC 1 and ANTIBIOTIC 2 out of refrigerator
- Pretreat with ALBUTEROL (inhaler)
- Prepare nebulizer medicines (7% SALINE, PULMOZME and CAYSTON)
- Begin percussion VEST treatment

- After 1st 10 minutes, administer 7% SALINE via nebulizer
- After 7% SALINE, administer PULMOZYME via nebulizer
- When VEST is done, administer CAYSTON via Altera disc unit

6:00 AM
ANTIBIOTIC 1 & ANTIBIOTIC 2
IV Line with blue clip ..

- Remove white cap from saline (don't let it touch fingers or surface) and remove air from syringe
- Replace white cap
- Using alcohol pad, clean IV line for at least 10 seconds
- Using saline syringe, pull back to try and get a blood return to make sure the line is open
- Once you get a blood return, flush saline through the line
- Attach TOBRAMYCIN and make sure both clips (on the line and on the medicine) are open

IV Line with white clip ..

- Remove white cap from saline (don't let it touch fingers or surface) and remove air from syringe
- Replace white cap
- Using alcohol pad, clean IV line for at least 10 seconds
- Using saline syringe, pull back to try and get a blood return to make sure the line is open
- Once you get a blood return, flush saline through the line
- Attach CEFEPIME and make sure both clips (on the line and on the medicine) are open

6:30-ish AM
When VEST and nebulizer meds are done, remove vest and give oral medications

VITAMIN D3	2 capsules/tablets
AZITHROMYCIN (M,W,F only)	1 tablet
OMEPRAZOLE	1 capsule
PERIACTIN	1 tablet
CETERIZINE	3 tablets
FLONASE	2 puffs each nostril

Place all nebulizer/altera cups in bottle washer and sterilize

6:40 AM
Unhook IV meds
IV Line with blue clip ..
- Remove white cap from saline (don't let it touch fingers or surface) and remove air from syringe
- Replace white cap
- "Pop" and remove blue cap from heparin (don't let it touch fingers or surface) and remove air from syringe
- Replace blue cap
- Remove TOBRAMYCIN from IV line
- Using alcohol pad, clean IV line for at least 10 seconds
- Flush saline through line
- Flush heparin through line and close blue clip

IV Line with white clip ..
- Remove white cap from saline (don't let it touch fingers or surface) and remove air from syringe
- Replace white cap
- "Pop" and remove blue cap from heparin (don't let it touch fingers or surface) and remove air from syringe
- Replace blue cap
- Remove CEFEPIM from IV line
- Using alcohol pad, clean IV line for at least 10 seconds
- Flush saline through line
- Flush heparin through line and close blue clip

Remove nebulizer/altera cups from bottle washer to air dry

10:00 AM
Repeat ALBUTEROL, nebulizer medicines and VEST treatment

1:00 – 2:40 PM
Repeat antibiotic procedure with ANTIBIOTIC 2

4:00 PM
Repeat ALBUTEROL and nebulizer medicines

5:00 – 6:00 PM
Repeat antibiotic procedure with ANTIBIOTIC 1

9:00 – 10:40 PM
Repeat antibiotic procedure with ANTIBIOTIC 2

After a minimum of two weeks of this schedule every single day, Faith and I were thoroughly exhausted. Each time IV antibiotics were needed to fight off a lung infection, the specific IV medications and the schedule might change slightly, but it was never less brutal. As rough as it was, though, I grew quite good at administering all the IV medications and was told on more than one occasion by various home health and hospital nurses that I had missed my calling.

When Faith was in daycare and elementary school, I would need to leave work several times a day to take care of all the medications and treatments. In elementary school, we devised a way to at least keep her in class while the IV antibiotics were being administered by putting the IV medication ball into a small camera bag clipped onto her belt while I waited in the teacher's office. When she hit middle school and beyond, she would administer her own medications in the nurse's office, including the IV medications, and take care of all her treatments. She didn't let it stop her from enjoying life as best she could. As she grew older, she continued to dance, continued to hang out with her friends, and would even attend sleepovers complete with IV medication pole, percussion vest, and all her other treatments.

And through it all, Faith continued to display a grace and maturity well beyond her years, which I knew must have been God-given in preparation for all of life's struggles and challenges she would be forced to face.

Faith did, of course, complain from time to time, and we went through a period of rebellion against her treatments that is apparently quite common with CF patients. But for the most part, she was a true inspiration and a wonderful example of accepting the "thorn in her flesh," as Paul talks about in 2 Corinthians:

> *"Concerning this thing I pleaded with the Lord three times that it might depart from me. And He said to me, 'My grace is sufficient for you, for My strength is made perfect in weakness.' Therefore most gladly I will rather boast in my infirmities, that the power of Christ may rest upon me. Therefore I take pleasure in infirmities, in reproaches, in needs, in persecutions, in distresses, for Christ's sake. For when I am weak, then I am strong."*
> 2 Corinthians 12:8-10, NKJV

I won't go so far as to say that Faith boasted in her infirmities, nor did she take pleasure in them, but she did handle them with an amazing tenacity.

She still, however, had many questions and struggles with the "thorn" with which she was saddled.

One day sitting on the couch while doing some IV treatments, Faith asked me through tears why God would allow her to live with this disease—why did she have to have CF? All I could say was that I could not even begin to understand why God would give her this burden, but that we could know for certain there was a reason for it and that we had to trust it was ultimately for His glory and for His kingdom. Although I wholeheartedly believe this to be true, this answer still seemed somehow sorely inadequate.

Another day, sitting in the car as I dropped her off at the bus stop, again through her tears, Faith was talking about how tired she was of being "the sick girl" at school. I told her to try and remember that cystic fibrosis was not who she was. It was something she had, but not who she was, and she needed to try very hard to not let it define her. From that point on, she did a great job (for the most part) of living with that in mind. She worked very hard at choosing what things in life *would* define her—her love for friends, family, the Lord, and dance being among the top of her life's loves!

In 2005, when Faith was four and my oldest daughter, Kelsey, was in sixth grade, Kelsey came home one afternoon obviously very distraught. She pulled me aside to ask me if what she had learned at school that day was true. They were studying genetics in science, and CF happened to be one of the genetic diseases discussed. Not realizing this was something Kelsey's sister had, the teacher went on to say that CF caused a shortened life span, and currently, the median age for people with CF was only twenty-five. As the color drained from my face, I pulled both her and her other sister, Jenni, together and said we would talk more after I put Faith to bed. Once Faith was asleep, I sat Kelsey and Jenni down and told them the whole story about cystic fibrosis and what that meant for their little sister. I did confirm that it was a life-ending illness but assured them the teacher had slightly outdated information, as the median age at the time was thirty-seven. Many tears were shed between all three of us as I shared the information and answered their many questions as best as I could. We talked and cried until 1:00 in the morning.

Not wanting Faith to find out about the full impact of her illness in the same manner as her sister, I realized it would be necessary to have a very serious and difficult conversation with her before *she* entered middle school. In the spring of 2011, when Faith was nine years old and nearing the end of her fourth-grade year, I arranged for Kelsey and Jenni to stay with a friend from church while Faith and I left to spend the weekend together near Asheville at the Ridgecrest Conference Center, a Billy Graham property. Kelsey had been there for youth camp a couple of times, and it was a very peaceful atmosphere complete with a little chapel and a beautiful prayer garden.

While combing through some of Faith's school work after she had passed away, I came across one of her fourth-grade morning journals, and her entry for March 11th, 2011, was heart-wrenching. She wrote, "I can't wait for this afternoon after lunch! My mom is picking me up so only we can go on a fun trip alone on the weekend! We're going to the mountains near Asheville! We're coming back on Sunday! I can't wait." Knowing what the weekend was to entail and seeing her excitement and her *not* knowing the devastating conversation that was about to take place completely crushed my heart.

When we arrived at Ridgecrest that Friday night, I was not yet prepared to have this horrible conversation with her, so we simply drove around the area looking at the sights. On Saturday after breakfast, I suggested we take a walk through the prayer garden. As we were walking and Faith was enjoying the beautiful day and stunning garden, my heart was in my throat, and I realized I could wait no longer. I sat her down on one of the benches and proceeded to tell her the full impact of her disease. Through many, many tears and hugs, she asked as many questions as she could think of, and I told her as much as I knew. We prayed together, then continued walking through the prayer garden, hand-in-hand, in silence. After lunch, we visited the Biltmore House, then stopped and picked up a couple of movies to watch in our room and just unwind from such an emotional day.

The next day before heading back home, I wanted to do something special for Faith to cheer her up a little bit. We visited a music store in Black Mountain, and I bought her a guitar, which she had been wanting to learn how to play for several years. We eventually got her guitar lessons for a couple of years. This guitar now hangs on my wall.

The Early Years

Faith (front, center) with sister, Jenni, mom, and sister,
Kelsey (back, from left to right), Christmas 2009

3

Family and Friends

Faith grew up in a very close-knit family with her two older sisters, Kelsey (eight years older) and Jenni (six years older), along with quite a few cats. Some of our family's favorite activities were Family Game Nights as well as Sofa Sleeper Night, where we would each pick out two movies from Blockbuster or Family Video, pull out the sofa sleeper in the living room, eat popcorn, and watch movies until we all fell asleep.

We loved binge-watching shows together, such as *Sherlock, Atlantis, Merlin, Reign,* and *Doctor Who.* Once, after spending the day watching all of *Sherlock* series 3, we spent the next day on a *Doctor Who* shopping spree, followed by an *Atlantis* marathon. Jenni fondly commented how much she loved our family and our "geeky TV show ways."

Faith and her sisters spent many summers in Florida at my mom's and stepdad's house for a week or two at a time, and it turned out the salt air was actually very good for Faith's lungs. They all learned to swim while in Florida, as well as gained their love for the beach. Faith loved the water so much that my mom called her a "little fish." If she couldn't live in a big city, Faith's desire was to live at the beach.

Kelsey and Faith had a beautiful bond together, and I think that Faith was Kelsey's favorite companion for make-believe games. Faith looked up to Kelsey and often viewed her as a second "mom." When Kelsey was old enough, there were many times I put her in charge of Jenni and Faith when I had to leave the house. I would always make sure they knew that Kelsey was "in charge" and to listen to her as they would to me. One day when Faith got in trouble and was showing me some sass, I very angrily reminded her that she had better listen to me. I asked her, "Who's the mom? Who's the boss?" to which she tearfully replied, "You are." So just to make sure she had the point, I asked again, "So who's in charge?" And bless her sweet heart, through her tears and in all seriousness she replied, "Kelsey." It took me completely off guard, and I found it so funny that the anger was immediately gone. It took everything in me not to burst out laughing.

Jenni and Faith also had a beautiful and loving relationship. For "Woman Crush Wednesday," a social media gimmick, Jenni once wrote:

"#wcw goes to my baby sister who definitely isn't a baby anymore. She's as beautiful as she is strong, and she's pretty much the strongest (and bravest) person I know. I love you, Faith! Stay strong and keep getting better!"

Because of Faith's love of dance, Jenni surprised her one year with tickets to see The Nutcracker, performed by the Charlotte Ballet, and in October of 2018, Faith would be Maid of Honor in Jenni's wedding. There's still a great sense of relief that Faith was able to participate in the wedding, as five days later, she would end up in the hospital which, unbeknownst to us at the time, would begin the downward spiral toward transplant.

Faith loved to read, had a keen interest in fashion, was very artistic, and was wonderful with small children. She loved horses and also had an overwhelming desire to travel. Faith never sneezed less than five times in a row, and she had a unique talent for being able to fall asleep anywhere and in any position! The girl could sleep—and sleep hard! Once when she was about five years old, she fell asleep at a talent show in one of the auditorium chairs, sideways, her cheek and her knees on the seat, mouth open and her bottom sticking up in the air. As she grew older, waking her up each morning became more and more of a challenge – at one time we even tried rousing her with the help of squirt bottles.

Faith also had a habit of talking—and walking—in her sleep. One evening, she fell asleep on the couch in the family room while Kelsey was playing video games. Suddenly, Faith bolted upright exclaiming, "I found it!" Kelsey asked, "Found what?" to which Faith excitedly answered, "I found the way to Hogwarts!" She then laid back down and continued sleeping. Another time when she had fallen asleep on the couch, she stood up, went all the way upstairs to use the bathroom, then returned to the couch downstairs, and laid back down. In trying to converse with her, it was clear she was still asleep.

Bizarre dreams sometimes plagued her sleep, as well. One evening after Faith had gone to bed, Jenni and I were sitting in my room talking when Faith suddenly started screaming. We ran to her room to find her lying in bed, staring straight up at the top of her canopy, mouth and eyes wide open, and just screaming. I glanced at the canopy expecting to see some large scary spider or something, but nothing was there. I said her name many times and shook her shoulder once before she finally came around and stopped screaming. She looked up at us and simply started crying, so I picked her up, carried her into my room, and all three of us sat down on the bed. After a few moments, she was able to share with us that she had dreamed Rabbit (from Winnie the Pooh) was on top of a hill and had gotten badly sunburned. That was it. Jenni and I glanced at each other in confusion, but this apparently had been a traumatic dream. I still wonder if there was more to the dream than Faith was able to remember and relay to us that evening.

Faith always wanted a dog and espsecially adored corgis. Unfortunately, it was just never in the cards given all we had going on. In the spring of 2014, however, when Faith was twelve years old and going through a period of depression, I got her a bunny so she could have something to look forward to when she came home from school each day—something to give her a little bit of joy. She named her bunny Pebbles and enjoyed her tremendously. Sadly, in the summer of 2015 when we left our house of twelve years and moved into an apartment, we had to re-home Pebbles as well as our cats. A good friend of Faith's from school was fortunately able to take Pebbles.

As much love as we had for each other, family life was not always easy, and siblings were as siblings typically are, with the older ones finding it very easy to pick on and aggravate their little sister—and vice versa. Sometimes there were "knock down drag out" fights with screaming, yelling, stomping feet, and slamming doors, whereas other times were simple aggravations that later became family favorite funny stories to retell.

Once while sitting in a Chinese restaurant, Faith was very excited about her fortune cookie and its perfect shape. She exclaimed, "Oh! Look at this *perfect* fortune cookie!!" to which Kelsey responded without missing a beat by smashing her fist down on top of the cookie and crushing it to pieces. Faith just sat there with her mouth open unable to believe what had just taken place. Then, the surprise turned to glares at me and Jenni as we burst out laughing before Faith reached over and hit Kelsey in the arm.

Another time, Jenni walked into Faith's room to find her with a finished bag of potato chips, the bag pulled all the way open flat, and Faith *licking* the inside of the bag. Faith was so embarrassed and begged Jenni not to tell anyone what she had seen. Jenni said, "Ok," then immediately went downstairs and proceeded to tell me and Kelsey what she had caught Faith doing.

Embarrassing and rough moments aside, we thoroughly enjoyed spending time together and doing fun and silly activities. We went to Carolina Panthers football games, had many fun-filled days at Carowinds Amusement Park over the years, loved going to movies, made sure meals were eaten together, and the day before Faith's sisters both headed off to college, we had a "Shaw Girls' Date Night" at Build-A-Bear.

Faith loved playing "Pokemon Go" with Kelsey, Jenni, and their husbands, Jarrett and James. They would often gather in the car together and go driving to different places looking for Pokemon. One of their favorite and most "productive" locations was the UNC Charlotte campus.

In December 2012, at age eleven, Faith became an aunt and would embrace her new title with her whole being. She and her nephew, Gabriel, became super little friends and bonded in an amazing and incredibly sweet way. Her niece, Kyla, was born four years later in August, and Faith was head over heels in love! For an English writing assignment, she once wrote,

"I can't wait to see my niece and nephew! I was supposed to see them this weekend, but that's not happening anymore. They are so funny, goofy, and I couldn't imagine my life without them! They may be crazy at times or sad or even a little testing but there's nothing I wouldn't do for them. There are so many great memories with them, more with my nephew, Gabriel, because he's older. He'll turn 5 in December and it just makes me feel like time has just flown by. He is such a good, happy, and silly little boy! He's also very smart and loves his family. He loves coming to 'Nana and Bae's house' (my mom and me) and playing the Wii, playing on my phone, or just running around the house acting crazy. But I think [one] of my favorite memories with him would be when my mom and I were watching the kids and he was in one of the silliest moods I've ever seen him in! We were going to play some Wii games but he just kept wanting to tickle me! We ended up having a tickle fight for about 20 minutes. All the tickling wore us out."

As is common with most children, there were also plenty of times when Faith could be somewhat aggravating. When she was younger, she would eat rice literally one grain at a time or corn one kernel at a time. She would be at the table for hours and would get so upset when everyone left her alone to finish her dinner by herself—but there really didn't seem to be any other choice. I initially had a rule that no one could leave the table until everyone was finished but soon realized it was not fair to make everyone sit there and stare at Faith while she ever-so-slowly ate her meal. She was also extremely picky about what she would eat, which made for very frustrating menu planning. One of her silly quirks was with her McDonald's Happy Meal. She would get a hamburger, ketchup only, take off the bun, making sure to wipe all the ketchup onto the burger, then fold the burger like a taco with the ketchup in the middle, and eat it that way. The bun would remain uneaten. Faith also loved mac 'n' cheese—*Kraft* mac 'n' cheese—*only* Kraft. She refused to eat any other mac 'n' cheese.

Her pickiness and quirky eating habits all changed, however, when she hit her teen years (except for McDonald's hamburgers). She became much more of a "foodie," so much so that I once told her she ate like a teen-age boy. Given her calorie requirements with cystic fibrosis (2500-4500 per day), that was actually a very good thing. In high school, she became well known for loving Taco Bell and chili cheese dogs at Sonic.

Another aggravating moment was when Jenni, Faith, and I were in the car together on our way to a dance competition, and Faith had brought along eight movies for the portable DVD player. She was in the back seat and asked me and Jenni which movie she should watch. We both replied that it didn't matter since, being in the front seat, we would only be able to hear it anyway, so it was up to her. She asked again and again, and we kept telling her it did not matter to us—that it was entirely up to her. This went on for a good five to ten minutes. Finally, out of sheer frustration, I chose a movie to which she replied, "Naw—I don't want to watch that one." I was tempted to pull the car over and let her out by the side of the road!

For the most part, though, Faith was extremely loving, thoughtful, and adored her family immensely. I love coming across some of her social media posts that express this love. For my birthday one year, she posted,

"Happy Birthday to this loving, beautiful, caring, awesome, strong, brave . . . sorry got carried away. But anyways . . . Happy Birthday to my wonderfully fantastic mom! She's been through so much to take care of me and [my] sisters and I could never thank her enough! She's been there when I needed her every time, loved me when I've felt un-loved, cared for me while I'm sick, and just was pretty freaking awesome at all of it! She is one of my big hero's! I love you mommy!"

That same year for Mother's Day she posted,

"Happy Mother's Day to the best mommy ever! She has helped me get through so much, especially recently! I could not make it without her even if she [can] be a little embarrassing. She's silly, loving, and very strong! Love having her as a mom!"

Faith also surprised me with a Father's Day gift one year, saying it was because I had been mom and dad to our family and deserved to be appreciated on both days.

Another amazing moment of Faith showing her love for family—as well as her indescribable strength and courage—happened in the fall of 2015 when she stood up for me while I was verbally attacked. In early October of that year, I had a total knee replacement and needed lots of extra care and assistance. Faith was only fourteen and could not yet drive, which required bringing other people in to help. About three weeks after the surgery, the family friend who came to stay with us disagreed with something I had said earlier that day and began to verbally attack me. Faith had already gone to bed but was not yet asleep. When she heard the conversation turning ugly, she crept out of her room and listened from around the corner for a bit. Then she suddenly popped out and told this person she had no right to speak to me the way she was and that I did not deserve the words that were being said. Faith stood her ground and did not back down, even when the verbal attacks then turned towards her. It was one of the bravest things I had ever seen her do, especially at just fourteen years old, and it filled my heart to the brim with pride and admiration—and appreciation! She later confessed that she was utterly terrified but was not about to let someone talk to her mom that way. It was a turning point for her, and from that point forward, she had just a little more fire in her personality and attitude! For the mom doing the raising, that was not always an easy thing. But for the most part, it gave her that edge and the spit-fire attitude she needed to face the many obstacles and struggles in her life.

After the confrontation, the woman who was supposed to be helping me packed her stuff and immediately left, leaving no one there but a fourteen-year-old to take care of things. Kelsey wound up coming in for a few days to cover the gap.

The following year would have some very difficult and emotional moments with family when Jenni moved to England for six months to study abroad, and Kelsey and her family moved an hour and a half away to Hickory, North Carolina. But that year also held some exciting moments. In the spring, I began teaching Faith how to drive, Jenni returned from England that summer, Kyla would be born, and we also moved into the rental house that would put Faith in the Hickory Ridge High School district, the school she wanted to attend. In January 2017, Faith got her learner's permit and officially got her driver's license on February 1, 2018. She loved being able to run errands for me, take her friends places, go to Hickory to see Kelsey and family, and drive Gabriel to Vacation Bible School at church in the summer.

Another one of my most cherished memories of our beautiful times together was on a snow day in mid-January 2018 (Faith, age sixteen). We played outside in the snow catching snowflakes, taking videos, tossing snowballs, etc. We had such a fun time that was thoroughly enhanced by the fact that the cold—for once—did not reduce Faith to wracking coughs, which would normally happen. I wholeheartedly believe that God gave us this beautiful day together as a special gift.

Yet not all family dynamics were what was desired and longed for. Faith did not meet her dad until she was eight years old. He visited a few times, once while she was in the hospital, and they emailed and called back and forth for a while. But somewhere along the way, her dad seemed to drop out of the picture once again. He would not answer her phone calls nor respond to any of her emails. Shortly before her thirteenth birthday, she sent him a scolding email in a last-ditch effort to try and establish a relationship with him. The subject line was "Read This!!!"

"Hey. Look, this is going to be a very important email so read and pay attention! Don't read it and push it to the side. I know you might be busy and I definitely know that time isn't always something someone has, but people always have a little time on their hands at some point. You need to know a heck of a whole lot of things! You never send me any emails. Even a 'Hi Faith, how are you doing?' would brighten my day, but no. You can't even send 6 words to me. You have no idea how it feels to think your own father doesn't think about you, care about you, or even love you! With all of the struggles that I'm going through, I need my dad to actually be a dad. You need to know how much it hurts me to never hear from you. You would always reply when I was younger, but you know what, people don't go through a stage of loving their dad and just growing out of it. I would still love getting emails from you. If you feel guilty right now, you should. I'm kind of glad because you need to open your eyes and pay attention to the world around you. I am not 9 years old anymore! I'm going to be 13 next month, which you probably didn't know. If you would have been sending me emails you would've known that your daughter was going through depression. How would you have felt if something had happened to me and you could've stopped it by just getting in touch with me? I would feel miserable if

I were you. People need their dads, no matter how easy their life may be. If a dad is in the army or a really, really important job like that, that would be understandable if they couldn't do much for their children, but they still try to send birthday cards or Christmas cards and you don't! If you had talked to me somehow you would know that I have a great doctor, have been gaining weight, and doing well with my treatments and that is fantastic, but you probably don't know how fantastic that is because you don't know how much of a struggle it is to live with CF every single day and how life threatening it really is. I'm done trying to be [a] thoughtful and caring and respectful daughter to you. It's your turn. Be a father, and do what God created you to do. ~Faith"

He never replied.

Friendship isn't about who you've known the longest,
it's about who walked into your life and said,
"I'm here for you" and proved it.
~Unknown

Ever since Faith was a tiny little girl, she had an uncanny knack for drawing people to her and, for the most part, always had a great group of friends who accepted her for who she was and all she had to endure.

Faith loved spending time outside playing with her neighborhood friends, riding bikes, jumping on their trampoline, and playing with their dogs. She had several sweet friends she grew up with from church and school that she would also spend a lot of time with doing the typical little girl activities—sleepovers, trick-or-treating in each other's neighborhoods, playing at one another's houses, building snow forts and snowmen in the rare snowfall, creating little "plays," enjoying birthday parties, etc. She joined Girl Scouts when she was eleven, went to summer camps, rode horses, etc. She worked hard at having a "typical" ordinary childhood in spite of the medical circumstances she had to face. She was sassy and silly and loved her friends deeply—and they loved her, even when making fun of each other. One time when she was in middle school, I took Faith and her friend, Cat, to Cici's Pizza. Cat asked Faith, "Have you ever had alfredo pizza?" to which Faith replied, "No.—Wait—what are alfredos again?" After Cat and I finished laughing, Faith had moved to another table. But Faith was without a doubt able to dish it out as well as she could take it! She was as sassy and sarcastic as she was sweet.

Unfortunately, as so often happens in life, not all her friendships were always at their healthiest. One day during middle school, Faith came into the house after the bus dropped her off, and she was visibly very upset. She went straight upstairs to her room without responding to me or Kelsey when we said hello, so we followed her upstairs to find out what was going on. Through her tears, we learned that there had been an argument she and a friend of hers had on the bus with two boys. There was some unfortunate language used during this argument, causing tempers to flare even hotter. When Faith angrily reached across one of the boys to grab her book bag, which he had been blocking from her, he said to her, "Get away from me, you diseased b***!" Through some more questioning, we were able to determine where this boy lived, so Kelsey and I went to pay his mom a visit. She was appalled and said she would definitely be having a conversation with him. Not too long after we returned home, he and his mom showed up at *our* door, and we were able to hear both sides of the story. He profusely apologized to Faith for what he had said and told her he hadn't meant it. His mom told me that on the way over to our house, he had told her, "I don't even know why I said that. I like Faith, and she's a friend of mine." But even though things had been worked out and the kids apologized to each other for their respective wrongs, those words hung very heavy in her heart and on her mind for a very long time.

Another instance happened when Faith was fifteen and a couple of long-time friends said some very cruel things that completely broke her heart. I recall having just picked her up after an event, and when I asked her how it was, she responded by breaking down in tears. When we got home, she was able to explain what had happened, and I simply held her for a long time as she continued crying. That night, after she had finally drifted off to sleep, I laid awake for hours with my mind spinning and my heart broken on behalf of my girl, praying that the love and peace of the Lord would surround her wounded heart and heal the pain from the insensitive, biting words that had been said.

Thankfully, instances like these were few and far between, and her friendships were primarily filled with mutual love and respect. Faith's friends were more often than not very supportive and kind. The way many of them went the extra mile to make sure she knew how awesome and special she was deeply touched this mama's heart!

When Faith was diligently working on getting through eighth grade after switching to online school, her young friend, Kyle, from church asked my permission to take her to his high school prom because he didn't know if she would ever have a chance to go since she was doing school online. I was moved to tears by the sweet offer as I told him of course! The prom took place on May 14th, 2016, one day before her fifteenth birthday. They went to prom with a group of five other people, and Faith had a magical time. Following the prom, they had a post-prom party at one of the kid's houses. By this time it was officially May 15th. When Faith emerged from the bathroom after changing out of her prom dress into more comfortable clothes, she was greeted by all the other kids waiting for her with a Cinnabon on a plate, topped with a candle, as they cheerfully sang "Happy Birthday."

Toward the end of 2017, I talked with Faith's competition dance team and the team moms about an idea I had to design some t-shirts in Faith's honor that we could all surprise her with by wearing at the same time. The team girls and moms were very excited about doing this for her, and we decided to surprise her with it at the stage rehearsal in January. The front of the t-shirts read, "Friends don't let friends fight Alone—Cystic Fibrosis Awareness." And the back read, "Lungs4Faith" and "I'm in the fight against cystic fibrosis." Everyone arrived at the Grady Cole Center in Charlotte wearing their team jackets zipped all the way up. Before her team's turn to go on stage, we pulled Faith off to the side. Everyone lined up in front of her and on the count of three, unzipped and removed their jackets to show the t-shirts. She was deeply touched by the outpouring of support and moved to tears as many hugs were shared.

When she reached high school and was able to discontinue online school, she again met some of the greatest groups of kids who would end up deeply touching not only Faith's heart but also mine and her sisters' in so many ways. Faith and her friends enjoyed many late nights on the phone, sleepovers, parties, cheering together in the student section at football games, followed by runs to Taco Bell or Sonic. A small group of them even accompanied her to Chapel Hill when she had to go for some tests, all of them wearing face masks in solidarity, since she had to wear one to appointments following her lung transplant due to the immune suppression medicine.

After Faith died, many of these friends continued to selflessly and graciously reach out to me and the family. One of her dear friends from school made a beautiful portrait with the silhouette of a dancer and the words "Dancing With Jesus," which I displayed at her Celebration of Life service and now proudly display on my wall at home. A few months after she passed, a small group of her school friends took me to lunch at Taco Bell; a month later, this same group took me out on a date night bowling, then to Cook Out afterward for dinner. A couple of Faith's friends from church also texted or called me quite often just to ask, "How are you doing?" They took me out to dinner several times or just came over to the house to hang out and make sure I was not alone. For the first couple of years following her death, many of us gathered on Faith's birthday to eat Taco Bell and light sparklers in her honor.

On my first Valentine's Day without Faith, two of her school friends brought me some chocolates along with a portrait they had made showing the silhouette of a dancer holding onto a large purple rose (purple being the color for CF) standing next to an oxygen tank with the oxygen tube from the tank becoming the stem of the rose. This portrait also hangs on my wall.

One of Faith's dance friends made a beautiful wreath with a small chalkboard in the middle that reads "Always Have Faith" along with pictures of Faith on a clothespin. It resides on my front door. At other times, I have received flowers, various gifts, cards, and sweet messages of love and encouragement. Another one of her precious friends, Glenn, and I went to a Rage Room where we could—legally and in a controlled environment—use bats, hammers, and axes to smash up bottles, mirrors, glass shelves, big screen tv's, etc., to release some of the grief and anger. It was very therapeutic, and I highly recommend it if you have never gone to one! There have been a multitude of social media posts and text messages as her friends continue to let us know they are thinking about us and remembering Faith.

A few days after what would have been Faith's nineteenth birthday, I celebrated her friends with the following post . . .

"A LASTING LEGACY — As I continue to focus on celebrating Faith throughout this month, I also continue to be overwhelmed at the impact she had on the lives of others and how many people she touched, from family and friends to groups and organizations like Snowbird, HISRadio, and the band for KING & COUNTRY, to people known and unknown to us all over the United States and even as far reaching as The Netherlands, Japan, the UK and more!

"So today I'd like to celebrate Faith's friends because the great group of friends she surrounded herself with says a lot about her; and the amazing way they rallied around her and have since rallied around me and my family after her passing says a lot about them! The way they have honored and celebrated Faith and her life has been nothing short of awe-inspiring.

"When Faith returned from Chapel Hill and victoriously arrived at school for the first day of her senior year, she was deeply touched to find a sweet 'Welcome Home' message painted on the school [spirit] rock. After she died, the

rock was painted again in her honor and remains painted to this day! The candle-light vigil held three days after she died was completely student-arranged and organized. One of her friends, writing a scholarship essay in which he had to describe a situation/event that shaped or influenced his understanding of himself and/or others, wrote about Faith and her impact on his and other's lives. I continue to periodically receive messages from many of her friends out of the blue letting me know they're thinking of and praying for me; some of them brought me gifts and flowers for Valentine's Day and Mother's Day; we also got together to light sparklers in her honor because, as one of her friends said, every time he sees sparklers he thinks of her because they are bright and shiny but brief. My heart is filled and warmed by all the social media posts and tributes, cap & gown pictures at the rock, memories, and remembrances shared; she was even written about in a blog by someone we never met. Thank you to all who have helped to keep her story alive, as was one of her final wishes, and for helping me feel not so alone. It all means more to me than you can possibly imagine!

"As always, my sweet Faith, I love you and miss you from the deepest depths of my heart and soul. And I'm so comforted to see you live on through the actions and words of your sweet friends. You are deeply loved and deeply missed."

Family and Friends

4

Spiritual Walk

Our faith in the Lord, our church, and our church family have always been a very important foundation of our family's life. As the girls were growing up, we attended church pretty much any time the doors were open. I was involved in the choir and praise teams, and the girls were all very active in AWANA, children's programs, youth groups, mission projects and activities, as well as various Christian summer camps.

Faith accepted Christ and was baptized when she was about six years old. Her faith played a huge role as one of her biggest inspirations and motivations for having to battle and be so strong against CF. She also once told me that watching my strength as I raised three kids completely on my own was an inspiration to her, which touched my heart deeply and was very humbling.

I came across a Bible Study writing assignment in which she described her background—

"I grew up middle class. I grew up in a Southern Baptist, Christian home with a single mom and 2 sisters. My mom comes from a liberal, non-Christian home, but having found Christ later in life, she did her best to teach us about Jesus. My dad is a Christian, too, but he's turned his back on Jesus a long time ago. He loves me, but he has often let me down, and he doesn't always live truthfully. I still do enjoy and love both my mom and dad, but I'm far closer to my mom."

In another journal entry I encountered, she referenced an article she read about a controversial law and what her thoughts were from a Christian viewpoint.

". . . We may have different beliefs but that doesn't mean Christians hate everyone that 'aren't like them'. If you see a 'Christian' discriminating [against] someone and just being awful to them, they're not a Christian. Christians will love and welcome you even if you have different beliefs. And if they try to talk to you about God and his word, they aren't attacking you or your beliefs, they're loving you. . . ."

Her love for the Lord gave her a strength unmatched by anyone I have ever met. She walked around with things on her mind that no young person should ever have to worry about. I discovered some of her thoughts one afternoon following a doctor's appointment when she was thirteen. We were sitting in McDonald's across from the doctor's office and she was talking about how much she wanted to travel before she ever had to get a lung transplant. *Really* travel—to places like Paris or Italy or back to Hawaii, where we had gone on her Make-A-Wish trip. I asked her if she wouldn't want to wait until *after* a transplant so she wouldn't have to worry about the oxygen, vest, nebulizers, and such, to which she replied, "But I may not even make it off the table." That thought had never before entered my mind, but those were the kinds of thoughts she lived with.

During times when a lung infection was suspected, Faith would have to undergo a procedure called a bronchoscopy, in which the doctor would put a scope into her lungs to see what was going on and take a sample to see what infection might be brewing to determine the appropriate antibiotic combination. Prior to one of these procedures, when Faith was very young, I asked the pastoral staff and deacon team of the church we were attending at the time if they would lay hands on her, and it was an amazing experience that I will never forget. Following service on the Sunday before her procedure, we gathered together, and they had me sit in a chair with Faith on my lap. Everyone gathered around and laid hands on both of us. The prayer time was so sweet, and I literally felt like the chair was lifting into the air! It was astonishingly beautiful.

At the procedure, they allowed me to stay with her right up until the time she went to sleep from the anesthesia. To help with anxiety, they pre-treated her with a drug called Versed, which made her quite loopy. She was so goofy and funny that my pastor, who had come to offer his support, prayers, and encouragement, laughed and asked if all of us could have some of what she was given. Whenever she was in recovery, however, she would wake up almost violently, sometimes trying to rip out the IV from her hand, her face twisted in anger and frustration. We later discovered this was an unfortunate side-effect of Versed, so we eventually stopped having that administered. After we stopped, she came around much more calmly and peacefully following the procedures.

While Faith was in these procedures, the waiting process for me was always an awful and tense time. Faith and I had to come packed and prepared to stay, arrangements made at work, and a place for Kelsey and Jenni lined up to stay in case they determined IV antibiotics were necessary, which would require hospital admission. The wait was always made easier by the presence of friends from church who would come to pray and just sit with me while I waited.

In the spring of 2015, when Faith was thirteen and a member of the youth group at our present church, she was facing another one of her many bronchoscopies. I again asked the pastoral staff and deacons if they would lay hands on Faith. Some of the young youth group men also stood by Faith's side to demonstrate their love and support for her as well. It was a sweet, sweet time of fellowship in the presence of Jesus. During this precious time of worshipful prayer, Pastor Mike anointed Faith's forehead with oil as he referenced the following Scripture from James:

> *"Is anyone among you sick? Let them call the elders of the church to*
> *pray over them and anoint them with oil in the name of the Lord."*
> James 5:14, NIV

Faith was so excited when she had reached the age to become part of the youth group. She remained very active, participating in several local mission trips and activities in which they helped paint, do repairs, clean up yards, pick up trash along the side of the road, etc. She loved attending concerts, such as "Winter Jam," which is where she first saw and fell in love with the Christian rock band *for KING & COUNTRY.*

One of her favorite activities with the church youth group was attending summer camp at Snowbird Wilderness Outfitters in Andrews, North Carolina. It was an amazing, spirit-filled week and a fun bonding experience among

the youth and with the Lord. She looked forward to going every year, and always came home so on fire for Christ. She even figured out how to make camp work with her vest, all her medicines, and her treatments. One summer, I received a picture from one of the youth leaders that showed Faith sitting in an office, early in the morning, percussion vest on, taking care of her nebulizer treatments, deep in her personal Bible study before the other campers were even awake.

The year we were in Chapel Hill as she recovered from her double-lung transplant, she was unable to attend summer camp, so she recorded a video message to the church for the youth group's annual fund-raiser (called a "Celebraiser") describing the benefits of the camp.

"So, first off, I would like to say thank you to everyone there for all of the support and encouragement that you guys have been giving me and my family. We wish we could be there right now, and we wish we could be there to kick off this Celebraiser for the youth to go to Snowbird, where they can really dive deep into God's Word, grow in their relationship with Him and with others and really find a part of themselves that they may have never known was there. It's a time to reflect and to have fun with each other and just enjoy each other's company and learn more about what Jesus did for us and why it's so important that we share that with everyone we know and share His love and how much He cares for everybody. The past years that I've been to Snowbird, it's been amazing, and it's hard to put into words. It's really challenged me to want to share my faith with everybody I know and to not be ashamed or embarrassed of my faith. And it's made me long for a deeper relationship with God. Snowbird is not just a camp with fun rides and loud music. It's a second home, and the staff there . . . we're not just campers to them . . . we . . . they want so much for us, and they care so deeply and put everything they have—all of their time and their energy—into making sure that we get at least one thing out of the week that we're there. They want all the campers that come to help be a part of the

future that turns towards God and loves God. And they . . . they care for each and every individual person there. An example of how much they care is when I was in the midst of some of the hardest times these past few months, they actually reached out to me and made sure that me and my family knew that they were thinking of us. They sent me some Snowbird merchandise, and they made sure that we knew all the staff that was there were praying for us, and they said that they can't wait to see me there again. Snowbird is just . . . it's truly a special place. You feel God's presence there all the time. You have so much fun in the process. You go to services and worship and fellowship and then you have . . . you go and ride rides and enjoy nature and God's amazing creations. And you grow so much spiritually, and you feel at home the whole time. I hope that this Celebraiser helps every one of the youth to get there. I hope you guys have fun. I hope that it's so exciting and amazing like always, but just don't have too much fun without me. Thank you. Bye."

But more than letting people know how wonderful camp was, she had a deep desire to let everyone, especially family, know how wonderful her Lord was. One day, while we were still living in Chapel Hill, she felt the need to have a very specific conversation with her Uncle Tim about her beliefs. She took a walk outside around our neighborhood and spoke with him on the phone for quite some time. I will probably never know the details or the content of the conversation they had, but I know she felt very good when she returned from her walk, and Tim sent me a text that said, "News Flash: Your youngest daughter is an amazing person." I replied that she had told me they'd had a really nice conversation, to which he answered, "We did. Most enjoyable conversation I've had in a long time."

Her love for the Lord also gave her incredible strength and peace at the *end* of her life, knowing exactly where she was going and that she was going to be more than okay. She wanted everyone to be happy for her. And she desperately wanted certain family members to understand where her faith was coming from and what it meant to her.

Even on her literal death bed, her final day alive, she was still witnessing to Uncle Tim via the board with which she used to communicate with everyone since she was unable to speak due to a tracheotomy. She had some very specific things she still felt she needed to say to her extended family that she wanted to be sure to say before she died. She and Tim carried on an entire private and intimate conversation on the writing board while the room was filled with people. By the end, she, unfortunately, did not have the strength to say all she had wanted to say to everyone, but I asked her if she had at least been able to say everything to Uncle Tim she had wanted, to which she nodded yes. He later made a post with the hashtag "#Ipromise." I can only assume that was related to their final conversation.

When I was going through Faith's things after she died, I came across a journal filled with many of her prayers and praises. Due to the personal nature of most of them, I have chosen not to share them here, but one of the last entries is a good representation of her love for the Lord and definitely worth sharing. She closed out the journal entry with,

"Thank you, Lord. I love you so much and love living in your light!
~Amen"

Spiritual Walk

Faith with her first-place winning
Motion and Design science project, 5th grade

5

School and Work

When Faith was born, we lived in a rental house in Concord, North Carolina, near the Kannapolis line. Faith initially stayed with my friend, Terri, during the day while I was at work. But after Faith's diagnosis, Terri was concerned about the medical circumstances and couldn't bear the thought of her own children potentially getting Faith sick causing her to be hospitalized, so Terri sadly asked me to make other arrangements. Faith began attending Kids' Korner in Kannapolis, which had a phenomenal staff who took wonderful care of Faith and looked out for the whole family. One time, when I was facing some pretty heavy-duty medical expenses, the staff at Kids' Korner put out a notice to their other families that one of their own was in trouble and, keeping my name anonymous, asked for donations. The generosity of these families was heartwarming as they donated just over $400 in a week to an unknown fellow daycare family.

A couple of years later, I was able to buy a house near the Concord/Harrisburg line. Due to the distance from our new home, we sadly left Kids' Korner, and Faith began attending King's Keep daycare, which was a part of the church we were attending at the time. When The Ruckus House, formed by several Carolina Panthers players, opened in Harrisburg, we moved Faith there as it was much closer to home. They, too, were phenomenal and took wonderful care of her, even handling many of her medical requirements and providing me with a much-needed break. As Faith entered elementary school, she began attending the KidsPlus before- and after-school program held on school property.

Faith was a very intelligent and bright child who did very well in school and actually enjoyed it. Early on, her favorite subjects were math and science, and at one time, she expressed interest in becoming a doctor. We would talk about how neat it would be if she one day found a cure for her own disease.

In her fifth-grade science fair, she won first place in the Motion and Design category. She made a roller coaster with pipe tubing and popsicle sticks. She then took different-sized marbles and rolled them down the rollercoaster to see if the size had any impact on the speed. I remember this roller coaster taking up my dining room table for many weeks as it was built and tested. In her sixth-grade year, she started the STEM program (science, technology, engineering, and mathematics) at JN Fries Middle School. She also began playing the flute as her sister, Jenni, had done for a few years. For the most part, she enjoyed the STEM program and enjoyed middle school. But things were not always easy.

At the beginning of seventh grade, because of hospital stays, doctor visits, and other times kept home from school from just plain feeling yucky, Faith began to feel like she was spending all her time playing catch up, which was causing a great deal of stress. Even with a 504 plan in place (a written plan outlining specific allowances for medical circumstances) to account for missed days and provide her extra time to complete missed assignments, it just did not help eliminate the stress. After much discussion and prayer, we decided beginning with the second semester to transfer her to a non-STEM middle school, hoping the curriculum would be a little more forgiving of her situation and schedule. But she was very unhappy there, having left her good friends and favorite teachers. She also still had a great deal of difficulty keeping up, given all the medical hurdles. Together we decided to have her try online school for eighth grade so she could work at her own pace without worrying about CF-related hurdles getting in the way. This ended up being more of a perfect solution than we realized it would be, especially since it was that December when she would end up in the hospital for a month (more on that in a subsequent chapter). And given that month-long stay in the hospital, all the follow-up appointments in Chapel Hill, physical therapy, etc., she lost about seven months of school. Because of this, she wound up taking two years to finish the eighth grade, which resulted in her starting high school a year late. She was at first very upset and discouraged about starting high school a year behind schedule but grew to accept it and be sort of excited about the fact that she would be one of the oldest in her class.

Faith's first day of high school was August 29th, 2016. She thoroughly loved her high school years and made wonderful friends. She was an active member of the Student Council, Beta Club, Leadership, the National Honors Society, National Society of High School Scholars (NSHSS), and theater. She also continued with her competition dance.

A month before turning sixteen, Faith had the joy of making her first visit to New York City with the theater group from both her school and another high school in the area. This was of course a challenge given her medical needs. We were able to arrange with an oxygen company in the NYC area to have some loaner oxygen tanks waiting for her at the hotel (which was paid for by a charitable organization arranged for through her Chapel Hill respiratory specialist), so she would not have to lug a bunch of them with her on the bus. She was able to use her small portable oxygen concentrator on the bus and in the hotel for sleeping.

Faith still missed a lot of school not only from doctor appointments and hospital stays but sometimes from just not feeling up to par, which is very common for CF patients. Fatigue, achiness, and fevers would periodically settle in for no apparent reason, without signs of infection. Many times when these instances would occur, her pediatric pulmonologist would prescribe oral antibiotics just to be on the safe side. There were many times when oral antibiotics were also prescribed as a preventative measure. For instance, when she came into contact with someone who had strep, even if she showed no signs of it herself. School days were a constant balancing act of medicines, appointments, homework, treatments, hospital stays, and work, all while still trying to live life like a normal girl. Fortunately, truancy rules took her illness and its associated challenges into account, and she always worked extremely hard, receiving exceptional grades.

On April 30th, 2018, a few weeks before turning seventeen, Faith began working her first job as a cashier at Lowes Foods in Harrisburg, NC. This would also end up being the only job she would ever hold. As much as any teenager can enjoy a job, Faith truly enjoyed working at Lowes. She loved her co-workers and really enjoyed her supervisors. They were all very supportive of and flexible with her circumstances and worked very well with her when the need arose. The staff and management at Lowes became some of her largest supporters when she ended up in the hospital waiting for new lungs, as well as during her recovery. Unfortunately, due to the immune suppression drugs she had to take following her lung transplant, she was unable to return as a cashier over concerns about germs with handling cash and the sheer number of people with whom she would be in contact.

Unable to return to Lowes Foods following her transplant, Faith set out to find some more creative ways to earn an income. She decided on tutoring, so in September 2019, she posted an "ad" on some Harrisburg community Facebook pages:

"NEED A TUTOR? Hi! My name is Faith Shaw. I'm 18 and a senior at Hickory Ridge High School. Now that school is back in session, I'm offering tutoring to kids up through 8th grade in a variety of subjects. Due to being on medications to suppress my immune system from a double lung transplant at the beginning of the year, it would be ideal for any tutoring sessions to be over Skype or FaceTime. I'm also currently on oxygen 24/7 from some recent complications, which somewhat limits my mobility, as well as my options for the 'typical' high school job. Throughout this past year, I have faced extreme challenges, spending much of my time in the hospital, yet still managed to complete my junior year through all of it with online classes while maintaining a 4.1 GPA. If you have a child who is struggling, or would just like some additional assistance as an added boost, I would love for the opportunity to share that determination and perseverance with them! Please PM me with any questions and for pricing information. (Also, as I'm trying to earn money to prepare for college, if you are aware of other job opportunities in the Harrisburg area for someone in my situation that can't do a retail or restaurant type job, please let me know!) Thank you! I look forward to hearing from you and working with your children!"

Sadly, she would never have the opportunity to take on any students.

School and Work

Faith doing her percussion vest and nebulizer treatments

6

CF Life

In addition to the many treatments and medicines Faith had to contend with daily, doctor's offices, hospitals, surgeries, and procedures were a very normal and very large part of her life. As painstakingly detailed in this chapter, living with CF is cumbersome, overwhelming, endless, and disruptive to day-to-day life. Each appointment—each hospital visit—each procedure—shows the roller coaster ride of the struggles with CF and, over time, the progressive downward spiraling nature of her disease. Much of the time, it felt very much like one step forward, two steps back.

Following Faith's diagnosis in 2001, we started with the doctor in Charlotte who had given us the diagnosis. Doctor B was an extremely competent and intelligent doctor who had received his training at UNC Chapel Hill, apparently the top CF clinic in the state of North Carolina and one of the best in the United States. But he did not have the best bedside manner and sometimes came across as very harsh and unsympathetic. This was difficult, at first, for a scared mother and terrified little girl, but I came to realize he was simply very direct and did not like to beat around the bush. I later grew to immensely appreciate that approach. So much so that when he was out of town on business and his colleague, Doctor A, was to perform one of Faith's bronchoscopies, I found myself a little frustrated with Doctor A's laid-back approach. He told me that if the bronchoscopy showed IV antibiotics were needed, they would bring us back a day or two later to get her admitted to the hospital. I told him under no uncertain terms that if IV medications were required, she needed to be admitted to the hospital that day—I had already made the necessary arrangements for my other daughters as well as at work in the event hospitalization was required, and I was not about to put it off. He was very cooperative and understanding, and Faith ended up being admitted to the hospital that day.

Sometime around 2008 or 2009, the doctor-patient/doctor-mom relationship with Doctor B unfortunately began to deteriorate, and visits became
very uncomfortable for both Faith and me. I had broken down in his office a
few times because as a single full-time working mom of three young children,
I was struggling to keep up with everything. I felt many times like I was failing
all three of my daughters, especially Faith's medical needs. I was in trouble a
lot at work for all the time I kept having to miss due to appointments and hospital stays, and I was dealing with depression that was steadily getting worse.
At first, Doctor B seemed compassionate and on one visit told me I was doing
better with Faith's treatments than a lot of two-parent households. But then I
think he grew frustrated with me and I felt he no longer took me seriously. He
did not even seem to believe me when I brought up the mediocre treatment
she had received from the respiratory team at the hospital. When Faith grew
increasingly uncomfortable with him, however, I started questioning whether
that was a good place for her to be because it was vitally important she be able
to open up fully with her doctor in order for him to know what was going on
and be able to treat her properly. It was a very uneasy time. But the last straw
came when the social worker said some things to Kelsey and Jenni that were
very divisive and caused problems between my daughters and me.

During one of the visits when I was at my wits' end, feeling very over-
loaded and overwhelmed, the social worker and I discussed all that I had going
on at home and work. She said to me, "Your other daughters should be helping
you! They are definitely old enough to help you! — Around the house, with
Faith — would you like me to speak with them about it?" I told her that would
be great, so we arranged to bring them with us to Faith's next appointment.
When we arrived for that appointment, the social worker took Kelsey and Jenni
into another room while Faith and I talked with Doctor B. About twenty minutes later, Kelsey and Jenni returned to the room where Faith and I were. As
they walked in looking very angry, they both shot glaring looks in my direction.
On the car ride home, I learned that the first thing the social worker had said
to them was, "Your mother wanted me to talk to you guys about doing your
chores, but that's not my job. So I'm going to talk to you about cystic fibrosis
and what your little sister is dealing with," and then proceeded in very harsh
tones to give them a lesson on CF. Kelsey and Jenni couldn't believe that I
would ask the social worker to talk to them about doing their chores, which
I hadn't—it had been her idea to talk to them about helping me more. Plus
they were under the impression the harsh tones of the social worker were also
stemming from me. Not only did this create a tremendous amount of tension
at home, but the tension this created at the doctor's office was detrimental to

Faith's care. So I began researching other pulmonologists in the area.

I discovered there was a pediatric pulmonologist in Concord (Doctor H), which there hadn't been when Faith was first diagnosed, and of course that was much closer to home. I had a consultation with him to discuss Faith, her medical situation, and the current environment at our present doctor's office. Because Doctor H's office was not an accredited CF facility, he agreed to take Faith on as a patient as long as we agreed to stay connected with a CF clinic. So, in late 2010 (Faith, age nine), we switched to Doctor H, and through his recommendation, we eventually got connected with the CF clinic at UNC Chapel Hill.

Although the Concord office was not an accredited CF facility, Doctor H had previously worked very closely with CF patients and came with wonderful reviews and recommendations. Faith adored him. And he adored her. The entire staff was great, and the environment was much more conducive to proper two-way communication. They spoke to Faith directly, not just to me, and encouraged her to own her illness and take full responsibility for it. Through his detailed and comprehensive explanations, he taught us many things about cystic fibrosis that we had not previously been told. It was without a doubt a good move.

Throughout her life, Faith also got to know several hospitals quite well. The most frequented hospitals were Levine Children's Hospital at CMC Main in Charlotte and the North Carolina Children's Hospital/UNC Medical Center in Chapel Hill. Because Faith typically spent a lot of time in the hospital, we would try and bring as many of the comforts of home as we possibly could, especially during the Christmas holidays. We would load her up with snacks and movies and even her PlayStation 4 console from home with her favorite games. Due to contact precautions, she was not allowed to go to the playroom when other kids were there, so craft activities and games had to be brought to her. Plus, she would get plenty of craft activities and goodies sent to her from friends and family.

When she was older, her favorite shows to watch while in the hospital were *Friends, The Office,* and *Impractical Jokers.*

Her favorite movie to watch when in the hospital was *Ratatouille.* This would also end up being the last movie we watched together on her final night before she passed away.

The other activity she had to do while in the hospital, which she did *not* particularly enjoy, was her schoolwork. As much as she loved school, doing it in the hospital was extremely difficult and burdensome. Before she was doing online school, I would go to the school office each day or every other day, pick up her schoolwork, and take it to her at the hospital. I would take the finished work back with me when I picked up the new.

Not only did Faith have to deal with an overwhelming number of appointments and hospital stays, but she also dealt with devices surgically placed in her body that had both positives and negatives. When Faith was six, Doctor B and I decided it was a good time to install a Port-A-Cath (port), which was a device placed under the skin on the right side of her chest attached to a thin, flexible tube called a catheter threaded into a large vein above the right side of her heart.[4] It was used for administering IV antibiotics as well as drawing blood for labs. This was a one-time surgery and would take the place of having to insert a PICC line in her arm every time she needed IV antibiotics. One of the other great advantages of having the port was whenever IV antibiotics were needed, we could immediately start them at home without the previously required hospital admission.

Other than the bump it caused under her skin, about which Faith was very self-conscious, the only other thing she hated about the port was that it had to be "accessed and flushed" once a month, when it was not being used for antibiotics, to keep it from becoming clogged. Access was gained by taking a small needle attached to the tubing, sticking it through her skin into the center of the port, and flushing it with saline. These monthly flushes were traumatic for her. The anticipation was always way worse than the procedure itself, but each month was a repeat of the emotional turmoil and tears.

The first port lasted about four years before it reached the end of its life. In late 2011, the first port was removed and replaced with a new port placed on the opposite side of her chest. Although Faith was frustrated with now having identical surgery scars on both sides, she was still thankful for the new port so she could continue not having the PICC lines put in her arm, which she hated even more than the monthly flushes of the port. Unfortunately, this new port began having issues a mere two months later, and we began struggling to get it to work properly. We made several trips back and forth to the hospital as they tried different procedures and drips to get it unclogged and working again. All to no avail. So even with a port, Faith wound up having to get PICC lines put in for her IV antibiotics and in December 2012, while she was already in the hospital dealing with a lung infection, we decided to have the port removed as it was just an infection waiting to happen.

A year after the first port was installed, Doctor B recommended Faith get a gastrostomy tube (G-tube), which was a surgically placed tube directly into the stomach for supplemental nutrition via high-calorie shakes. This decision was based upon the extremely high daily calorie needs, which Faith found exceedingly difficult to consume — especially given her picky and slow eating habits.

On the outside of the abdomen, there was a little button called a Mickey button that looked similar to the air nozzle on a blow-up pool floaty. Using a very large and wide syringe (called a bolus) attached to the Mickey button via some thin tubing, these high-calorie shakes were literally poured straight into her stomach. These were in addition to regular meals and would many times make her feel so full she felt sick. The Mickey button needed to be replaced every six months, which was another traumatic experience for her — and for me as I was the one who had to replace the button.

The button was held in place by a "balloon" filled with water on the inside of her stomach. Replacing the button entailed using a syringe through the button to remove the water, which would "deflate" the balloon, pulling the button out, inserting a new button into the hole in her abdomen and stomach as quickly as possible, and then using the syringe to fill the new balloon with water to hold the button in place. It caused quite a bit of discomfort and anxiety and was usually a thirty to forty-five-minute process when it should have only taken less than a minute to perform.

At first, we would do her shakes several times a day between meals but found they interfered with her regular meals, defeating the purpose of the extra calories. So, as Faith got older, we decided to try overnight feedings while she slept. Using an electric pump called a kangaroo pump, the shakes were slowly administered through a flexible tube hooked up to the Mickey button over many hours throughout the night. Although it did still tend to interfere with breakfast, it at least no longer interfered with her other meals, and she was able to benefit from the added calories—at first.

One of the issues with the G-tube was that it would leak from around the base of the Mickey button. It got to the point that every time Faith would eat or drink anything, the button would leak. Many of her shirts became ruined as the leaking would cause them to be stained. The leaking also caused the area around the button to become very irritated without an opportunity to heal since it was always wet. The irritation grew worse, which pulled the skin further away from the button, causing the leaking to become worse, causing the irritation to become worse . . . It was a vicious cycle that created a lot of pain and frustration for Faith, and nothing we did seemed to help. We tried changing out the button to a different size, tried a different kind of button called a Mini One button, and tried all kinds of ointments and creams around the area to try and heal the irritated skin—all to no avail. One of Faith's nutritionists even said the irritation around Faith's button was the worst she had ever seen.

The final straw for Faith came when the leaking grew so bad that she would wake up in the morning drenched in a puddle of shake. She eventually got to the point that she was afraid to eat or drink anything, let alone do her shakes at night, and she began to lose weight. We even tried gauze to keep the leaking from reaching her shirts or from leaking out overnight. But, again, nothing seemed to work. She had pleaded with her doctor on numerous occasions to have the button removed entirely, but now she became fiercely adamant that it had to go! Doctor D, her Chapel Hill pulmonologist, was afraid that if the G-tube was removed, Faith would not be getting the nutrition she needed. But Faith guaranteed Doctor D that she would eat enough and agreed to have another one put back in after a year if she could not maintain or improve her BMI. So, in 2015, Doctor D reluctantly agreed to let Faith remove the G-tube. Over the next year, as Faith promised, she diligently focused on her nutrition and actually *gained* weight.

The only complication she faced with having the G-tube removed was that the hole in her abdomen, which was supposed to close on its own within a couple of weeks, did not close due to the severe irritation in the skin, and it became clear it was going to need to be closed surgically. Because Faith was in the midst of her dance competition season and given the fact that the hole in the stomach itself had properly closed, she opted to wait until after competition season was over to have the surgery so as not to interfere with any competitions. On August 3rd, 2016, a few weeks after the Nationals dance competition was over and before the new season began, Faith had a successful surgery to close the hole in her skin and, much to her relief, was finally done with all aspects of the G-tube.

    One thing we certainly learned over the years of Faith's life with CF was that things could change drastically in a very short amount of time, unfortunately, usually for the worse.

    Pulmonary Function Testing (PFTs) was a standard procedure that was done at every doctor's appointment to determine Faith's lung function. She would inhale as much air as she possibly could to fill her lungs, then she would blow out as quickly and as forcefully as possible into a tube and keep blowing out as long as she could until her lungs were emptied. This would give us the FEV1 score (Forced Expiratory Volume in 1 second) as well as a whole slew of other numbers that I unfortunately never did quite understand. The FEV1 score (lung function) would give us a picture of the health of her airways and how much air she was moving in her lungs. They would then compare her number to a predicted number based on her size, age, etc., resulting in a percentage. In August of 2009, at the age of eight, Faith was on top of the world with an FEV1 score of 104%!

    In October 2009, Faith had the swine flu, which quickly turned into pneumonia, with her fever spiking to 104 (I also had the swine flu which turned into bronchitis, and at the same time, was dealing with fleas in the house from our cats). Following IV antibiotics and defeating that round of pneumonia, her FEV1 score peaked at 74%, which would become her new baseline and would never again reach outside the 70's.

    Randomly spiking a fever at times also became a new way of life and interrupted many things such as school and time with friends and family. In December 2009, we were on our way to Portland, Maine, to spend Christmas with my brother, Tim, and his family. We stopped in Richmond, Virginia, to spend the night with my dad and stepmom and thought we were going to have to cancel the trip. That evening Faith developed a fever of 102 for no apparent reason, so we put her to bed early and prepared ourselves for the return trip home the next day. Fortunately, it turned out to be one of the mysterious random fever spikes, and she was perfectly fine the next day, so we were able to continue our journey. She thankfully had no further difficulties the rest of the trip.

    Another random occurrence Faith had to deal with was suddenly and unexpectedly throwing up. It would come out of nowhere with no other symptoms leading up to or after. It resulted in spoiling many activities and school days for her. One such activity was a back-to-school pool party with the youth group from church. I was driving Faith and two other youths to the party when she suddenly told me I needed to pull over—*now*! She quickly got out of the car and proceeded to get sick on the side of the road. Some paramedics happened to be driving by and stopped to see if we needed assistance. Faith and I assured them she was okay and that this sometimes occurred. They still wanted to help in some way, so they went to a nearby grocery store and brought back a bottle of Sprite for Faith. In the meantime, I made a phone call to Aaron, the youth pastor, to see if he could come pick up the other two youths since I had to take Faith home. Faith was very discouraged and disappointed as she had to miss yet another activity due to something "random and stupid" with her health.

In early February 2010, Faith's doctor's appointment did not go very well, as her lung function was way down. They scheduled her for a bronchoscopy the following week (reporting to the hospital at 6 am!), and the result was a hospital admission and a two-week regimen of IV antibiotics. After a few days in the hospital to make sure they had the correct antibiotic combination and to make sure her IV port was properly working, they sent us home to continue the brutal IV schedule for two weeks.

In late February 2010, we reported back to Doctor B hoping for the news that Faith could discontinue the IV antibiotics. Sadly, even after just over two weeks of IV treatments, her lung function was actually *down*. He gave us a two-week break to get some rest and regain our strength, but then we were to restart another two weeks of IV antibiotics. He also decided to admit her for the full two weeks at Levine Children's Hospital in Charlotte so she could receive a focused intensity of airway clearance treatments that would be physically impossible to provide in the home environment by one person. Following this two-week segment, her lung function showed a slight improvement, so in late March 2010, she was discharged.

Faith did fairly well for the remainder of 2010—until December. The week before Christmas, she developed another infection and was once again placed on IV antibiotics. Fortunately, she was able to celebrate Christmas at home, although we did have to deal with the merciless IV schedule. A week into 2011, she was able to discontinue the IV antibiotics—and *I* was able to get some sleep.

In mid-May 2011, Faith developed a 102.4 fever. When I took her to the pediatrician, they discovered her white blood cell count to be such that they feared pneumonia yet again, so we went to see her new pulmonologist, Doctor H. She again wound up in the hospital on IV antibiotics that would continue through the beginning of June.

Faith would have another several months of reprieve with relatively no difficulties—again, until December. In early December 2011, Faith's FEV1 score was a dismal 55%, so she was scheduled for a two-week hospital stay at Jeff Gordon Children's Hospital in Concord. With the date of admission, we were now looking at her spending Christmas in the hospital, much to the dismay of her and the entire family. The doctor talked about the possibility of "breaking her out" for Christmas and then having her return to complete the IV therapy, but that was a long shot. An added complication to this admission was that her IV port was no longer working, so they had to put a PICC line in her arm, which the port was supposed to help her avoid. In the meantime, I would report to work at 4:30 each morning so I could get off early to spend as much time at the hospital with her as I could.

While she was in the hospital, they tried several measures to get her port to work. All proved unsuccessful, and Faith was devastated. The next step would be to put her under general anesthesia and go in to see if they could clean out the tubing that went into the vein from the inside. She was terrified. While in the hospital, they also had to draw blood several times a day to run tests and check glucose levels, and because they were unable to access the port, she was getting stuck multiple times in multiple places. When her sister, Jenni, and I tried to encourage her that God had everything all worked out and He had a plan, her tearful reply was, "Well this doesn't seem like a very good plan!" She did try, however, to be in good spirits and put on a happy face but would randomly break into tears. My heart broke for all that this precious ten-year-old had to deal with. It just did not seem fair.

A few days later, Faith was blessed with a day in which no blood draws were required, and she was paid a visit by her good friend, Makenzie, whom she didn't get to see much anymore due to differing schedules. It was a welcome emotional lift during a miserable storm.

After a week of IV therapy and intensified airway clearance, they performed another PFT to see how Faith's lungs were responding. We were very discouraged and disheartened to find out her FEV1 score was now 53% — lower than when she had been admitted. And Christmas was only five days away.

The following day, Kelsey and Jenni gave me the "day off" from hospital duty so I could get Christmas shopping done, buy groceries, and get some much-needed sleep! I somehow managed to get all my Christmas shopping done in one day, even in "zombie" mode. Two days later, to help create another special moment and add some Christmas cheer, a sweet lady from church arranged for Faith to get a ride in both a firetruck and a police car. In the police car, the officer even let her push the buttons for lights and sirens. It was a very nice distraction to an otherwise frustrating and discouraging time. But the best news came when they decided to discharge her on Christmas Eve—and she would *not* have to return after Christmas!

In addition to all the CF-related complications, life also happened. In January of 2012, as if Faith didn't have enough to deal with or had missed enough school already, we spent an evening at Urgent Care getting her ankle X-rayed following a kickball injury at school. Fortunately, there were no broken bones. But her ankle was sprained, and she had to stay off her feet for several days.

When she was older and had been dancing for a little while, she began to deal with some knee pain and other joint issues which were exacerbated by her CF. She required several rounds of physical therapy, adding more to her already overwhelming schedule.

In February 2012, at a regularly scheduled doctor appointment, we were excited to see her lung function at 68%. It saddened me deeply to think that there was a time we would have been devastated to see her score that low, but it was the highest we had seen it in quite a while. So we took it as a positive. In August, she was back down to 53%. Doctor H put her on oral antibiotics and asked us to return in two weeks.

Faith spent the next two weeks working extremely hard to make sure she got all her treatments and medicines in. At that time, she had been intentionally trying to take much more ownership of her illness and hold herself accountable. Through that effort, along with lots of prayers and encouragement, she was rewarded with an FEV1 score of 79%. She had gained just shy of four pounds, which was another huge victory in the face of CF, and when Doctor H listened to her lungs from the back, he said for the first time *ever* since he had been treating her, he heard nothing!—No crackling, no wheezing—just moving air. It was a wonderful praise and answer to prayers!

But, as previously mentioned, things turn on a dime when dealing with cystic fibrosis, even when being 100% (or close) compliant. One month later, Faith ended up back in Jeff Gordon Children's Hospital with her lung function at a never-before-seen 39%. Because by this time her port had been removed, they had to put in a PICC line. She was such a strong, brave, young lady, and, even in the midst of all the issues and complications, she continued to face everything with a strength, grace, and maturity that were well beyond her tender age of eleven. Doctor H also decided it was past time to get connected with an accredited CF clinic, as we had discussed a little over a year prior. So he reached out to the CF Clinic in Chapel Hill and got Faith on their radar.

Our first appointment in Chapel Hill was January 10th, 2013, and took the *entire* day, as the appointment turned into a revolving door of medical personnel from different departments—nutritionist, social worker, pulmonologist (Doctor G), GI doctor, financial services, nurse for vitals, and respiratory specialist for PFTs—as each had their turn speaking with Faith. It was a wealth of great information, a wonderful team of medical personnel, and I was duly impressed. Faith, however, was very aggravated with how long it took.

After that initial visit, we began alternating appointments between Concord and Chapel Hill. Subsequent appointments in Chapel Hill were still always very long (four to five hours) but not quite as long as that first visit. Faith was always very exhausted and very hungry following these appointments. We got in the habit of bringing snacks along with us since we were always there through the lunch hour and beyond. Following these appointments, we made it a ritual to stop at Panda Garden on US Hwy 15-501 for dinner on the way out of town. It was something Faith and I always looked forward to.

On the five-hour drives to and from Chapel Hill (two-and-a-half hours each way), we would pass the time playing the alphabet game, in which you try to find all the letters of the alphabet—in order—on billboards, street signs, building signs, etc. We would play it over and over and over again. She would get so frustrated because I won about 98% of the time. As soon as I said "z," she immediately was saying "a" to start the next game. Kelsey called once when we were both on "q," so we paused the game to talk with her. No sooner had we said, "time out," than we passed through a little town with "q's" all over the place. By the time we got off the phone with Kelsey, we had passed beyond the little town, and there wasn't a "q" to be found for miles. But, of course, I was the first to find the next one that showed up. Another favorite pastime in the car was to sing loudly, including silly songs such as "A Hole in the Bottom of the Sea." Or Faith would simply watch movies on the portable DVD player.

Faith's first admission into the Chapel Hill Children's Hospital took place in mid-July 2013, when she was admitted for what was called a "tune-up"—a two-week therapy of IV antibiotics and intensified airway clearance just to give her lungs a boost. It was incredibly difficult being so far away from our network of family and friends. And because I could not take the prescribed two weeks off work, I was forced to drive back and forth between Concord and Chapel Hill several times, having to remain in Concord for a couple of days at a time. This would be the first time I ever had to leave Faith alone in the hospital for more than just overnight, especially so far away, and it was a huge adjustment for both of us! After a little over a week—and several back-and-forth trips for me—she appeared to be responding fairly well to the IV treatments, so they decided we could continue them at home for the next week or two. By the end of this tune-up, her lung function was back up to 78%. This would prove to be the last time her FEV1 would be this high and only the beginning of many, many trips to Chapel Hill.

Faith's hospital room, December 2014

7

A Devastating Turn of Events

Ever since Faith was a little girl, she had a passion for dance and wanted to join a studio. As a single mom struggling financially, I was unfortunately unable to afford it for a long time. Finally, when she was almost thirteen years old, I was able to get her signed up for a ballet class with a studio in Charlotte. Being January, half the season was already gone, but they agreed to let her join as long as she could catch up with the routine they were rehearsing. She did great! She danced from the heart with a passion that gave voice to her movements and brought tears to my eyes. The studio also recognized her natural talent and recommended her for their Production Team for the following year.

After that year, however, we moved her to another studio that was closer to home, and where we knew some of the other students through our church. Faith tried out for and made the Competition team, which was the beginning of her amazing journey in the world of competition dance. Her love for dance was dramatically intensified, and it became a huge part of our world. Having not started until she was almost thirteen years old, Faith did not have the benefit of years of technique training, so she had a lot of ground to make up. But her raw talent and her passion were not lost on any of the instructors or the director at the new studio.

In early November of 2014, she went to her first dance convention, called Jump, which would end up being the only convention she would ever attend without the need for oxygen.

A few weeks before the convention, Faith began struggling with a lung infection that just would not respond to antibiotics. She was having difficulty making it through her dance routines without being reduced to wracking coughs. After multiple trips to the local doctor and several rounds of oral antibiotics, things did not seem to be getting any better. And then things took an even more drastic downward spiral.

The Saturday before Thanksgiving, Faith walked in the Concord Christmas Parade with her dance studio. It was a little over two miles and, although it was difficult and tiring on her lungs, she was so excited to have made it the whole way. By Thanksgiving, however, she was feeling extremely fatigued and struggling to even walk up the stairs to the second floor of our house. She would have to stop at the top of the stairs and catch her breath before continuing to her room. By the following Saturday, for the Mt. Pleasant Christmas parade, she was unable to walk it, even though it was a shorter route and she had to ride in the back of the studio's pickup truck. After consulting with Doctor G in Chapel Hill, we scheduled an appointment for December 5th, and it was believed she would most likely need to be admitted to the hospital there to get started on IV antibiotics. I remember telling the director of her dance studio that following a hospital stay and a good round of IV treatments, she would be a completely different person when she returned. I had no idea just how very different things would be.

On December 4th, 2014, the night before going to Chapel Hill, Faith and Jenni met one of Faith's favorite authors, John Greene (author of *The Fault in Our Stars*), who was filming parts of "Paper Towns" at Central Cabarrus High School across from our house. She was able to get his autograph and get a picture together with him.

On December 5th, 2014, we left for Chapel Hill, expecting the typical two-week "tune-up," but things took a dramatic turn for the worse the first night there, following an already extremely stressful and ridiculous day.

When we arrived at the clinic, we faced a series of errors that compounded one on top of the other culminating in Faith being transferred to the Pediatric Intensive Care Unit (PICU) for the next six days due to her oxygen levels being dangerously low.

At check-in, we were given the armband for some ten-year-old boy. When I brought it to the attention of the lady who checked us in, she took the armband back, told us to go on to our appointment, and someone would bring us the correct armband. At the appointment, it was discovered that Faith had lost *fifteen* pounds since her last visit, and her oxygen level was found to be so low that the rest of the appointment did not even take place. Instead, they immediately admitted her and transferred her into a room, so they could get her on a couple liters of oxygen, get her started on airway clearance as soon as possible, and arrange for a PICC line to be placed to begin her IV antibiotics—the sooner the better.

Hours later, after repeated requests, we still had not seen anyone from respiratory to get her airway clearance started. We were also told that, due to Faith's low oxygen levels, someone from anesthesia would be stopping by to check her over before she was taken to have the PICC line put in to ensure her lungs could handle the anesthesia. We still had not received the correct armband.

Eventually, they came to take Faith to have the PICC line put in. No one from anesthesia had been by, no one from respiratory had been by, and still no armband. In my stressed state of mind and assuming that the anesthesiologist was merely going to check her over wherever it was they put in the PICC line, I didn't speak up.

After the procedure, when Faith's lungs were more compromised from the anesthesia that she probably should not have had, it still took hours before anyone from respiratory came to get her started on her airway clearance. Having gotten to the clinic before 8:00 am, it was now well into the evening. While she was finally getting her airway clearance, her oxygen numbers remained way too low. The nurse kept pushing on Faith's fingers to see how quickly the color returned, and Faith's lips were also slightly blue.

The nurse called a "Rapid Response" in which what seemed like thirty people from different departments came pouring into the room to give their assessment and make sure everyone was on the same page for proper action and treatment. There was no warning before the Rapid Response was called, so Faith and I were both very shocked and scared by what was going on.

One of the members of the Rapid Response team included the hospital clergy, who sat down next to me and proceeded to ask what she could do for me. As soon as she started speaking to me, I broke down. And right at that moment, Faith—with her nebulizer sticking out of her mouth—glanced over at me. Seeing me in tears, a wave of fear flashed across her face, and she quickly looked away. Nobody was telling us anything, and we both continued to grow more terrified.

After the doctors and residents from each department had checked her over and given their own assessments to each other, without much fanfare or explanation, Faith was whisked away to the PICU and placed on high levels of high-flow oxygen.

The respiratory therapist who accompanied us unsuccessfully tried to calm Faith's fears by saying she'd had a friend with CF who had gone through this very same thing. She then proceeded to say, "He died when he was nineteen." I was flabbergasted that she would be so insensitive to say such a thing to a scared thirteen-year-old and mom! I requested that this individual have nothing more to do with Faith's care.

After Faith was settled into her PICU room, frightened and upset, she asked me through her tears if she was about to be getting a lung transplant. I told her of course not, that we were not yet at that stage of the game. I assured her there was also a whole lot more that went into getting a transplant, and this was just a complication she would get through.

All our stuff was still upstairs in her previous room, so I had to go and deal with it. What I instead proceeded to do was scream at the poor, sweet nurse who just happened to be there. She got the brunt of my frustration as I exclaimed how poorly everything had been handled from the check-in process to the transfer to PICU (I later profusely apologized to her and baked her a batch of Christmas cookies during one of my treks back home to Concord).

I talked them into letting me keep our personal belongings in that room with the hope that Faith would not be in PICU long — plus, it was one of the biggest rooms, and we wanted to be sure we did not lose it since hospital stays for Faith were typically long and uncomfortable. Again, little did I know just how long this stay would end up being.

I fell asleep in a chair in Faith's PICU room. Early the next morning before the sun was up, I awoke from a fitful sleep to discover all our personal belongings piled up in a corner of the room. I went upstairs to find out what had happened and was told they needed the room for another patient. This, of course, made perfect sense, but I found myself irrationally upset about losing the room. At the same time, I couldn't understand why I was letting myself get so upset about a hospital room while my terrified daughter was on thirteen liters of high-flow oxygen downstairs in the PICU with fevers spiking as high as 103 degrees. I would later conclude that it was only because that seemed to be something I could try and control in a situation of uncontrollable circumstances. A room was the only thing that made any sense to me at the time in a whirlwind of a situation that made no sense.

Faith would remain in PICU for six days until her oxygen levels were stable enough to be moved to a regular room, meaning she had to be off high-flow and in need of no more than four liters.

The company I worked for had just been sold and in an effort to keep my job and hopefully not upset the new management, I had to spend quite a bit of time going back and forth between Chapel Hill and Concord so I could spend some time at the office. When I was not at the office, I was up at 4:00 in the morning in Faith's hospital room working on paperwork so I could spend her waking hours with her. My oldest daughter, Kelsey, worked for me at the time, so we would alternate working in Concord and spending time in Chapel Hill with Faith.

On the fourth day of Faith being in the PICU, I finally found some time to catch my breath and took a few minutes to bring everybody up to speed through a social media post. I found this to be the easiest way to inform multiple people with the latest information at one time without having to make numerous phone calls and texts, which was exhausting and overwhelming.

"To those who have been keeping abreast of the situation with Faith . . . on behalf of her, myself, Kelsey and Jenni, thank you so very much for your prayers, support, words of encouragement, and love! This has been a trying and at times frightening experience, and feeling the arms of the Lord wrapped around us along with the love and prayers from a multitude of people across the country has provided a peace, comfort and strength that I never would've been able to find on my own."

After filling in the details of what was going on with Faith, I concluded the post:

"I had to return to Concord today in order to work, and Kelsey has taken over watch in Chapel Hill for a couple days. I received word from Kelsey a short while ago that they've lowered the oxygen to 5 liters and Faith's saturation is at 97%! This is very good news indeed and an awesome answer to prayer! Please continue to pray for her, the doctors and our family as we still face an uphill battle in restoring her to healthier levels. She's an amazing young lady and has exhibited a phenomenal amount of strength and maturity throughout all of this. God is good . . . all the time . . . even when times are bad and scary and uncertain. Jeremiah 29:11-12 [NIV] – 'For I know the plans I have for you,' declares the Lord, 'plans to prosper you and not to harm you, plans to

give you a hope and a future. Then you will call upon Me and come and pray to Me and I will listen to you.'"

Following five days in PICU, Faith was deemed stable enough to move to a regular room, but there were no beds available. It took an extra day before that would happen, but she was thankfully no longer considered an ICU patient.

After being transferred to a regular room, Faith showed small signs of improvement. However, it was very slow going, and the need for oxygen continued to be a problem. They tried to wean her off the oxygen, but she just couldn't seem to get below four liters before her O2 saturation levels would drop too low. She also developed a blood clot in her arm related to the PICC line, so they had to remove the first PICC line and replace it with a new one in the opposite arm. Faith and I were very apprehensive about the procedure because we believed the PICC line procedure when she was first admitted con-tributed greatly to the crisis that resulted in her being whisked down to the PICU. The difference this time would of course be the near week and a half of IV antibiotics and intensive airway clearance behind her, putting her lungs in a much better place than they had been when she was first admitted. She was also in much better spirits, having received a visit from her friends, Lance and Roz, the day before, and was in a slightly better frame of mind to handle concerning news. Fortunately, the procedure went well.

Unfortunately, however, Faith had to be placed on blood thinner injec-tions in her stomach twice a day for the next three months to ensure the blood clot went away as well as keep more from forming. These were very painful and would prove to be quite traumatic for her.

On December 20th, 2014—day fifteen in the hospital—it began to snow in Chapel Hill, as Faith's hospital stay continued with no end in sight. She was doing better but still on oxygen, and they told us she would need to be off oxygen for at least twenty-four hours before they would send her home. She had gotten down to one-and-a-half liters for most of the previous day but had to be put back up to three liters overnight. Christmas in the hospital was looking more and more like a high possibility.

Sadly, we were unable to get Faith home for Christmas which devastat-ed her. So, in order to try and bring as much Christmas cheer as we could, we decided to bring Christmas to Faith! Kelsey and Jenni bought a small artificial tree, brought some of our ornaments and our stockings from home, decorated the room with lights and Christmas decorations, and brought in all the gifts, placing them under the tree. As Jenni would point out in a social media post, the Shaw family wasn't going to let a hospital stay get in the way of our Christmas! We had our traditional Christmas morning coffee cake baked at the Ronald McDonald House where I was staying. We also enjoyed a complete ham dinner with all the fixings selflessly provided by Kelsey's and Jenni's dad, my ex-husband, Roger. The nursing staff and doctors all told us it was their favorite room to visit because it was so festive. We spent the day with several family members, opening gifts, enjoying wonderful food, and playing games. Under the circumstances, it turned out to be a beautiful Christmas filled with lots of joy, fun, and love.

On December 29th, when it became apparent that the only thing now keeping Faith in the hospital was the oxygen need, the medical team decided she could be discharged. Faith and I could not contain our excitement that we would get to ring in the New Year at home! She was still on oxygen (less than 1 liter during the day!) and would require several more weeks of IV antibiotics, physical therapy, and other treatments. But they felt she was stable enough to continue in the comfort of our own home where we would finally get to sleep in our own beds, be with family and friends, gradually return to a somewhat normal life, and I would no longer have to drive two hours one way to get to work.

So, on December 30th, 2014, Faith was finally able to come home. In addition to the IV medications, she was also still on blood thinner injections in her stomach twice a day and oxygen 24/7 with a new large piece of equipment called an oxygen concentrator. Even given all the challenges and stress of the preceding month, it was wonderful to finally be home in our own beds. The following night, we had a "sleepover" in my room and watched the ball drop, hoping and praying the new year would bring rapid healing and much better times ahead.

We drove back and forth to Chapel Hill once a week for the next couple of months as they continued to monitor her progress. Because of the severe lung infection, her lung function had now dropped to 32% from the 78% it had been before November. She continued to attend dance so she would not fall any further behind on the competition routines. She would stand in the back of the room tethered to her oxygen tank doing as much of the dances as she could.

Around the third week of January, the first battle since leaving the hospital was conquered as they determined that Faith could discontinue the IV antibiotics. Her white blood cell count was normal, meaning the antibiotics had completed their mission, and the PICC line was removed. Her FEV1 score, however, was still very low, which surprised Doctor G given her apparent improvement otherwise.

The following week at her hematology appointment, Faith was devastated to find out that the blood clot wasn't completely gone, and she would need to continue the blood thinner injections for the time being.

In early February, battle number two was done and won. Faith's blood clot was shown to be completely gone, so they discontinued the blood thinner injections. They also decided that the weekly follow-up visits we had been doing since her discharge at the end of December could be dropped back to monthly visits. But along with the victories came some crushing news. Because Faith's lung function was still in the low thirties, Doctor G informed her that she would most likely not be up to competition level that year. Faith refused to accept not being able to dance, no matter what. After all the years she had wanted to dance but couldn't because of finances, she was not about to let "something like stupid CF" keep her from dancing now that she was finally at a studio she loved and part of the competition team.

While she continued her dance classes at the back of the room, she and her physical therapist also worked extremely hard with very specific goals in mind to see if they could get her to where she could dance. Her physical therapist cleared her to dance *ONE WEEK* before the first performance! She was still on oxygen full-time, so she would have to wear it right up to the point they were to go on stage, dance her heart out without her supplied oxygen, then put it back on immediately after dancing to recover. I will never forget how, at that first performance, she flew across the stage with the biggest smile on her face. In some small way, on some small level, she had beaten cystic fibrosis, at least temporarily.

At the next month's follow-up appointment, with the improvements

Faith seemed to be making and the fact that she was cleared to dance, Doctor G was expecting to see vast improvement in her FEV1 score. However, after seeing it still in the low thirties, Doctor G pulled me into another room, while Faith talked to another member of the medical team, to give me the devastating news there now appeared to be permanent lung damage. Her lung function was probably as good as it was ever going to get again, and the words "lung transplant" were tossed out for the first time as a reality. Most of that conversation remains foggy to me now. I remember asking many questions, but can't remember a single one. The only thing that remains clear is the pit in my gut knowing we had to go back into the other room and broach the subject of an eventual lung transplant with Faith.

Faith and I spent the next week talking and praying with the family before finally putting out a call for fervent prayer via social media on March 14th, 2015. Even though Faith had been gradually improving over the past months, growing stronger and overcoming challenges one by one, the challenge of coming off oxygen was slower than hoped for or anticipated. That, combined with her FEV1 score and permanent lung damage placing her in the transplant range, had me crying out for a miracle. Firmly believing in the power of prayer, I asked anyone and everyone to join us in that cry. I knew I served an awesome God who was the Great Physician and knew that, even when I couldn't begin to understand, He had His hand all over the situation and was still in the business of miracles. A couple of dear sweet friends reminded me that these miracles don't always come in the way we may envision, ask, or expect. But they are miracles, nonetheless. And although the unknown, uncertain future was scary, I was also excited to see how God would work in and through the situation.

One such miracle was that Faith would spend the next *four* years dancing with 32-34% lung function, continuing to press on and fight to live the life she felt worthwhile.

Following World's Dance Championship, August 2018

8

Saved By Dance

Faith's favorite genre of dance was contemporary, closely followed by lyrical. She also participated in jazz, hip-hop, and pointe, although hip-hop proved to be more difficult for her given the condition of her lungs. The only genre she did not do was tap.

Each year in February, Faith's studio would hold a Showcase, which was very similar to a recital. They would perform all their dances for the upcoming competition season before an audience of family and friends. It was a great way to work out any bugs, adjustments, and nerves about performing on stage before the actual competitions began. It was also a great way for the studio to show love to the community. They would hold a raffle where half the proceeds would go to the competition team to help cover that year's competition expenses, and the other half would be donated to a charity or cause. In 2015, they chose Faith to be the recipient of the charitable half of the proceeds to help cover medical expenses related to her battle with CF. It was a beautiful and much-appreciated gesture.

For the Showcase and the first competition the following week, Faith was still saddled with being on oxygen full time. But she performed amazingly and with such an indescribable joy that was evident in her every movement and by the smile brightening up the entire room. That overwhelming joy was shared by me, her sisters, and all who knew her as we watched her sail victoriously across the stage and virtually fly through the air with each leap. Her resilience and consistent ability to always push through and press on was nothing short of awe-inspiring.

In early April 2015, we experienced the joy of battles being won once again. At her appointment in Chapel Hill, Faith's weight was up five pounds, no small feat for her as her body now used most of its calories just to try and breathe. The oxygen requirements also netted a huge victory — she was still required to be on two liters for sleeping until they could schedule her for another sleep study, but other than needing to be on one liter for exercise and physical therapy, she could discontinue using oxygen during the day while at rest! Her new pulmonologist, Doctor D (Doctor G had sadly moved to another state), was very pleasantly surprised by this turn of events and attributed the improvement to Faith's dancing. They were not expecting this kind of improvement to happen. In fact, Doctor D shared with me that they had fully expected Faith to be back in the hospital within six months following her month-long stay. But her fight and determination were too great to let that happen.

This fight and determination got her through that very challenging first year of competition, and she proved herself in many ways—not only to others but to herself as well. Toward the end of the season, when one of the dancers left the studio shortly before the Nationals competition, Faith's confidence and skill had grown so much that she asked to fill in on one of the dances that would otherwise have to be completely reworked. So, while everyone else on the team had been performing the routine the entire season, Faith learned the dance in just four weeks, and she killed it at Nationals! It was so exciting to have a victory that was unrelated to just her health, but also with something she so deeply loved!

But as hard as she tried to not let her health get in the way of her dancing, she also knew her body so well that she was fully aware when it needed rest, or her lungs were struggling more than normal. At one competition during her third year of dance, she sadly pulled herself out of one of the group dances because she did not feel her lungs could handle it. We later discovered the portable oxygen concentrator had not been working properly, and she wasn't getting enough oxygen delivered overnight, adversely affecting her lung capacity the following day.

In the spring of 2016, I put together a press release as I attempted to make Faith's incredible story known.

NORTH CAROLINA TEEN LITERALLY DANCES FOR HER LIFE

Faith, a 14-year-old from North Carolina, loves to dance. She dances on her studio's Competition Team and dreams of one day dancing professionally.

But Faith also has Cystic Fibrosis, a genetic disease affecting the lungs and pancreas causing poor weight gain and frequent lung infections, and for which there is presently no cure. In December 2014, she got a lung infection so severe that she was in the hospital for the entire month and wound up with permanent lung damage.

With her lung function at a new norm of 32-34% and nearing lung transplant range, Faith was told by doctors in early 2015 that she would not be up to competition level that year. At first, devastated by this news, Faith grew more and more determined to not let CF keep her from pursuing her dreams. After working very hard with her physical therapist, she was cleared for the 2015 Competition season one week before the team's first performance. In July her doctor expressed pleasant surprise that Faith hadn't been back in the hospital by then, as had been fully expected, and attributed a lot of it to dance, at which point Faith turned to her mother and said, "Dance saved my life!"

Although the lung function remains a struggle, Faith continues to dance with the Competition Team. This year she and her instructor even choreographed a solo for her—with her oxygen tank built into the choreography—so that, through dance, she could tell her story and share her struggles with CF. She still requires oxygen to sleep at night, as well as for recovery during rehearsals and following routines at Competitions; but through her perseverance and continuing to be active with dance, she has been able to keep her lung function from dipping any lower, thereby holding off a lung transplant as long as possible.

But even with her diligence and determination, the day will still come when the damage in her lungs catches up with her and the transplant will be inevitable. And dance will once again prove to be paramount in saving her life. The strength in her body that she has been building through her hours and hours of dance will be vital in the surgery, recovery, and potentially anti-rejection process. And looking forward to the opportunity to dance freely, able to breathe through healthy lungs, gives her the strength of mind to keep pressing on towards her dreams.

For the 2015/2016 Competition season, her second year on the competition team, Faith wanted to use dance to tell her story of living with cystic fibrosis. Choosing a song called "Breathe" by *Superchick*, she and her dance instructor, Heather, put together a solo complete with her oxygen tank built into the choreography. It was beautiful and heartfelt and brought many people to tears as she danced her story on the stage. Even without the years of technique training, she had a natural talent and passion pouring forth from her heart that was truly unmatched. At one of the competitions that season called "Star Power," she was awarded the "True Inspiration" Judges' Special Award, as well as a score of 4 ¾ stars out of 5. At the end of that year, she was also awarded a scholarship from her studio for the next competition season.

Faith's tenacity and perseverance were also evident at the Showstoppers Convention we attended in Myrtle Beach each January. The convention consisted of back-to-back classes in the different dance genres taught by an array of fabulous instructors, some of whom had been on shows like "Dancing With the Stars" or "So You Think You Can Dance." Faith would push herself to her limits out on the dance floor. When she would feel her oxygen levels start to drop, she would step off to the side of the room and put her oxygen on to recover, many times while continuing to dance the choreography with the rest of the class. This was yet another example of her sheer determination and perseverance as well as her love for dance. She had every excuse to simply sit while she recovered, but she continued to press on. One of her instructors, Fikshun (2012 winner of "So You Think You Can Dance"), had some very inspiring words to say that deeply touched both Faith and me. He said that no matter what hurdles you face in life and what you may be going through, you are **stronger than the struggle**. That really struck a chord with both of us and was something that Faith demonstrated daily in her battle with cystic fibrosis. From that moment on, *"stronger than the struggle"* became one of her mantras and one of our hashtags in all our social media posts and updates.

Faith would continue to prove she was stronger than the struggle as she continued to push on and excel with her dancing. In June of 2016 at Nationals in Myrtle Beach, for the final performance of her solo, "Breathe," Faith received a Platinum award! In December of that year, she gave a beautiful performance, on pointe shoes, as the Dew Drop Fairy in her studio's production of "The Nutcracker."

In the summer of 2017, Faith and I thought it would be fun to enter a pageant together, so on June 30th, we participated in the Harrisburg Miss 4th of July Pageant. Faith decided to also enter the talent competition portion of the pageant and chose to choreograph her own dance. She ended up winning the talent competition and became the "2017 Talent Miss 4th of July Harrisburg!" She was first runner-up in her age category and was awarded the "Best On-Stage Answer" to the question they asked. I, sadly, do not recall either the question that was asked or her answer (for what it's worth, I was also first runner-up in the Sr. Miss category and was awarded "Best Smile.").

For the 2017/2018 competition season, Faith changed to a new studio where many of her high school friends danced. Doctor D came to one of her competitions in Raleigh, and by the end of Faith's solo, Doctor D was sobbing because she understood exactly what it took and how hard Faith had to fight to dance so beautifully with only 32% lung function. The studio owner, seeing Faith's doctor in tears, leaned over to me and asked if that was one of Faith's sisters. I told her no, that was one of Faith's doctors, to which she replied, "*I want a doctor like that!*"

In January 2018, when we attended the Showstoppers Convention again, Faith posted on social media,

"Had such an amazing time this weekend with amazing choreographers! They always inspire me and challenge me to push past my limits. Can't wait for next year!"

Sadly, this would be Faith's final year attending the convention.

In June of 2018, Faith had the pleasure and honor of dancing on the Belk Theater stage in uptown Charlotte for her studio's four recitals throughout an entire weekend! Having seen many plays and performances on that stage over the years, it was such a neat experience for Faith to get to dance on it herself.

In addition to her solo, Faith was involved in the studio's ninety-seven-member production routine and several smaller group dances. She continued to dance her heart out on the stage, giving it everything she had, while someone waited in the wings with her oxygen tank where she would immediately sit down after dancing and put on her oxygen to recover. In some dances in which the choreography had some of the girls briefly leave the stage during the routine, she would put her oxygen on to give herself a quick burst. Sometimes, their group dances were almost back-to-back, and she barely had time to recover and change costumes before having to go right back on stage and give it her all once again. More evidence that her perseverance and determination were truly unmatched.

At one of the competitions, their production number received an invitation to the World's Dance Competition to be held later that year in Secaucus, New Jersey. There was no question that we were going to go! Due to all of Faith's medications, oxygen concentrator, oxygen tanks, percussion vest, and other equipment, flying was not an option, so we decided to make a road trip out of it. On the way, we stopped in Luray, Virginia, and spent a day visiting the Luray Caverns, the Garden Maze, the Cars & Carriage Museum, Toy Town Junction which was a museum of the "toys of yesteryear," and just having an all-around great time together. On the way back, we would take another route and spend a day visiting the sites in Washington, DC.

Day one in The Big Apple was a little overwhelming for me, having never been there, so I relied on my "tour guide," Faith. She did a fantastic job of helping us get around, and we never once got lost!

The following day, their production number competed for the World Championship. They were definitely up against some very stiff competition, and our nerves were quite on edge. The first time they performed their routine would be to qualify for the "Final Five," and they brought down the house! Later that day, the final five routines competed for the title of World's Dance Champion. The fifth-place studio name was read, and our girls were still standing. The fourth-place studio was called out, and Faith's team remained in the running. My heart began pounding faster and harder as the third-place studio was read, and our team was now included in the final two remaining. After a drum roll, the 2018 World's Dance Champion was announced. As Faith's studio's name was read as the winner, the auditorium erupted in cheers and applause. I screamed and clapped so hard that I literally bruised my hand. We celebrated that evening with a wonderful dinner in New York City, and the next day enjoyed taking in a Broadway show with many from her team, as we went to see "The Lion King," my first ever Broadway show actually *on* Broadway.

It was an amazing way to end that competition season, and unbeknownst to us, would be her final bow.

Youtube.com: Piano Tiles 2 Cystic Fibrosis Fundraiser for Faith

9

Fundraising Efforts

The Cystic Fibrosis Foundation holds a number of different fundraisers every year to raise awareness and raise funds for the organization to go towards research, trials, and new treatments. Cystic Fibrosis is considered an orphan disease since there is no government assistance, even though more than 40,000 people in the United States are living with the disease (over 70,000 worldwide), with more than 1,000 new cases every year (If you are interested in learning more about cystic fibrosis and how you can help, please visit cff.org).

In addition to the "65 Roses" campaign, another one of their fundraisers that we as a family participated in for several years is their "Great Strides for Cystic Fibrosis" walk. The first year we took part, in 2009 (Faith, age eight), I signed up very late but managed to raise around $1,500 in just five days! The following year, we surpassed our goal of $7,000 and raised $7,250 (The Concord Great Strides Walk, as a whole, raised more than $30,000!). Each year, we raised a little bit more and had a few more walkers join us until our team went from the original five to well over thirty-five people.

In May of 2018, Faith and I were asked to man the rest stop/water station at the Charlotte Great Strides Walk as representatives for both the Miss Harrisburg 4th of July Court and the Cystic Fibrosis community. The weather started a little gloomy but turned into an absolutely beautiful day for a walk. Faith's competition dance team had initially been scheduled to perform one of their dances, fittingly called "The Cure," to kick off the walk. But the uncertainty of the weather, unfortunately, caused us to take a "better safe than sorry" approach.

The rest stop, located at about the halfway point of the walk, was quiet and peaceful as Faith and I prepared to hand out drinks to the walkers. We even got a great picture with an unexpected passer-by totally unrelated to Great

Strides—Ron Rivera, then head coach of the Carolina Panthers! who was very pleasant, humble, and gracious. I do believe it was more exciting for me than for Faith, but she enjoyed it as well.

Then the chaos ensued. As the walkers began to appear, the quiet and peace were quickly overtaken by more than 1,000 thirsty participants converging on me and Faith all at once! However, through the chaos (and unfortunately running out of drinks before everyone was able to get some), it was amazing and heart-warming to see the sheer number of people who were there to support Cystic Fibrosis, either because they were CFers themselves or were there in honor—or in memory—of someone afflicted by this disease. It touched me deeply to know that each and every person who walked by that table was affected in some way—directly or indirectly—by this disease, and like us, had their own stories of pain and victories, ups and downs, joys and sorrows, and daily struggles! The sense of camaraderie I suddenly felt for this overwhelmingly large group of strangers was uncanny. I wanted to hug them all. But, seeing as I could not even keep up with handing the drinks out, that wasn't quite feasible. Upon returning to "base," it was exciting to find out that this walk had raised $312,382 for cystic fibrosis!

That evening, Faith posted on social media,

"I stride until CF stands for cure found . . . Went to the great strides walk today for Cystic Fibrosis awareness month. Most people know that I have CF, but some of you don't. It is a chronic lung/pancreas disease that makes it difficult to breathe, leads to frequent lung infections and hospital stays, and makes it hard for people to gain weight. Currently, I have 32-34% lung function and use oxygen frequently when dancing and to sleep. There can be many challenges and rough patches, but there are also many blessings that have come from having CF. And I am so lucky for the support I have from all my friends and family."

Another fundraiser Faith got to be a special part of was the 2010 "Kick CF with Jordan Gross" annual kickball tournament, in which many of the Carolina Panthers would play a kickball match against another kickball team and raise funds for the cystic fibrosis foundation. Faith was invited to throw in the "first pitch." It was a beautiful and fun-filled day of meeting Panthers players and getting their autographs. She took pictures with Steve Smith, Sr., Jordan Gross, DeAngelo Williams, Jonathan Stewart, and more. It was so exciting as they announced her name over the loud-speaker and she ran out to the pitcher's mound to roll the ball, which was a straight roll right over home plate. Most of the players autographed the ball and gave it to her as a souvenir. I still have it to this day.

In the spring of 2011, Ms. Smith, the theater teacher at Central Cabarrus High School where my older daughters attended, decided she wanted to do something unique to raise money for our Great Strides team. She decided to hold a two-day camp for young students from fourth through eighth grade. Students from within the high school's theater department along with Ms. Smith offered several workshops on topics such as improvisation, creating a play, making masks, and stage combat. The cost of the camp was $25 per student which included lunch on the second day, with a goal of raising $1,250. The campers were split into two groups, and each group created their own play that was presented to family and friends at the end of the second day.

In 2012, Faith's final year at Rocky River Elementary School, her principal, Principal Lamm, wanted to do something special to honor Faith and her fight with cystic fibrosis. So, after a meeting with him and the local chapter's representative, Gwyn, we decided to have a week-long event called "Change for Cystic Fibrosis." During this week, each classroom would collect change from the students. The student in each grade that brought in the most change by the end of the week would get to join Faith in a kickball game against the teachers, and the teacher of the classroom that raised the most money overall would get to wear jeans the following week. During the fundraiser, the school raised $637.60 in loose change for cystic fibrosis.

In 2015, my oldest brother, David, came up with a unique fundraiser idea to benefit not only the Cystic Fibrosis Foundation but Faith directly. He had discovered the phone application called Piano Tiles, to which he had become quite addicted and grown quite good. He wanted to come up with a way that, as he called it, his new-found skill could benefit his niece. So he decided to put on an online "concert," playing each of the Piano Tiles songs he knew once through and see how far he could get—no matter how long it took him. Donors could give a lump-sum donation or make a pledge based on the number of notes David successfully played. Half the money raised from his Piano Tiles "concert" would go to the Cystic Fibrosis Foundation, and half would be used for setting up a medical fund to help cover the costs of Faith's eventual double-lung transplant.

In December 2015, we made a video so Faith could introduce herself and tell her story in her own words, and Uncle David could explain how the fundraiser would work (to view the complete video, reference the YouTube link in the Appendix).

In the video, after Faith and Uncle David introduced themselves, Faith went on to explain what cystic fibrosis was and how it affected her. She shared that the simple act of breathing, which most people take for granted, was a daily struggle for her and felt like she was breathing through a straw. She then described the never-ending cycle of doctor visits, hospital stays, multiple daily medications and treatments, and the daily nutritional requirements. She then discussed how CF affected her daily life, most notably dance, followed by interviews with her dance studio's owner and her dance instructor:

FAITH: *"Living with CF makes many of the most ordinary activities much more difficult—Such as simply walking around the mall with friends or joining in on recreation activities at church, school, or camp. But, for me, one of the most devastating activities CF complicates is dance. Dance is my passion and brings me a lot of joy! I've been especially involved in competitions, recitals,* *showcases, and conventions through this past year. I typically spend three to four nights a week at the studio and hope to pursue dance as a career!"*

LAUREN, OWNER/DIRECTOR/INSTRUCTOR AT DANCE TRAP STU-, **DIO:** *"The first time that I heard about Faith, one of the moms from the studio that knew her and her mom from church told me about Faith and told me about—kind of told me about her story and told me that she had cystic fibrosis and that she just wanted to dance! And I said right then and there if that—if she wants to dance, then this little girl will dance! She pushed herself so hard, and she worked so hard. It was just very evident that she had a drive within her and a passion within her to dance; and so, it's just been truly an honor to be a part of her story."*

HEATHER, INSTRUCTOR AT DANCE TRAP STUDIO: *"I've been a dance teacher for a really long time, and have taught for many, many years. I have to say that I am really inspired and really impressed with how she deals with her cystic fibrosis. She pushes no matter what, and then she'll take a minute, she'll put on her oxygen, and then she'll come right back as soon as she's ready."*

FAITH: *"Although I'm doing much better now, and only need oxygen at night and during exercise, at one of the appointments in February, they realized I had irreversible lung damage. With my lung function at around 32-34%, I was told I'm now in lung transplant range and could potentially need to be placed on the donor list in the very near future. At this time, we were nearing our first performance of competition season for dance. And the doctor said I would not be up to competition level this year. That was a crushing blow and completely broke my heart. But I decided I was not willing to accept that. I had worked too hard to get where I was and became determined to not let CF keep me from pursuing my dreams. I worked very closely with my physical therapist and set very specific goals. I kept dancing even when I wasn't fully off of oxygen yet. I'd still go to class and do what I could in the back while still on my oxygen. Then as I got stronger, I started dancing without my oxygen and put it on for recovery. My physical therapist cleared me for the competition season one week before the first performance. During competitions, someone waits backstage with my oxygen, so I can recover following a routine. At an appointment in July, my doctor said she was surprised I hadn't been back in the hospital yet and actually attributed a lot of that to dance."*

HEATHER, INSTRUCTOR AT DANCE TRAP STUDIO: *"It's so inspiring* *to see somebody who is going through such an ordeal . . . She makes it look so easy when she's here. She literally dances, she puts on her oxygen, then she goes back. While at home, she has like a million treatments a day. She has all these things that she has to do, all these medications she has to do, and she's always in good spirits. She always is happy, and she always comes in with a smile on her face. And that's really awesome and inspiring. I am really honored and excited to be able to teach her, and we've decided we're going to put together a solo for her so that we can tell her story through dance because she loves to dance so much. And I can't wait for us to finish it and put it out there and share who she is and share what an awesome and amazing young girl she is."*

LAUREN, OWNER/DIRECTOR/INSTRUCTOR AT DANCE TRAP STUDIO: *"I know that God brought her here to us to build our faith—no pun intended—but to build our faith in Him and what He can do and what He will do. It's been an honor to stand with her and her mom in prayers and to see God work in her life and to see how God works through her to touch other people's lives. It's just really awesome to see how she has progressed in the setbacks that she has had and how she has pushed through and overcome those and kind of gone against the odds and come out with her head held high. And it's just amazing. It's such a cool thing to watch and to be a part of."*

FAITH: *"Although I've made a lot of progress and improved since December, my lung function continues to remain very low. My doctor says although I'm not quite sick enough yet to be placed on the donor list for a lung transplant, she says it could realistically happen within the next 6-12 months. Once I'm on the list and we receive the call that lungs are available, which could happen at any time day or night, we have to be at the hospital in Chapel Hill within two hours. Following the lung transplant, we must also remain local for three months, which means my mom will have to take a leave of absence from work, and we will have to find a temporary place to live. But—through it all . . . I continue to dream . . . and I continue to live . . . and continue to pursue my goals . . . and continue to hope and pray for a cure."*

This was followed by Uncle David explaining how the Piano Tiles "concert" would work and when it was going to take place. His goal was to reach 100,000 points—or notes—in one sitting, which he said could take up to 7 hours or more to accomplish, and he was taking pledges based on that goal. He introduced the GoFundMe page we had set up for Faith, explaining that 50% of the proceeds would go to help with the overwhelming medical expenses and potential double-lung transplant for Faith, and 50% would go to the CF Foundation. He started things off by making a $500 pledge himself.

A couple of days after the fundraiser, and after Uncle David was able to get some much-needed rest, he posted the following message on Facebook,

> *"It was admittedly a lot tougher than I had thought it would be, but we made it. The 'Piano Tiles 2 Marathon for Faith Shaw and the Cystic Fibrosis Foundation' ended up lasting 19 hours and 7 minutes. . . . [W]e raised (about) $8,000 for Faith and CF and I wanted to thank everyone that contributed to this very worthy and needed cause.*

> *"After CFF has been given their [portion] of the proceeds raised from the marathon, www.gofundme.com/lungs4faith will remain open for further contributions, all of which will be for Faith when the time comes that those funds will be needed. . . .*

> *"And a special thanks to Faith. Thank you for openly sharing your story and for helping to bring awareness to a disease that affects thousands of young people and is desperately in need of a cure. Good luck with the Nationals in your dance competition coming up soon here. You are an amazing dancer and a wonderful person. I hope this is only the beginning of the long and beautiful dancing career that you dream of. And I sincerely believe that you will make that dream come true. I am so proud of you."*

Thus, "**Lungs4Faith**" was born.

Following the Piano Tiles fundraiser and the CF Foundation being given their portion, **Lungs4Faith** became our family's fundraising campaign to help offset the costs of medical expenses associated with cystic fibrosis and the double-lung transplant that was undoubtedly on the horizon—and eventually the trip to Hawaii to spread Faith's ashes, honoring one of her final wishes after she had passed away.

In the spring of 2017, Faith's ninth-grade year, the Student Council at her high school put together a fundraiser led by Faith's dear friend, Abby, selling "Breathe" t-shirts and "Team Faith" wristbands. Donations made by local businesses helped cover the cost of the shirts, and Abby covered the cost of the wristbands. By the end of the semester, they had raised a total of $1,712.00 for Faith.

On March 3rd, 2019, a hair salon in Palm Coast, Florida, called Reflections Hair Salon, gave up their day off for a fundraiser to benefit Faith. As explained by my stepdad in a Facebook post, Reflections Salon *"featured $15 haircuts, raffled items donated by local businesses, and baked goods, with all proceeds going to Faith's cause. Many customers gave additional donations. In four hours, Reflections raised $1,747. Words CANNOT fully express our gratitude."*

In April of 2019, three months after Faith's double-lung transplant, North Carolina State's Alpha Phi Omega (APO) chapter hosted a three-hour event called "Pie-A-Brother," in which anyone could throw a pie at the face of an APO member for just $3. In addition to the pie throwing, they also sold succulents for $2 each. All proceeds went to **Lungs4Faith** to help cover the ever-growing medical expenses and costs associated with living in Chapel Hill. In just three hours, they raised $342. With Raleigh being so close to where we were in Chapel Hill, Faith was allowed to attend this event and even got to throw one of the pies herself.

Following Faith's death, one of Faith's friends from church, Taylor, designed a t-shirt that had "Faith" on the front with "Faith is Bigger than Fear" on the back. She made these shirts, in either purple or gray, available to anyone wanting to buy one. From the sale of these t-shirts, she raised $900 which I was able to put toward the remaining medical bills.

Although many of the fundraisers mentioned here benefitted Faith and the family directly, the CF Foundation fundraisers benefit the thousands of patients and families affected by this deadly disease in phenomenal ways. Today, because of people like you and your generous support, significant progress has been made toward new medicines and treatments, helping those with CF live longer and longer. If you are interested in finding a Great Strides Walk near you or finding other ways in which you can help, visit cff.org and click the "Get Involved" or "Donate" button. We can't stop until CF stands for "cure found!"

PART TWO

Faith's Final Journey

Early December 2018

10

The Road to Transplant

The years 2015 and most of 2016 proved to be victory years for Faith, maintaining her new baseline of 32% lung function, no hospital stays, and doing very well in dance, especially under the current medical circumstances. In early December 2015, through a social media post, she recalled how drastically these medical circumstances changed her life.

"One year ago, my life changed a whole bunch. I had been feeling sick and then eventually I couldn't walk for two minutes without getting way out of breath. Eventually, I was admitted into the hospital, December 5th, 2014. I was going in for a little extra boost with treatments and antibiotics .. little did we know that 'little boost' was going to be for a whole month (through Christmas), a week in PICU, and several months on oxygen. Living with CF, I knew of dangers of getting sick and going to the hospital and everything but I never expected that. So many days, so much pain (physically and mentally), and not a thing to do but just push through it. I know you may see me and think 'Ok, cool she's just a regular girl.' But on the inside, I'm much different. I can't even remember how it feels to get a nice deep breath of fresh air anymore .. but you know what? This is my life. I was given this life for a reason and even though I don't see that reason sometimes and I feel like giving up I also remind myself that I can have a chance, I just need to let loose and give myself to God and let him guide me. Right now I'm in possible double lung transplant range and we're seeing if that is a path I should go down. . . . I also want to say thank you for anyone who has helped me through this in the past and anyone who is now. God bless!"

But in late 2016, the victory years would come to a close as Faith would begin another once-a-year series of hospital stays and IV treatments, which would ultimately lead to meeting the transplant team in Chapel Hill.

Throughout her life, dealing with constant infections and challenges, Faith had grown very skilled at being in tune with and "reading" her body, and she could tell when it felt like an infection was brewing. Late October 2016, upon recognizing the beginnings of some of the feelings she'd had two years earlier that had put her in PICU and the month-long hospital stay, Faith felt it might be a good idea to get some additional treatments and IV therapy to keep things from taking a turn for the worse. After consulting with Doctor D in Chapel Hill, we all agreed that taking some aggressive, proactive measures would definitely be the best course of action. Fortunately, at that time, Doctor D was able to coordinate with Doctor H, Faith's Concord pulmonologist, who then coordinated with Levine Children's Hospital in Charlotte, so we could have her treated locally instead of going all the way to Chapel Hill. With her compromised lung function, time was never wasted, and she was admitted the next day to get started on IV antibiotics and intensified airway clearance. She was discharged a week later to continue the treatments and therapies at home.

Even after these treatments and therapies, things quickly took another downward turn just a few short weeks later. Faith's lung function was back down, even though she'd been diligently on top of her airway clearance. Her weight was down, even though she'd been consuming a large quantity of calories. Her ability to absorb oxygen appeared to be deteriorating, and she was facing the possibility of being back on supplied oxygen full-time.

Over the next few weeks, we tried oral antibiotics, increased airway clearance, added oxygen use during at least one of Faith's vest treatments as well as during the half-hour car ride to dance, all in hopes of bringing all her numbers back up. Doctor D told me that if Faith weren't Faith and didn't do all she did and work as hard as she did trying to keep herself healthy and active, we would have more than likely seen her on the transplant list a year and a half prior. Doctor D pointed out how proud she was of Faith and that this was just the nature of CF and the severity of Faith's lung disease. Eventually, no matter what one does and how hard one works to do everything right, there comes a time when things continue to go in the wrong direction. She was hopeful things could still be turned around but said it was a reminder of how precarious a ledge upon which Faith resided. Faith was very down about the circumstances and the potential of having to once again lug around an oxygen tank.

But on January 3rd, 2017, after the follow-up appointment in Chapel Hill, I was excited to post,

"There will be a day when Faith has to go back on oxygen full time, but TODAY IS NOT THAT DAY!! Her lung function was still lower than hoped for but was acceptable. Her weight was way up—higher than it's ever been—and her O2 saturation was back to baseline!"

Following some chest X-rays at an appointment in August 2017, Faith and I were very concerned with how they looked. I reached out to Doctor D wondering if this signified a new "turn" in her condition and meant we would be seeing a more rapid decline in her lungs. Faith was also wondering if it could be turned around. Doctor D's reply was encouraging even given the current state of Faith's lungs.

". . . To me, her Xray looks quite similar to last year's . . . I don't expect more rapid decline based on Faith's Xray, and while she's had some more bumps in the road over the past year, she is remarkably stable given her current lung function. Everybody is different, but many people with FEV1 in the 30s are in the hospital/on IV antibiotics 3-4 times per year or more. She is working hard to take great care of herself, and, importantly, living her life and embracing all the great things that come along with being a teenager. . . . I feel like Faith has many other indicators of relative stability, and honestly thriving given that she has a serious illness . . . There's so much accommodation that happens with CF – Faith's 'norm' has changed dramatically over the past few years, and she has adapted to her current baseline. So have you. And so have I. . . ."

In September of that year, she did start to feel less than stellar once again and expressed some of her frustration regarding her medical circumstances in an English writing assignment.

"I hate storms. They terrify me and are pretty annoying. Whenever there's a storm, I cuddle under the blankets in my bed and turn Netflix on to distract me. That's usually what I do if there's a storm in my life, physically or emotionally. I feel it's easier to just pull up the covers and not think about it. But this storm is different. I have to think about it. I have to think about what I would do in certain emergent situations. But what if I don't want to think about it? Can't I just hold on to the hope that it won't come my way?"

Unfortunately, her medical storms were unavoidable. At the beginning of October, she was once again admitted to Levine Children's Hospital for IV antibiotics and increased airway clearance treatments.

Other than being much closer to home, another positive to being at Levine (and something that was much more appreciated by me than by Faith) was that her floor was the Carolina Panthers floor. The day after Faith's admission, Graham Gano and Michael Palardy of the Carolina Panthers paid a visit to the patients on the floor. Unfortunately, due to contact precautions, they were not allowed to go into Faith's room. But I was more than happy to make the "sacrifice" of getting a picture with them! I even happened to be wearing one of my Panthers T-shirts that day. They then gave me some Panthers merchandise to give to Faith which, again, I appeared to appreciate more than she did.

A few days later, Faith was visited by her Youth pastor, Aaron, his wife, Jenna, and a large group of the youth for an impromptu "hospital room party," along with Faith's sisters and her niece and nephew. Thirteen people in all. Jenna picked up Taco Bell for everyone on the way so Faith could get a break from hospital food. The following day, Faith was discharged to continue IV therapy and treatments at home.

The following week at her follow-up appointment in Chapel Hill, Faith was thrilled to have her IV treatments done, her annual labs completed, her numbers looking good, and the PICC line removed. She was even more excited to finally get to eat as she'd had to fast for her annual glucose test. And mom was no less hungry! Whenever Faith would have to fast, I would always fast too because I didn't feel right eating anything in front of her. So onward we went to our favorite post-Chapel Hill doctor visit restaurant, Panda Garden.

In February 2018, after a few good months, Faith spiked a fever of 103, and her oxygen saturation was too low for comfort. I took her to Urgent Care where we were immediately redirected to the ER. The doctors at first thought she was once again going to have to be admitted to the hospital, but after consulting with Doctor D, they decided admission would not be necessary. Her fever came down, her oxygen came up a little, and they put her on Tamiflu and an oral antibiotic.

At the beginning of September 2018, I ended up at the ER thinking I was having a heart attack. After several tests and an ultrasound, they discovered I had gallstones that were causing such intense pain I needed two doses of morphine before I felt any relief. After getting home several hours later, Faith and I discussed the pain I had felt and its location. She realized it was almost identical in severity and location to her pains which had made us previously think she was dealing with an ulcer. I contacted Doctor D, and we agreed to further dive into the possibility of potential gallstones at Faith's next appointment.

In October 2018, however, the gallstone issue was forgotten as Faith told me her chest was starting to "feel tight," and that it was probably time to check in with Chapel Hill for another tune-up. She wanted to wait until after the end of October, however, because she was a maid of honor in Jenni's upcoming wedding. She also wanted to enjoy the Trunk or Treat/Fall Festival at our church the weekend after the wedding as well as trick-or-treating with friends on the 31st. I touched base with Doctor D to get the ball rolling for a potential November 1st admission.

The wedding proved to be an incredibly beautiful, fun-filled, and eventful weekend with lots of activity and very little sleep. This appeared to take more of a toll on Faith than she had anticipated, and she realized going to the hospital sooner rather than later was in her best interest, even if it meant foregoing the other activities she had wanted to enjoy. After another consultation with Doctor D, she was admitted into the hospital on October 25th. Little did we know, this would be the beginning of the path that would lead to her need for a double-lung transplant.

Faith's first night in the hospital was very rough as she unexpectedly had a respiratory distress event, and her oxygen numbers took a drastic dip. They placed her on high levels of oxygen and called in a Rapid Response, which brought back way too many memories from the last time a Rapid Response had been called. She was very close to once again being admitted to PICU -- an all-too-familiar scene from four years prior that remained devastatingly fresh in our minds. With the high-flow oxygen at its highest level allowed on the regular floor, she thankfully stabilized enough to stave off relocation to PICU but remained under close watch by the PICU team. She felt somewhat better the following day but remained on oxygen even when awake, much to her disappointment, anger, and dismay. Given the complications, they delayed putting in a PICC line for a few days until she had become stable enough to tolerate the procedure.

Faith remained in the hospital until the early part of November, at which point she was discharged to continue IV medications at home. But even after two weeks of IV antibiotics, things were not only *not* getting better, they had gotten worse. Her white blood cell count was elevated, she began spiking fevers, and she had a terrible rash and itching all over her body. Plus, she was still on four liters of oxygen 24/7. Doctor D thought that perhaps an additional week of IV medications might be needed. To avoid the trek back to Chapel Hill, Doctor D arranged to have Faith admitted into the Levine Children's Hospital in Charlotte to see if they could determine the cause of her medical condition heading in the wrong direction and if a changeup in the medication was necessary. On a phone call with me, through both of our tears, Doctor D confided in me that we might have now reached the point where we needed to seriously think about a lung transplant.

I reached out to the school administration and Faith's teachers to alert them to what we were facing in hopes of seeking their advice and help in how it all related to her schooling. The homework output had been less than desired, and I felt they needed to know that not only was the lung infection alone very draining, leaving her with limited energy, but the IV medications and medication schedule had also taken a heavy toll—on both her and me! But the emotional toll it took on her was heartbreaking. She was very anxious to get back into school, dance, church, time with friends—to all of life's normal activities. She was very discouraged and more than a little afraid of what the future was looking like.

The supplemental oxygen situation was another area of concern I needed to discuss with the school, since she was currently on oxygen 24/7. If it was going to be the new norm, we would need to figure out if there was a way for her to continue school *on* campus with multiple oxygen tanks, since one tank lasted only about 90 minutes.

The largest concern brought about by the inability for her to wean off the supplemental oxygen, however, was what it meant regarding the progression of her disease. Doctor D was afraid Faith's disease was finally catching up with her, and we would be facing the most difficult time she'd ever had to face—physically *and* emotionally. Doctor D stated that if her oxygen needs remained unchanged by Faith's next appointment, which was only a few days away, it would probably be time to begin talking with the transplant team. She believed a lung transplant was realistically in Faith's future before she was done with high school—a very sobering thought given the fact that Faith was at that point a junior.

The team at Levine, however, concluded that Faith was having an allergic reaction to one of the IV antibiotics. Once they stopped that medicine, there was an almost immediate improvement, and she was able to leave the hospital two days later with no PICC line, no IV medication, and NO OXYGEN! I confidently—and, admittedly, almost smugly—felt that Doctor D was "obviously" incorrect about it being time to consider a transplant.

The week of Thanksgiving, Faith started having the belly pain we had previously thought was consistent with an ulcer but now believed could be gallstones. The pain was so bad this time, she wasn't even able to enjoy Thanksgiving dinner. The Sunday after Thanksgiving I noticed that she was looking jaundiced. We were fortunate to have an ER across from our neighborhood, so I took her there right away where it was discovered she did indeed have gallstones, as well as a blockage and infection in her bile duct. They told me that if I had waited even one more day, we would have been looking at a very different story.

Faith was once again transferred to Levine—making it the third hospital admission in five weeks—so they could perform an endoscopy and remove the gallstones. They also began discussions about potential surgery to remove her gallbladder to hopefully stave off any future gallstone complications.

Earlier that year, I had surprised Faith with November 30th VIP tickets to see *for KING & COUNTRY*, one of her all-time favorite Christian bands. Seeing as the concert was only four days away, we made sure that everyone from nurses to doctors to respiratory to anesthesiologists—everyone with whom we came in contact—knew we had a very big day on Friday. We were assured that since the endoscopy was so early in the week and would be a quick recovery, attending the concert should not be a problem. The endoscopy went very well, and they were able to successfully clear out what had been causing the blockage and the jaundice. I found myself oddly praising the Lord for the jaundice that had prompted me to take her to the ER because the doctor said there was an infection beginning and had the procedure not been done that day, Faith would have become very sick very quickly over the next day or two and would have been in a *very* bad situation. The surgeon was then scheduled to come and speak with us the next day to discuss when we could bring her back in to remove her gallbladder, most likely within the next week or two. But, again, things did not always go according to plan.

The next morning while I was at work, I received a call from the surgeon telling me they had determined Faith's gallbladder actually needed to come out right away. So less than twelve hours after putting her under anesthesia for the endoscopy, they put her under again for a second surgery. When Faith expressed concern about the *for KING & COUNTRY* concert, she was told that the recovery from this surgery should also be pretty quick, and the concert should still be a go. We would quickly discover, however, that putting her under anesthesia twice in less than twelve hours would prove to be too much for her already damaged lungs.

Following the surgery, Faith posted on social media,

"This past month has been a roller coaster. I've been admitted to the hospital 3 times in a 5 week period and have had 2 surgeries in the last 2 days. As most of you know I have cystic fibrosis which sometimes results in having to go to the hospital for IV antibiotics to take care of lung infections. I usually start the IV antibiotics in the hospital for about a week then finish them at home for another week. This time when I left the hospital I was still on oxygen full time and seemed to be getting worse instead of better over the next couple weeks. This led to the second hospital stay where they found I was having an allergic reaction to the antibiotics. When we stopped the antibiotics, my oxygen levels went back to normal and I was discharged from the hospital again. A couple days after the second hospital stay I started feeling a lot of pain. The pain wasn't going away and I became jaundiced on Sunday so went to the ER. They then sent me to the hospital where we discovered I would need a procedure the next day to take care of what was causing the pain. During this procedure, they discovered I would need immediate surgery to remove my gallbladder. Currently, I'm still at the hospital recovering from surgery but hope to be able to go home tomorrow. It's been a very difficult 5 weeks and I really appreciate all the thoughts and prayers."

The following day, even though she was told she could go home if she chose, Faith decided it would be best to stay one more night to get the extra airway clearance since it was hard to use her percussion vest due to the pain following the gallbladder surgery. Being discharged on Thursday would still allow us to make the *for* KING & COUNTRY concert on Friday, so we were feeling pretty excited about that. Using social media, I updated the "masses" with details regarding the two procedures and how Faith was doing, then went on to say:

"She'll be in the hospital one more night to help with balancing her airway clearance and pain management, then should get to go home tomorrow (Thursday)! Thanks again and again for all the prayers, visits, and sweet messages of encouragement. She has been through MORE than her 'fair share' of . . . well . . . crap and it just doesn't make sense. But I know God has a perfect plan and we are only seeing one small 'screenshot' at a time. That doesn't mean we like it or even remotely understand it and that we don't get angry with Him

about it. But even so, we trust Him and know His love for us far exceeds our understanding of the present circumstances. . . . [I]t has truly been a very trying time made more bearable by your love and support! God bless you all."

The decision to stay that extra night turned out to be a very good thing, as Faith's oxygen once again plummeted, and a high fever set in. Had we left, we would have been right back in the ER that night. When I arrived at her hospital room after putting in a few hours at work, Faith was in tears. With her oxygen needs not diminishing and her continuing to spike fevers, she told me through her tears that they decided they wanted to keep her in the hospital for several more days to figure out what was going on and that attending the *for KING & COUNTRY* concert was now officially off the table. On top of all the sudden medical concerns, this was devastating news for her as she had been looking forward to this concert for months.

Because we had told everyone daily how much we were looking forward to this concert, many, many people in and out of the hospital knew about the excitement and then the sheer disappointment surrounding not getting to go. They wanted to try and do something very special for Faith and bring her some cheer during this difficult time. Separately, without knowing each other was doing the same thing, church members, hospital staff, and my brother, Tim, all reached out to anyone they could in connection with the band to try and see if they could visit Faith in the hospital while they were in Charlotte ... AND THEY DID!

It was such a beautiful moment the afternoon of November 30th when Joel and Luke Smallbone from *for KING & COUNTRY*, their brother Joshua Smallbone, and Joel's wife, Moriah walked into the hospital room and surprised Faith! She threw her hands up to her mouth and cried as they all poured into the

room. Surrounded by her family, a whole slew of the nursing staff, and one of her doctors, Faith was showered with merchandise, told she would have free tickets to their June 1st concert at Carowinds Amusement Park, given a small private "concert" as they sang a little bit from "Little Drummer Boy," and had plenty of videos and pictures taken together. After spending quite a bit

of time talking with her, praying with her, and saying their goodbyes, I walked out of the room with them where they proceeded to ask me many questions about Faith and her situation. I shared with them her story, her journey, and her struggles. They were the most gracious and humble artists I had ever met. Their sweet, generous spirits were a true reflection of God's grace, mercy, and love. The fact that they took the time out of their schedule to come to see Faith before their concert to talk with her, love on her, and pray with her was beyond selfless and so incredibly special! They asked me to keep in touch with them as they wanted to keep up to date on Faith's journey, so Josh and I exchanged numbers.

They gave free tickets to any of the nursing staff who wanted to go to the concert that night. We also found out later from some of Faith's friends who attended the concert, as well as from a social media post by *for KING & COUNTRY* themselves, that they even dedicated their song, "God Only Knows," to Faith that night. When I later texted Josh to thank them all again for such a selfless and special act, he thanked *me* for letting *them* get to meet Faith and for the opportunity to learn about her and her story. He said they were all deeply impacted and touched by her. And there began their involvement in Faith's journey and the beginning of a very special friendship!

It was such a great uplifting moment and memory for Faith in an otherwise very difficult and trying time. Faith, in her excitement, posted on social media,

"After finding out that I would be in the hospital longer than expected because of some lung complications, I was devastated to realize I wouldn't be able to go to the Little Drummer Boy concert by one of my favorite bands, for KING & COUNTRY. I had been looking forward to it for months and was so excited. I had no idea however that an even greater surprise was ahead of me! Levine Children's hospital was able to contact the band, get them to the hospital to see me, and they even sang a verse of The Little Drummer Boy. I cannot thank Levine Children's and for KING & COUNTRY enough for making this happen! I will never forget it. #godisgood"

Uncle Tim arrived in Charlotte from Maine that evening to help out with Faith's care and give me a much-needed break. Faith and Uncle Tim had an amazing time together during his visit and became very close. The bond that grew between them was truly a beautiful thing to witness. It felt like it had been so long since I had seen Faith laugh as much as she did while Uncle Tim was there. So that Tim might be able to speak with the doctors about Faith's medical circumstances when they made their rounds, I added him to the list of those allowed to be included in the sharing of Faith's medical information. I also introduced him over the phone to Doctor D and gave him the same permissions with the Chapel Hill facilities. He stayed for about five days before needing to return home. Faith and Uncle Tim continued to communicate via text, and Faith was at that time in pretty good spirits.

We also later found out that the morning crew at HISRadio, a Christian radio station located in Greenville, South Carolina, aired a segment entitled "*for KING & COUNTRY* performs in Hospital for local girl" about Faith's visit from *for KING & COUNTRY*. They played some of the footage from our Lungs4Faith Facebook page as well as from *for KING & COUNTRY's* social media post talking about their wonderful visit.

It was a very special time in the middle of a very disappointing part of Faith's journey and gave her some cherished memories to hang onto when things began to spiral in the wrong direction.

Early in December, thinking Faith would be discharged around the second week of the month, I bought a beautiful little Christmas tree. Before Uncle Tim returned to Maine on the 5th, I was hoping for the chance to get the tree and the house all decorated as a surprise for Faith when she got home. The tree and the house would sadly remain bare.

Faith remained in the hospital, and every night she would spike a fever causing her oxygen levels to drastically dip. After having spent one afternoon and evening on only 1 liter of oxygen, her O2 saturation levels took a huge hit due to the spike in fever overnight, and she ended up on 15 liters. Her oxygen would also drastically dip whenever she did her airway clearance, bumping up her oxygen requirements even more. The medical team had been trying to wean her off the oxygen little by little, but the fever spikes kept standing in the way of any significant change. And there was still no clear reason for these fever spikes. They had her on three different antibiotics to cover as many possibilities as they could and even discussed adding a fourth. They felt that if they could identify the cause of the fevers and treat it specifically, her oxygen needs would begin to decrease, and things would turn more quickly back in the right direction. But no answers seemed to come.

These dips in oxygen by themselves were concerning, but her medical team also began to fear her heart was being compromised from her lungs working so hard just to breathe. They performed an ultrasound on her heart and found one side to be enlarged. One of the first distressed calls I made was to Pastor Mike. He immediately dropped everything, and along with his wife, Susan, arrived at the hospital in record time to pray with us and offer as much encouragement as possible. Her medical team and I also discussed a plan to give Faith Tylenol as soon as her fevers reached 99 to try to keep them from getting as high as 103, thereby also hopefully keeping her oxygen saturation from tanking.

Two weeks into Faith's hospital stay, which also made it the longest of the three she'd had since October 25th, the discouragement was intense. Every time she seemed to be making good progress, she had another setback and any discharge talks returned to up-in-the-air status. Even though she had recovered from the surgery from just a surgery standpoint, her lungs continued to struggle. And although her strength, courage, and resilience continued to amaze and impress me, her spirits also began to take a serious hit. She was at nearly her seventh week of missing school, had missed a couple of months of dance, missed her friends, going to church, spending time with her youth group, and eating a home-cooked meal. She missed sleeping in her own bed and just overall *not* being in the hospital!

I, again, put out a plea to my prayer warriors to pray hard for Faith's physical, emotional, and spiritual health to be touched by the healing Hands of the Great Physician. I pleaded with everyone to also pray for wisdom for the doctors to quickly discover the cause of the fevers, so they could be eliminated and we could get Faith home! I welcomed prayers for my own peace and the comfort of His presence as I, too, was emotionally and physically drained and feeling helpless that I couldn't help my precious child feel better.

For the weekend of December 8th and 9th, Faith and I found ourselves slightly apprehensive as we were informed that Doctor B would be on call for the weekend. Having left his practice on not the best of terms, we did not know how the weekend would go. But we found ourselves very pleasantly surprised. The weekend went very well, and we were able to re-establish a good rapport with Doctor B. He was very gentle and compassionate—he even hugged me when he entered the room—and he was very comprehensive in his explanations. Sadly though, Faith was still spiking fevers overnight and remained on fifteen liters of high-flow oxygen. When I arrived at her hospital room on the 9th, she burst into tears and said she was really scared.

Because the fever spikes and the drop in O2 saturation seemed so closely related, occurring primarily when Faith slept, her medical team and I decided that it would be best to not try and wean her oxygen at night while she slept, as they had been doing for several nights. The next day, I discovered they had still turned down her oxygen overnight, causing her O2 to drop and high fevers to set in once again. So I wrote a note on a piece of paper stating, "Do NOT turn down Faith's oxygen while she sleeps," and taped it to the front of the oxygen unit before I left for the night. When I came in the next day, Faith was feeling horrible, had spiked high fevers again overnight, and was on higher levels of oxygen than she had been the previous day. I found out that the night respiratory therapist had not only ignored the note on the oxygen unit but had to actually *lift up* the note to turn down the oxygen while Faith was sleeping. I was livid.

I immediately went in search of Faith's nurse to talk to her about it. As I walked out the door, her nurse was walking in, and I stopped her in the doorway. I proceeded to ask her why on earth the instructions to not turn down Faith's oxygen overnight were so blatantly ignored. The more I questioned her and the more I spoke, the louder and higher pitched my voice became until I found myself yelling so loudly that everyone around had stopped what they were doing to watch the scene I was making. I was exhausted and upset and had lost all sense of control. With tears streaming down my face, I asked them if they were trying to make my daughter worse and threatened to call a lawyer over their mishandling of her medical situation. I was a complete wreck. I turned in a huff back into the room to find Faith also sitting there with tears streaming down her face. She was afraid that because I had said the "L" word, it was going to adversely affect the care they were giving her. I felt so small and horrible and ashamed of my awful behavior. We both sat there and cried together as I apologized to her for losing control . . . then supervisors and staff began visiting us one by one.

The nurse manager was the first to come in and graciously listened to me as I first apologized for flying off the handle, then tearfully expressed my concerns. She assured me that Faith's oxygen would not be turned down again while she slept and that her proper care was their utmost priority. A respiratory department manager came to speak with me next and apologized profusely for what had happened, also assuring me that it would not happen again. A couple of the nurses and additional staff visited us just to let us know we had their support, and they would all do their part to make sure things were handled properly. The entire medical team and staff were nothing but generous, gracious, and kind, completely understanding that I was exhausted, frustrated, and scared. Nobody held my outburst against me—or Faith—and they even gave me some extra meal tickets as a small way of saying sorry.

Because of the fever spikes, increases in oxygen needs, and all the "chaos," I saw Faith begin to lose her fighting spirit for the first time. Her health was making a steady decline as was our emotional state.

That afternoon, I had an hour-and-a-half meeting with the pulmonary team with Doctor D on the phone. All of them were very concerned about Faith's progress—or lack thereof. We were back to talks of a transplant, and the team opened up talks of transferring her to Chapel Hill for a transplant evaluation. Faith grew even more depressed and angry.

After a few days of the oxygen unit being untouched at night and the Tylenol successfully keeping the fever spikes to a minimum, the team of doctors decided that the Tylenol plan of action was, in reality, doing Faith a disservice. After much discussion, they decided it was better to let the fevers run their course so they could see if the fevers continued to get high and address the cause instead of merely tackling the symptoms. I reluctantly agreed, and thankfully, Faith's fever spikes slowed down. Her oxygen needs, however, continued to take a hit.

Every time it looked like Faith was close to getting discharged, something would happen, and she would take another turn for the worse. Faith's spirits began to decline, as did mine. I would get up very early each morning, put in a full day of work, spend all evening at the hospital until Faith was asleep, then drive home after midnight sobbing and crying out to the Lord to not take my daughter from me.

By mid-December 2018, it was evident that Faith was rapidly declining into respiratory failure, and her only hope for survival now was a lung transplant. This piece of information had not yet been discussed with Faith. I didn't know how I was going to tell her, so Uncle Tim offered to come back to town and help. He flew back in on December 12th. He had many phone conversations with Doctor D, as I was not in a mental state to objectively carry on a conversation regarding the direction things were heading. Nor was my memory working very well, and I was afraid I would miss something important. Tim and I also had many conversations with the local medical team, getting as much information as possible before having this all-important conversation with Faith. The final conversation I felt I needed to have before I could talk to Faith was with Pastor Mike and Susan. On December 13th, they graciously met me and Tim at the Ronald McDonald House, where Tim was staying. Tim filled us all in on his conversation with Doctor D, explaining the path we were now headed down. I don't remember a whole lot about the conversation, other than that we wept together and prayed together. Pastor Mike also quoted Genesis 18:25 (NIV), which says, "Will not the Judge of all the earth do right?" Meaning, we may not understand God's actions or what He allows to happen in life, but He is the One true righteous Judge. Whatever He does for whatever reason is ultimately right and ultimately for His glory.

Faith, in the meantime, was not only spiraling medically but was also spiraling emotionally and withdrawing into herself more and more. I was hoping that Tim's presence would brighten her days, but she was so deeply upset and angry, not even Tim's presence could bring up her spirits. Tim and I decided we would try to talk to her together on December 16th about the next step needing to be a lung transplant.

On December 15th, Tim gently prodded Faith to see if there was anything she wanted to talk about, such as the possibility of a transplant. She said she wasn't ready to talk about that yet. He told her we needed to talk about it very, very soon to which she replied, "I know. That's what my mom said." She then turned back to her phone and shut him out.

That evening, she had a visit from some school friends which improved her mood greatly. While she was visiting with her friends, I used that opportunity to text Doctor D about the transplant evaluation process. Since Faith was still a minor, I asked if I was able to give the go-ahead to share her information with the transplant team to review her eligibility for evaluation *while* we talked with her about it. Doctor D said it was certainly within my authority, and she would be happy to get the ball rolling if that was my wish. My reply was a resounding, "Yes!" In the meantime, Tim took this time to call the family, letting them know what was now going to be taking place.

On Sunday, December 16th, 2018, Tim and I had the dreaded, difficult, and daunting conversation with Faith and filled her in on all the details of where she was at and what the logical next steps were, if she wanted to live. But the talk did not go well at all. She had primarily shut herself off from any kind of conversation from either one of us, other than to say she wasn't sure she even wanted to go down that road. But she would mainly just sit silently and solemnly in her hospital bed with her earphones in listening to music and ignoring any attempts at discussion. She wouldn't even make eye contact with either one of us. Later that day, during a time when it was just me and her in the room, her mood was understandably very down, and she shared with me that she wished God would just go ahead and take her. My heart shattered.

Since I had already gotten the ball rolling with the transplant evaluation process and recognizing that we were quickly running out of time, Faith eventually agreed to at least go through the evaluation process, but she was still unsure if she wanted to go through a transplant. She was also hoping that following the evaluation, she could return to the Charlotte area for Christmas, even if still in the hospital. She just wanted to be close to home. This, of course, would not be feasible.

Once the decision had been made to transfer her to Chapel Hill's adult ICU to meet up with the transplant team, Faith posted on social media,

"Today is day 24 of being in the hospital, after being told this stay should've only been a few days. I've been out of school, dance, work, and church for almost 8 weeks. And now, I will be transferring to Chapel Hill's ICU very soon. These past four years I have fought and strived to keep my lungs as healthy as they could be, even with the condition they've been in. But that couldn't last forever. I am now having to face reality and the fact that my lungs are failing and they can't get much better. Once I get to Chapel Hill, they are going to start evaluating me to determine whether or not I can go on the list for a lung transplant. We don't know how long I will have to be there or what the outcome will be. I'm not going to lie, it is very scary and the timing sucks with Christmas just around the corner. However, no matter how difficult this process may be, or how scary it will be, the outcome will hopefully be even better than I can imagine. And now I just ask for your encouragement and support, whether through prayer or other means. My family has set up a GoFundMe for anyone who would like to contribute to the associated expenses, such as the transplant itself, recovery efforts, and the temporary move to Chapel Hill where my mom and I will have to live for several months leading up to and following the surgery. Thank you all for your love, prayers, and support."

On December 19th, less than two months since her sister's wedding but feeling much longer, following a brief visit from another small group of friends from school, Faith was transferred via ambulance from Levine Children's Hospital in Charlotte to the adult Transplant team at UNC Chapel Hill. In one fell swoop without any kind of transition, she was ripped from pediatrics and whisked right into the adult world.

The first day of the evaluation process was a whirlwind of meetings where Faith and the family were interviewed by the transplant doctors, pre- and post-transplant coordinators, social workers, dieticians, finance and insurance coordinators, and more, in an effort to prepare us for what the evaluation would entail, what we could expect pre- and post-transplant, as well as ensure that

Faith had an adequate support system to get her through the surgery and recovery process should they decide to move forward with a transplant. As succinctly summed up by Jenni,

"We learned that what lies ahead is no small task. It will most likely tap out all our family's resources: time, emotional, financial, spiritual, etc. So much is involved in making sure Faith has the best possible support for the evaluation, the transplant itself, 3-4 months of in-Chapel Hill recovery, and then continuous recovery/maintaining efforts at home for the following months (and years). While this is unfamiliar and somewhat daunting, we are so excited for the incredible impact a brand new pair of lungs can have on Faith's life!"

I began to see Faith's fighting spirit return. Before agreeing to the evaluation process, she was struggling just to get better and not getting anywhere, which was totally draining her fight. Now she was facing something tangible to fight *for.*

The following days would be filled with tests and procedures to see if she met the medical requirements for placing her on the transplant list. As Faith continued to ask about the possibility of returning to Charlotte for Christmas, Doctor C of the transplant team replied that they were focusing on getting her to all the many Christmases of the future for years to come.

At the request of the HISRadio morning crew, I had been keeping them abreast of Faith's circumstances. When she was transferred to Chapel Hill, they reached out to me and asked if they could interview Faith on their morning program. Faith was very excited and willing to participate. Being thoroughly exhausted, however, she asked if I could do the interview instead. So on the morning of December 21st, 2018, I "sat down" with Rob Dempsey over Skype and shared Faith's story and her wait to be put on the transplant list.

ROB DEMPSEY: *"Sometimes life can get really rough during Christmas for some families, and right now there's a family that could use your prayers. You may have heard us tell you about 17-year-old Faith, who has cystic fibrosis, just a few days ago. She lives in Charlotte, she's been transferred to Chapel Hill's ICU right now, and she's being evaluated for a lung transplant. Now her mom,*

Susan, is along with us this morning. . . ."

After discussing what transpired over the previous several months, bringing Faith to her current circumstance, and witnessing the return of her fighting spirit, we talked quite a bit about *for KING & COUNTRY*, their wonderful visit to Faith in the hospital in Charlotte, and what that visit meant to her. We then discussed the transplant evaluation process, what Christmas was going to look like for us that year with spending it in the hospital, and Faith's love of and involvement in competition dance. The interview concluded with a brief discussion about our GoFundMe page and the impact of having to temporarily relocate to Chapel Hill. He asked me to continue keeping HisRadio abreast of Faith's situation and assured me we had lots of prayers between the HisRadio family and their many listeners.

In the meantime, Uncle Tim reached out again to his contact with *for KING & COUNTRY* to express his profound gratitude for Joel's and Luke's visit to Faith at the end of November. He talked about what an impact it had on Faith's spirits and that she still talked about it every day. Tim updated him on Faith's current condition and that she was undergoing evaluation for a life-saving double lung transplant. He closed by stating, "this part of Faith's journey with Cystic Fibrosis is going to be the toughest she's had to endure. But every little show of love and support gives her that much more strength to fight this disease, and the visit from *for KING & COUNTRY* meant everything to her. Everything. I cannot thank you, Joel, Luke, Moriah, and the rest of the band enough. What you've done for this very special person just goes beyond words."

The reply was heartwarming and showed not only what an impact *for KING & COUNTRY* had on Faith, but the impact *she* had on *them* and others touched by her story:

"We are all so very grateful for the opportunity to share even a brief few moments of joy with Faith. Even though I was not there, I've watched video clips and seen pictures. No doubt, she is tremendously special. We continue to pray for her, for her mother, for you and your whole family as you are walking this journey with her. To see the extent to which her story has touched so many others thru our visit is truly remarkable. I was just noticing that the video clip we shared was also shared by multiple social media outlets, including the producers of the Bible miniseries. It's wonderful to know that there are now countless more people joining all of us in our prayers for Faith! Please share our continued prayers and support with everyone and keep us posted! God bless you!

About three days following the initial meetings and interviews with the Chapel Hill transplant team, I posted on social media,

> *"The evaluation process to determine Faith's eligibility to be placed on the lung transplant list is well underway. We've met the entire team -- and they absolutely LOVE her!! She is handling everything asked of her like a champ! The team feels at this point the evaluation is more of a formality to fulfill the data requirements for UNOS but don't see that there will be anything keeping her from being placed on the list and that she is an excellent candidate!! The average wait time for Chapel Hill in-patients is about 2 months, followed by at least 3 months of in-Chapel Hill recovery and rehabilitation. Thanks to all for your prayers and support!"*

Because we were now facing Christmas in the hospital yet again, everyone was working hard at getting Faith transferred out of the teeny tiny ICU room into a larger room in the Medical Progressive Care Unit (MPCU), which was one step up from the ICU. Even though she was now on very high levels of oxygen, they felt she was certainly stable enough that she didn't need to remain in the ICU. The only problem was that there were no beds available in MPCU, so it looked as though Christmas would be celebrated in extremely tight and uncomfortable quarters, which was a source of great distress for Faith and the family.

As I left for my room at the SECU (State Employees Credit Union) house on Christmas Eve, which was lodging similar to the Ronald McDonald House, we resigned ourselves to the fact that we would be celebrating Christmas in extremely limited space. But at 1:20 in the morning on Christmas day, I was awakened by a phone call from a very excited Faith telling me they were moving her right then and there to the MPCU, and her room was going to be *much* bigger than what she had in the ICU! I was so excited that I never did get back to sleep that day but laid there praising Jesus until it was time to get up and go to the hospital.

Jenni and her husband, James, arrived early that morning so we could get the room decorated and all set up for Christmas. Kelsey and her husband, Jarrett, arrived later in the day, sadly, without Faith's niece and nephew due to visitation age restrictions. We had a very beautiful and very special Christmas celebration, continuing our family traditions of coffee cake in the morning and a ham meal that afternoon, hoping beyond hope that it would be the last Christmas we would have to spend in the hospital—little did any of us know, it would wind up being the last Christmas we would spend with Faith this side of Heaven.

The day after Christmas, the evaluation process to determine Faith's eligibility for placement on the lung transplant list was finally complete. As always, she handled the process with a strength, courage, and maturity well beyond her years, and her determination continued to be awe-inspiring. The wait would then begin for results to come in, data to be recorded, and a score to be tallied to determine how high, if eligible, her placement on the transplant list would be. Preliminary results looked positive and promising, and the hope was that Faith would be listed by the end of the week. By this time, she was on twenty-five to thirty liters of high-flow oxygen, which ironically was a very good thing when hoping for placement on the transplant list.

As we continued to wait, our support system back home continued to pray and encourage us from afar. A social media post by Mike, one of the worship leaders at our church, encouraged our hearts tremendously.

"Today we shared [the] song entitled 'Shoulders' by the group for KING & COUNTRY in honor of our worship team sister, Susan, and her daughter Faith. We've all been praying for their struggles and praising good news of advancement through the donor list recipient process. They inspire us in how they continue to rely on God as they face this challenge head on and I pray that they'll continue to let God carry their burdens as the fight continues! We love you both and miss you greatly! . . . Thank you for being such power pictures of relying on God and letting Him carry your burdens."

On December 28th, as the wait continued, the transplant team informed me and Faith that they wanted us to relocate to Chapel Hill for at least a year following the transplant. This came as quite a shock to both of us, as we had always been told the post-transplant relocation was around three months . . . potentially a little longer, but typically three months. Faith expressed her overwhelming desire and hope to be back in time for senior year and her final year of dance, all of which began in August. The transplant team said that was certainly possible, but we needed to be in a mindset of planning for the worst and hoping for the best.

By December 30th, 2018, the transplant team had received all the results and data from the evaluation, had completed their review, and was ready to list her, pending insurance approval. Other than a weekend and holiday, the team was not anticipating any complications with insurance and fully expected her to be listed by Thursday or Friday the following week. Her score, as it turned out, was seventy-eight. They shared with us that people with a score of eighty and above are typically on ECMO (extracorporeal membrane oxygenation), in which "blood is pumped outside of [the] body to a heart-lung machine that removes carbon dioxide and sends oxygen-filled blood back to tissues in the body . . . This method allows the blood to 'bypass' the heart and lungs, allowing these organs to rest and heal."[5] So because of her high score, we were told that she would more than likely be *extremely* high on the list. By the middle of the following week, we still had not heard from insurance. The pre-transplant coordinator approached the CEO of the hospital to obtain an emergency override since Faith's score was so high, and they did not want to risk putting off getting her on the list any longer.

On Friday, January 4th, 2019, it became official! We received the necessary CEO override approval, and Faith was officially on the transplant list. Based on the evaluation and her extremely high score, she was, as expected, placed very high on the list so they didn't anticipate her wait to be very long.

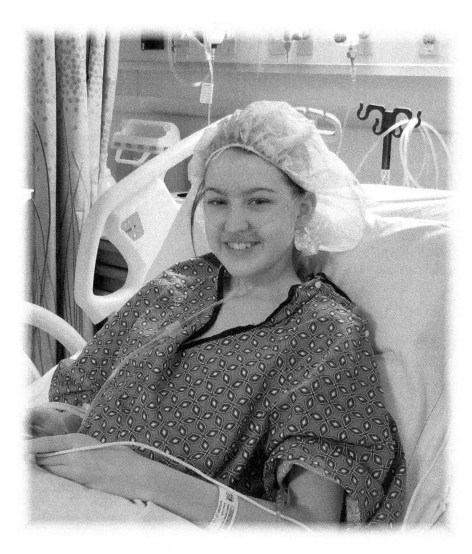

Preparing for transplant surgery, January 14, 2019

11

Lungs 4 Faith

Waiting for something to happen in the hospital is anything but simply waiting. In hospital terms, the "waiting game" continues to be a flurry of activity, treatments, tests, and procedures, a constant flow of people in and out of the room, overloads of information thrown at you, and a vast array of emotional ups and downs.

In the early part of January 2019, while waiting for the call for lungs, in a matter of just a few days, we went from thinking Faith had developed pneumonia to thinking instead she had a blood clot in her lungs, which required blood thinners through an additional IV line. Relief came with being told there was not a blood clot after all, but the relief quickly faded when Faith was told that prevention of blood clots would be necessary by starting her on blood thinner injections in her belly three times a day -- something she'd had to do before which had proven to be quite a traumatic experience for her.

On January 8th, 2019, we got the exciting and all-at-once terrifying news that she potentially had new lungs available. They would not know for sure until the surgeon was able to examine them in person the following day, but everything on paper looked very promising. Faith immediately began to cry, assuring me they were not sad tears. She was certainly nervous, but the sense of relief she felt was also very evident . . . along with being cautiously hopeful and optimis-

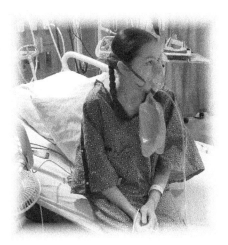

tic. Uncle Tim boarded a flight from Maine to be with us for the potential transplant surgery.

Around 3:00 pm on the afternoon of January 9th, thinking it was a go, they began to get Faith ready. Right as they were about to wheel her down to the operating room, excitement once again turned quickly to disappointment when they canceled the call, stating the lungs were not good after all. It was what they called a "dry run," something we had been warned about during the evaluation period. Although very disappointing, we also rested in the knowledge that it simply meant God had something better for her around the corner, and we now had a much better idea of what to expect with "the call" process. So we would continue the wait. Uncle Tim flew back to Maine on January 12th.

The wait was excruciating. We were also told that Faith received two to three offers for lungs each day that we never heard about because they were not up to par, the knowledge of which made the wait that much more excruciating. But on January 13th, 2019, we received the next call, although we would not find out until the following day after the donor surgery. As we anxiously awaited to hear if this would be another dry run or if the lungs were good, the flurry of activity once again began for getting Faith ready for potential surgery. At 2:52 pm on January 14th, 2019, we received the joyous news that the lungs were a "go!" After the surgical team wheeled her into the operating room, I was extremely overjoyed to post,

"WE HAVE NEW LUNGS 4 FAITH!!!! She is on her way to surgery right now to be gifted with her brand new, CF-free lungs!! Please join us in prayer for a successful surgery (expected to last 8-12 hours), as well as for a smooth recovery and rehabilitation (3-12 months!). This will undoubtedly be one of the hardest legs on this life-long journey with Cystic Fibrosis that Faith has ever had to face, but the blessings on the other side are enormous and beautiful! Please also say a special prayer for the donor's family who, when faced with one of the darkest days in their lives, still selflessly thought of others and allowed their loved one's legacy to live on through the precious gift of organ donation. Although I have no idea who the donor or the family are, God certainly knows, and they will always hold a very special place in my heart for the gift they've given my daughter!"

Uncle Tim once again boarded a flight out of Maine and arrived in Chapel Hill while Faith was in surgery. Kelsey, Jenni, James, Tim, and I were also joined by Faith's youth pastor, Aaron, and his wife, Jenna. Due to the surprisingly large number of people in the OR waiting room, we all decided to wait in the Children's Chapel, which was much more comfortable and empty except for us.

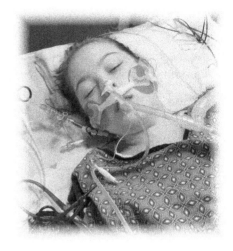

Since the surgery was scheduled to last anywhere from eight to twelve hours, at just shy of the eight-hour mark, we decided it would be a good idea to relocate to the OR waiting room so we would be available when someone informed us the surgery was done. Aaron, Uncle Tim, and I headed to Starbucks on the other side of the hospital to get everyone coffee, while the rest of the group proceeded to the OR waiting room. While on the way to Starbucks, I received a call from Jenni that they had just run into Doctor BH, Faith's surgeon, and her surgery was already complete! We immediately redirected to the waiting room to await being able to go in and see Faith. As we waited, Pastor Aaron and Jenna made a trip to Cookout to get us all something to eat since none of us had eaten since very early in the day.

When we were all in the waiting room, Doctor BH came in and told us that Faith's surgery went extremely well and lasted just under eight hours. He told us she had done great, and they fully expected her recovery to go well, although she would have tough days ahead of her as they weaned her off some of the support mechanisms such as the chest tubes, IVs, etc. He told us he believed the new lungs to be the most beautiful set of lungs he had seen come through there in a long time and expected these lungs to give her at least thirty, forty, or even fifty more years. Over

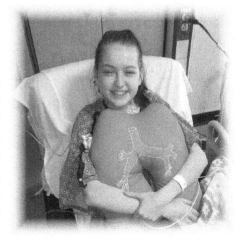

the following weeks, the medical team would get her moving and used to her new lungs, then hopefully allow her to leave the hospital for what would be the first time in months. We would now remain in Chapel Hill for anywhere from three months to a year during the recovery process due to the frequent follow-up appointments, tests, physical therapy, potential rejections, and to ensure everything was progressing as it should.

One by one, Kelsey, Jenni, Tim, and I were allowed to go to Faith's room to see her for the first time while she still slept from the surgery. At my request, the nurse gently pulled her hospital gown back a little bit showing me the scars from the surgery and the chest tubes. It was truly an awe-inspiring thing to see all that went into giving her this second chance at life. With all the tubes and wires she was currently hooked up to, it was hard to get a feel for what life would truly be like for her now, but we were all simply over the moon about when Faith could get out of the hospital and begin fully living her new life with her new set of beautiful lungs. Uncle Tim stayed overnight in her room that first night just to be there in case anything was needed, and her nurse for that night would have no other patients other than Faith.

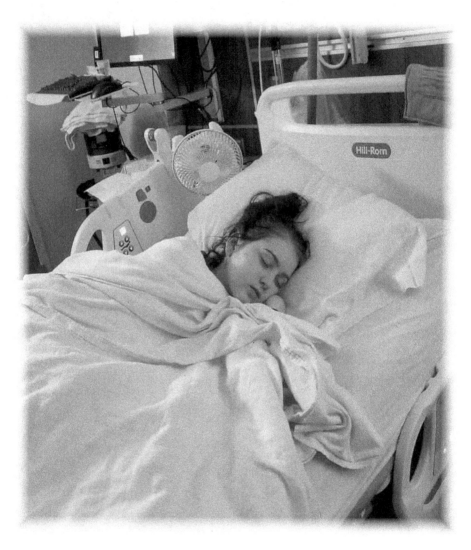

Back in the hospital, February 2019

12

Bumps in the Road

Due to the amount of time we would be required to stay in Chapel Hill, I rented an apartment for me and Faith to live in when she was finally released from the hospital. This, of course, put quite a burden on finances, as I was still paying rent for our home in Charlotte, along with all the utilities at both places. Much of the strain was thankfully alleviated, however, through the generosity of those who donated to our GoFundMe page as well as the generous donations received frequently from our church family. It certainly was bound to be a long, yet exciting, road.

Two days after Faith's transplant, Faith took her first post-transplant walk around the hospital unit. It was very, very painful and uncomfortable for her, but she did great. To keep all of our family, friends, and followers closely informed of her progress and specific prayer needs, I posted following update,

"POST-TRANSPLANT RECOVERY, DAY TWO . . . It's hard to believe only two days have passed since Faith received her new lungs . . . one, because these days have been extremely long with little to no sleep; but, also because so much has happened and Faith has already progressed so far! She has gone from having to use her finger to spell out words in the palm of our hands in order to communicate as she began coming out of sedation, to taking her first walk this afternoon! She has surpassed expected and typical timelines with certain recovery 'checkpoints,' such as being taken off the breathing tube, having two different arterial lines and an IV line removed, already breathing on room air without the need for supplied oxygen, and getting out of bed to sit in a recliner or walk up and down the hallway!! Her doctors have said she is not just hours ahead in her progress, but days!! As one of her surgeons put it, Faith is winning!!

"But this progress comes not because it's easy, but because Faith is determined, diligent, and motivated to push herself beyond what most people could even imagine. Her journey to recovery is HARD. The pain is intense and, at times, unmanageable. And while Faith is incredibly strong, it's still difficult to deal with. So much so that she hasn't yet been able to enjoy the beauty of the breath her new lungs have given her because she's too focused on pushing through the pain. This beauty is not lost on us, however, as we see her O2 sats at 98-99% while on room air!

"On top of the pain and discomfort, she also can't eat anything until it's determined she will be able to keep food down. She's going on 72 hours of no food, and she has been hungry since day one. Even when they do start introducing food, it will be a slow, baby-step process of soft foods for several days before she can eat 'real' food. She can't even drink water for the time being and is only allowed to occasionally swab her mouth to maintain enough moisture. The constant flow of people coming in to draw blood, give medicines, take vitals, assess, etc. continues through all hours of the night and day. Dressings need to be changed and surgery sites checked and cleaned. And the real work hasn't even begun. Please keep the prayers coming (they're obviously working!)."

The next day, after seeing a picture of Faith walking the hallway in her hospital gown using a walker, still attached to chest tubes, followed by someone pushing along her IV pole and a chair just in case she needed to rest during the walk, a dear friend wrote the following post,

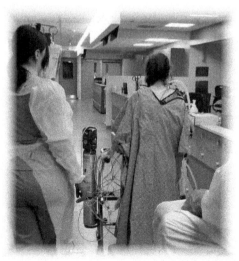

"Instagram is an interesting place. I was scrolling through this morning and saw a video of Dwayne Johnson working out, muscles rippling all over the place, and I thought 'Wow, that's a strong person right there.' And then the next picture I saw brought tears to my eyes. It was a shot of Faith Shaw taking her first excruciating steps two days after a double lung transplant. And I thought, 'No, with all due respect to The Rock, he's got nothing on this girl.' She looks so tiny and fragile,

but she is the perfect picture of strength and courage. Faith Shaw, you are a miracle and a hero and you continue to be in my prayers."

Just under a week after her transplant, Faith continued doing very well and continued to surpass expectations for her recovery. She was down to only one chest tube, which they hoped to remove the following day, and one central line in her neck, scheduled to be replaced with a PICC line in her arm also the following day. She was walking three to four times per day, and she scored another victory a few days earlier when she was given the green light to eat real food. She did not even have to go through the previously mentioned "baby steps." Her first post-transplant meal consisted of two peanut butter and jelly sandwiches, pretzels, a chocolate chip cookie, a brownie, and milk. She was so thrilled to be able to eat without restriction and within a few days had already surpassed her pre-transplant weight.

On January 21st, 2019, Faith took her first walk without the walker, and on January 22nd, she took her first walk free of ALL tubes, IV poles, etc. We were told a few days later by the transplant team they had an unusually large amount of transplant patients at that point in time, and *none* of them were doing as well as Faith!

Even with all the wins and exciting progress, however, Faith continued to face several challenges and frustrations. She was still dealing with a fair amount of pain and discomfort, she still had the constant flow of doctors, nurses, and techs in and out of her room for assessments, including chest X-rays, blood draws, medicines, treatments, etc.

But the biggest frustration came with the news that one of her IV medications could only be done on an *IN-patient* basis. And being a six-week regimen (with one week already behind her, at least), it meant she would have to remain in the hospital for an additional five weeks instead of one, even though her recovery itself had been noted by many to be on a "fast-track." This news, of course, did not sit too well with any of us, least of all Faith who had endured more than one could imagine—and with a grace, strength, and maturity few of us would probably be able to equal. This was an experimental drug, so there was currently not a lot of data on it. It had to be kept at a very specific temperature, which was why it needed to be done in the hospital.

Several days later, Faith was finally feeling up to posting her own update.

"Well, it's been 13 days since my double lung transplant and I feel amazing! There have been ups and downs, both physically and mentally, but

my recovery has been a lot faster than the doctors were expecting. Right after surgery, I had a breathing tube in my throat, a tube in my nose, 4 chest tubes, 3 catheters, and a central line in my neck. During the first couple of hours of me waking up, I was off of the breathing tube and breathing on my own! Throughout the first week, all of the various tubes were taken out one or two at a time until I was just down to a central line for the IV antibiotics, which I'll be on for another month. While I'm still in some pain and am pretty stiff sometimes, I'm amazed at how much easier I can breathe. I could've never even imagined how it would feel and now I know. I am so lucky to have been given a new chance at life. Even though I am doing very well, there's still a lot of work ahead of me over the next year to get as healthy as possible! But I know I can do it! I also want to thank the donor and their family. Organ donation is one of the greatest gifts someone could ever give and I am so blessed to have received this gift. Lastly, I want to say thank you to everyone for all of the love, support, and encouragement! I wouldn't have been able to get through this without you all!"

Faith was also experiencing mild headaches every day. She made sure to alert the transplant team about the headaches whenever they occurred but it was believed to just be from all the stress her body had undergone recently and was still undergoing. She was given Tylenol, which seemed to help for the most part.

On January 31st, 2019, in a surprising turn of events, the long-anticipated and long-awaited discharge day finally arrived! Faith would be leaving the hospital for the first time since November. She had continued to surpass all expectations in her recovery following the transplant, working extremely hard—mind and body—to push through every challenge set before her!

The strength and determination Faith exhibited gave the transplant team confidence in her commitment to do all that was required of her, prompting them to go above and beyond as well. After thinking she needed to stay in the hospital another month due to the experimental IV antibiotic, the team worked diligently, almost non-stop, with the drug manufacturer (located in Japan!), home infusion, and pharmacy to figure out a way to have it administered from home. The final piece of the puzzle needed to make it possible fit into place the previous day, so for the first time in over two months, Faith was able to leave the hospital, now with beautiful new lungs and the ability to breathe deeply without complication or limitation.

This strength and determination would continue to be called upon as Faith now faced adjustments to post-transplant "life on the outside," pulmonary rehab, new dietary restrictions, and extra precautions to avoid infections since her anti-rejection medicine severely suppressed her immune system. She also had to adjust to the new daily regimen. Pre-transplant, Faith had her vest therapy two to three times per day, each lasting thirty minutes, three different nebulizer treatments multiple times a day, along with what we considered a "vast" array of pills and medicines she had to take. We did not know the meaning of the word "vast" until post-transplant. She was victoriously no longer required to do vest or nebulizer

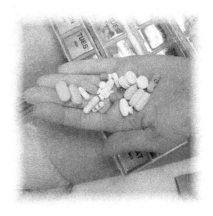

treatments, but her medicine regimen, on top of the experimental IV antibiotic, was over thirty pills taken in the morning, a few mid-day, and close to thirty pills at night.

Faith was also still experiencing headaches, so they instructed her to keep a headache journal to determine the frequency, severity, and any noticeable patterns. Her first entry dated February 2nd, 2019, read,

"About 10 after 7 — woke up with severe headache, on scale 1-10 pain was 6/7. Took Tylenol. Pain kept getting worse, on scale of 1-10 it was 8/9. Hour later took oxycodone & tried to eat but threw up – After throwing up took Zofran. Around 8:30 pain was getting better, nausea was also better. Went to hospital for labs, head & nausea was better. At home—10:18—pain is better but still lingering, just took daily meds but didn't feel nauseous. Head hurts more when writing, but not as much when watching tv, hurts more in certain positions. Didn't really hurt when looking at phone."

The following day she woke up with a headache again, but the Tylenol seemed to help. So we did what any teenage girl who had just spent more than two months in the hospital would do for her post-transplant required daily physical therapy—we went shopping at the mall! As the day progressed, however, her headache returned with a vengeance. Her headache journal entry read,

*"Woke up around 9, headache w/pain around 4 or 5. Took migraine meds in about 20 minutes it was getting better, still lingering but not completely there. Worse with light & when writing. *Took lassix day before. Hurt more when head/neck were in certain positions (leaning forward or back). Hurt when looking @ phone. Head started hurting again around 8, took migraine med. 40*

mins later pain got to 9/10. Pulsing, dull, achy pain." So we called the trans-
plant coordinator on call, who instructed us to go to the ER. After 5 hours at the
ER, some pain medication that seemed to help somewhat, and the ER doctor's
consultation with the transplant team, they sent us home.

The next morning, February 4th, 2019, I was awakened by Faith who was clearly in great distress. Her headache was worse than it had ever been, she was nauseous, having trouble breathing, and the pain was getting unbearable. We again called the transplant coordinator who instructed us to return to the ER. We later found out they were supposed to have admitted her the night before, and no one could tell us why they had sent her home instead. This time, they got her admitted, but only after an additional nine hours spent in the ER. While in the ER, they performed another MRI and a spinal tap to rule out any neurological issues or spinal meningitis. The MRI was inconclusive, and the spinal tap showed no concerns from that front.

After finally getting settled in a room and having gotten some relief from a magnesium drip, Faith wrote what would be her final entry in her headache journal,

"Woke up around 7 from severe migraine. Pain @ a 10, nauseous, slightly short of breath. Took Zofran, took 2 puffs of albuterol, took migraine med (didn't work). Went to ER. Pain was severe, still a 10 until getting pain med. Something helped temporarily but didn't last long. IV magnesium helped with pain & lasted longer as well. Neck slightly stiff. First day migraine/headache was constant all day. Pain comes in waves. Pulsing, throbbing, dull pain."

Over the next many days, the pain would become so severe that any thoughts of a headache journal were far from Faith's mind. All she could do was curl up in a fetal position with her eyes tightly shut and cry out in pain, as well as throw up many times. On several occasions I had to quickly sit her up when I could tell she was getting ready to throw up because she was too out of it to sit up by herself. Had I not been there, she very easily could have aspirated, which refers to the "accidental breathing in of food or fluids into the lungs. This can cause serious problems, such as pneumonia and other lung problems."[6] When I was telling Doctor D about this, she dubbed me the "vomit monitor."

After one of her bouts of throwing up, we managed to move Faith to a chair where she curled up in a ball in excruciating pain while the nursing staff changed the sheets on her bed. She told me that it felt like her brain was swelling. Doctor C from the transplant team came in, and the look on his face when he saw her level of pain was devastating. I was later told by another member of the transplant team that he had been deeply scarred walking in and seeing her in that much pain and never ever wanted to see that again. There began the task of trying to figure out the best course of action, which would prove to be a very daunting task indeed.

And Doctor C was not the only one scarred by watching Faith writhe and cry out in sheer agony. I discovered very quickly that the hardest part about being a parent was watching your child go through something so incredibly tough and not being able to fix it for them. I felt more helpless than I had ever felt in my life. Especially several days later, when her doctor called me early in the morning to say that Faith needed me to come in as soon as I could. I immediately got up and dressed, not knowing what to expect. When I walked into the room and said her name, Faith was sitting up with tears streaming down her face, and exclaimed, "*I can't see you! I can't see you! **I can't see!**"* No one was yet able to tell me why her vision was being impacted, and her pain was still the worst pain she had ever felt. All I could do was sit and hold her hand and cry with her as we both begged the medical team to figure something out. I ended up staying the night in her room as I did not want to leave her side.

At one point the next day, I was sitting in the hospital room following the medical team finally getting Faith's migraine pain to subside at least for a little while, but her vision was still gone. She was so quiet in her hospital bed that I thought she had finally fallen asleep, until this small quiet voice asked with an almost resigned tone, "So am I blind now?" My heart broke into a million pieces. I assured her that it was temporary, based on what everyone was telling us. According to the second MRI they had performed, the condition they found in her brain was something called PRES, which stood for "Posterior Reversible Encephalopathy Syndrome." It is a rare but known potential side effect from Tacrolimus, the anti-rejection medicine she was taking, and affected the part of the brain that controlled sight. It was amazing to think how in tune she still was with her body because, with PRES, her brain was indeed swelling. However, we clung to and counted on the word "reversible!" In the meantime, they discontinued Tacrolimus to hopefully help her brain recover and began the search for an alternative anti-rejection drug.

At another point, after she had been given an IV pain "cocktail," she woke up from a short sleep and sat up with a blank stare, her shoulder moving oddly back and forth. I asked her what she was doing, and she replied in a strange monotone voice that she wasn't doing anything. Fearing some sort of seizure, I called in the nurse to explain what I had seen. The shoulder movement had stopped by then, but she called one of the doctors anyway who came in and asked Faith several questions. Did she know where she was, in what city, and why? Faith answered everything in that same monotone voice, and I was so scared this was what my daughter was now going to be . . . that the swelling in her brain had caused permanent damage and she was no longer going to be the same.

The next day, in a rare moment of quiet, I called out to my prayer warriors the world over with a social media post,

"PRAYERS FOR THIS COURAGEOUS CF WARRIOR—The week has become more than just a 'bump in the road' along Faith's CF/Lung transplant journey. It's a huge barrier we're trying to break thru brick by painful brick. As her headaches steadily worsened, radiating down her neck, shoulders & back, multiple doctors dug deep into their 'toolbox' trying different options, with limited success, to provide her relief from the endless pain. Anything providing even the smallest amount of relief was short-lived & the pain returned with a vengeance. Her vision also began to change and she now can't see anything other than light, which has obviously terrified her."

"Yesterday was probably the single most difficult day in my life as a mom, as all I could do was hold her hand & stroke her head trying to offer comfort while she cried out in agony repeatedly begging for it to stop & asking me "Why?" Eventually, something the doctors tried seemed to work & she was able to get some sleep. When she woke, tho not in pain, the side effects were heart-wrenching. She was lethargic, stared 'off into space,' answered questions with a monotone voice, & did not hold my hand back as I held hers. She knew her birthday but not the year; didn't know how old she was; knew we were in Chapel Hill but didn't know where; knew the woman holding her hand was her mom and that Trump was president, but didn't know what year it was. Another MRI this a.m. revealed a complication due to one of her anti-rejection meds that has caused swelling in her brain in the area that also happens to control vision, explaining why she can't see."

"She's slept pretty much all of today, giving her brain & body much needed rest. The few times she's awoken, the pain has been less severe but she's still unable to see. They stopped the drug in question and as it works its way out of her system, the swelling should resolve, her symptoms should diminish & things should return to normal. We fully understood there'd be good days & bad days, but no one could've prepared us for this! She's fought thru so much, but when is enough enough? I find myself echoing her questions of "Why?"

Please pray for the Great Physician's healing touch!!!"

That evening, February 9th, a few of the youth gathered at Pastor Aaron's and Jenna's house to have some intentional prayer time for Faith.

Thankfully the following day, Faith was able to feel some pain relief, and was becoming more like herself. So on February 10th, 2019, I was able to post an update,

"THE AMAZING POWER OF PRAYER — God is, and always will be, in the healing and miracle business!! Yesterday as the day wore on, Faith began to show significant improvement! Pain was still there but bearable; her vision slowly began to creep back in, at first still extremely blurry and with no color but eventually with some colors coming through. This morning she was sitting up eating her breakfast, some lights on, TV on, pain down to a 3, and her vision getting better by the hour. As I left the room to get something to eat myself, she was even looking at her phone for the first time in I think 4 or 5 days.

"I am truly overwhelmed and deeply grateful for the outpouring of support, love and prayers from everyone near and far, known to us and unknown! During one of our darkest, scariest times as fear, doubt and questioning crept in, your standing in the gap for us held us lifted and enveloped in His care.

"Please keep the prayers going strong as she continues to recover and as they slowly introduce a different anti-rejection med. Hopefully, she can leave the hospital again soon and get back to enjoying her beautiful new lungs. Recognizing that there will still be both good and bad days throughout this transplant recovery process, please join us in praying that any future bad days we face will NEVER be as bad as these last days have been!"

That same day, Faith even felt well enough to make her own post,

"Well, this past week has been a whirlwind. I finally got discharged from the hospital after being there for two months (yay!) only to have to go to the ER Sunday night and again Monday morning for severe migraines. I was then admitted to the hospital later that day. The next few days my pain started to increase tremendously but the doctors couldn't find the cause. I was getting nauseous and sick multiple times a day, my pain was even worse than it was after my transplant, and by Thursday my brain was swelling in the area that controls my vision, leaving me temporarily blind. The last week was probably

the most painful and most terrifying week of my life. But the doctors, my family, and my amazing God got me through it. We found the cause of the migraines, which was due to one of my anti-rejection medications, and I'm getting better every day! My headaches are still there but are pretty minor and my vision isn't back to normal but is also improving every day. Thank you for all of the thoughts and prayers from everyone!! Please continue praying as I still have a ways to go in the transplant recovery process."

This relief would be short-lived. Over that weekend, Faith's severe migraines came back in full force, and at about 4:00 in the morning on February 12th, I received a call from one of the doctors telling me that Faith was very upset, in pain, and wanted me there just as soon as I could get there. I immediately got dressed and went to the hospital.

Her pain was so severe and she was utilizing such a large amount of everyone's time, the medical team decided to move her back to MPCU where they could monitor her more closely since the nurse-to-patient ratio was smaller. An MRI two days later showed the swelling in her brain, though still significant, improving. Throughout the day, her pain levels also improved, and the team felt pain management was under control enough for her to return to the regular floor.

Before the move, a box was delivered that contained a HUGE Valentine's Day card and lots of smaller handmade cards from our phenomenal church family. Faith and I sobbed as we read the cards and messages, and she said it arrived right when she needed it. Having been feeling incredibly discouraged, reading these sweet messages made her feel like everyone from church

and God had their arms wrapped tightly around her. The day before, I asked a very dear friend to pray SPECIFICALLY that we would feel God's presence because, although intellectually I knew it not to be the case, emotionally and spiritually we felt like God had left us on our own. And as always, God did not disappoint! Not only did He make it clear He was continually by our side, but He did so in a very big way. Not to mention that on that whole day, Faith was pain-free!

A few years later, after Faith passed away, I had the difficult and daunting task of sifting through the multitude of pictures and videos on her phone. It was sad and beautiful all in one as I traveled through many different fun, silly, happy, difficult, and significant moments of her life. They have all, of course, become quite treasured to me. One small set of videos I discovered was a vlog (a video blog) that Faith was apparently going to do to share her transplant recovery journey. There ended up being only a couple of these videos, and I don't believe she ever posted them. The first one happened to be on that same Valentine's Day she received the box with the wonderful cards and messages from our church. She must have recorded it after I, feeling confident she was stable, had returned to the apartment. As Faith discusses the difficulty she was facing at the time, she also ends up giving a sweet testimony of her faith and trust in God, even in the midst of her pain, her questions, and times of wavering hope.

"Hi. . . . I don't really know what to say. I guess this is kind of day one. I don't know how many of these I'll be doing or how often. But just a little video—a vlog—or a documentation of my journey {of my} transplant."

"Today is officially one month since I had my transplant. Things were going really well, I was recovering amazingly, I was ahead of the game. I was on a study drug, which they thought I would have to stay in the hospital for six weeks for, and we were able to get it at home. Of course, now you may be asking why am I back in the hospital because, obviously, with all the 'beautiful' plugs and 'accessories' behind me, I am not in a regular room or place. That is because one of my anti-rejection medicines was causing something called PRES—I'm not going to try and say what that means—all I know is that the 'R' means 'reversible,' which is a good thing. But basically, my brain was swelling, and—I mean, it's going down, but it's not gone away yet. This is an unfortunate side effect that not everybody deals with and it's, unfortunately, happening to me and, unfortunately, it's taking a while to go away. But today has been a good day. I'm hoping that it continues to be a good day. I kind of wanted to make this

to document my emotional status throughout the day, my—it hasn't been a bad day, it's been an eye-opening day. And what I mean by that is this whole time I've been hearing of people praying for me and God's gonna get me through this and He's gonna make me stronger and I'm—I've got Him through this. But it hasn't necessarily always felt like that. When you're in so much pain and when you're so terrified, it's hard to see that He's actually there. It's hard to— hard to imagine that He is really around me and that He's really around in general. But today I got a Valentine's card from my church, and I opened it up and I saw all these notes from so many people, young and old, and—well, not old. I'm sorry if I offend anyone by saying that—older—younger and older—and I just felt God's presence and I felt my church family's presence. When I was done reading the cards—well, the big—they got me a really giant card which was probably one of the biggest cards I've ever seen, and I didn't know they made them that big, which is pretty cool—but they—once I was done reading that, I could feel every single one of them wrapping their arms around me. And I could feel God wrapping His arms around me, too. And to be so far away from home yet still feel that—it's been amazing. And it really gives me hope. When all this was happening—starting to happen—not getting—well, getting better and then not getting better again, having another relapse, I couldn't see the light at the end of the tunnel, I couldn't see what the purpose was for any of this. And I still don't see the purpose, but I see in my heart that it will end soon -- well that it will end. This won't be my life. I won't let it be my life. And then back to the card—I get all these cards, too, from little kids ranging from 7 to 12, and the younger ones may not completely understand, but they're so genuine and they're so caring, even though they're young, they don't really . . . they may not get the entire picture, but they, they care, and they know that this is for someone that is one of their brothers and sisters in Christ, and they love them, and I think that's amazing. And then I also listened to some for KING & COUNTRY songs, which you should totally check out. Just the message that they have in those songs is amazing and . . . I guess what I'm trying to say is that everything today has made me find my courage again in God, and has made me trust Him again, even though it is so hard, and it's—it seems impossible sometimes. But if you do, you trust Him, and if you put all your faith in Him, He will bring you through it, no matter what it is. No matter if it's a stubbed toe, which also is not fun, or a lung transplant, or a family member who's died, or just anything that's been going on in your life financially, health wise, family wise, anything... He wouldn't give it to you if He knew you couldn't handle it. He brings us through everything, and He will ultimately bring us home to Him. I just want to say thank you to everybody who has been supporting me, and encouraging me, and praying for me through everything. It's definitely helped. I know I said I was losing hope but seeing what everyone has been doing for me has helped that hope stay there—at least a little bit—and it's helped it grow. So, yeah, just thank you."

The following day, back in a regular room and feeling pretty good, she again felt up to making her own post:

"Well, not out of the hospital yet. We were expecting a mid-week discharge because I had gotten better, but over the weekend the migraines and vision problems came back. Luckily it didn't get as bad this time and I'm feeling better again. Hoping and praying that it actually lasts this time, however! Next step is to try another anti-rejection medication and make sure it doesn't have the same reactions. Thanks to all of the thoughts and prayers and I ask that they keep coming!"

They began to *very* slowly introduce Cyclosporin, the new anti-rejection medicine, with the plan of gradually increasing the dose until it reached therapeutic levels, hoping no further complications arose. This new medication was of the same class as Tacrolimus, so there was a little trepidation among the medical team about continued difficulties, which is why they decided to introduce it very, very slowly.

A few days later, on February 17th, Faith was resting peacefully, so I thought it would be a good time to go get something to eat in the cafeteria. The nurse had left a few moments earlier after administering medicines, so I knew Faith should be able to rest undisturbed for at least a little while. Before I left, I remembered I had a text from Jenni to which I hadn't yet responded, so I sat back down deciding to respond to the text before leaving the room. Halfway through my response, Faith started to shake, and I quickly realized she was having a seizure. I immediately ran to the other side of the bed (to this day, I am not sure why), shouting out the door for help as I pulled Faith up into a sitting position. No one seemed to hear me, so I pressed the nurse call button and screamed into the intercom, "She's seizing!" "She's sleeping?" came the reply. "No! She's seizing! She's having a seizure!" In what seemed like forever, but in reality was not very long, the room became rapidly crowded with a throng of medical personnel and a crash cart as a code was called over the loudspeaker announcing Faith's room number. More medical personnel came pouring into the room. I don't even recall who was there. I just remember it being a virtual army. They administered a drug called Ativan and eventually the seizures stopped. Through a series of their questions and my trying to recreate the timeline, we were able to determine that Faith's seizure had lasted approximately two and a half minutes. They decided to immediately take her down for a CT scan to try and understand what was happening and what may have caused the seizure. As we headed down the hallway towards the scan, she began having another seizure. They quickly rolled her gurney into the closest unit (one in which she had spent most of her time post-transplant), and proceeded to administer more Ativan to control the seizure. As I stood with my back against the wall feeling helpless, tears streaming down my face, one of the unit nurses, who had previously helped care for Faith, asked me if I was okay, to which I replied, "No. Not even the slightest little bit." With concern in her eyes, she simply reached out and stroked my arm in sympathy.

Once the seizure was under control, they proceeded to the scan, then admitted her back to MPCU rather than her room on the regular floor. I was tasked with going back upstairs and gathering all of her belongings from the regular floor, but all I could do was sit on her bed and cry. I spoke with Doctor D on the phone for a while as she tried to help me regain a sense of calm. It took me a long time, much to the chagrin of housekeeping who was waiting to clean the room for another patient, but I was finally able to gather everything together and proceed to Faith's room in MPCU. When Jenni came, she brought an air mattress for me to sleep on in Faith's room, and I bought some clothes from the gift store because at that point, there was no way I was leaving the hospital or Faith's side unless other family was there.

That evening, as Jenni sat with Faith, Pastors Mike and Aaron dropped everything to make the two-and-a-half-hour drive to Chapel Hill to sit with me while I filled them in on all that had happened. They spent a few hours with me in the hospital's Children's Chapel, praying with me before turning around and driving back—saying they would do it all again the next day if I needed them to.

Faith would later tell me that, although she didn't remember the second seizure, she did indeed remember the first one and knew that she was having a seizure. She remembered trying to will herself to stay calm hoping that would help the seizure stop. She could hear me screaming out in the background and wanted to tell me it would be okay.

Doctor K from the transplant team immediately discontinued the Cyclosporine, feeling sure that it had led to the seizures. The team then began the tedious work of trying to figure out what anti-rejection medicine Faith would be able to tolerate. Because Tacrolimus and Cyclosporine were the best options for lung transplant recipients, they struggled with finding one that would give her the immunosuppressant coverage she needed and even reached out to many colleagues at various other hospitals for advice, suggestions, and ideas. Meanwhile, because Faith was not currently receiving any immunosuppressant coverage and unbeknownst to any of us, the T cells awoke and began slowly recognizing the lungs as foreign.

The following day, when we had a moment to breathe, with Jenni's help since my brain was exhausted and foggy, we posted an update on social media:

"Recovery continues to be a roller coaster. Faith had two medicine-induced seizures yesterday as complications of the swelling in her brain (a condition called PRES), one episode in her room and another while being wheeled down for a CT scan. This was obviously terrifying for all of us (especially since Faith has no history of seizures) and continues to be as she tries to bounce back from this.

"Since the episodes, Faith has had a CT scan, spinal tap, MRI, continuous monitoring by EEG, and a myriad of medicines/procedures to suppress any other seizures as well as help with pain and nausea, as her migraines have come back full force. She has been in severe pain since last night, only just now seeming to get some restful sleep after the chronic pain team at the hospital administered a lidocaine procedure through her nose meant to numb the nerves that may be responsible for the migraines.

"After speaking with her doctors, it's been confirmed that all of this (the headaches, nausea, seizures) are due to the PRES developed from her anti-rejection medicine. She was introduced to a new anti-rejection medicine on Saturday, which is thought to have spiked these severe reactions. She's since been taken off of it and will not be given a new one until the PRES looks like it is completely gone. They are also going to ensure she receives a different "class" of anti-rejection medicine since she has proved an intolerance to the ones they've been trying so far.

"All the doctors and teams here are confident Faith will get through

this just fine, and we know that too. But right now in the thick of it, it is still very hard to experience. Understandably, Faith's spirits are completely shot. She's in pain, exhausted, scared, angry, asking a lot of "why" questions and just wanting all of this to be over. Please continue to wrap her in your prayers and your thoughts, and please continue to share her story and contribute to the ever-growing financial burden that comes with prolonged hospital stays, new medications, and everything else involved in this process."

The next day, Faith showed some good improvement. She was much more awake and herself, talking, laughing, and even working on some of her homework. She was still exhausted and dealing with pain and discomfort, but overall, showed a huge change from the day before. Since she was showing such promising signs of improvement, the day consisted of managing the pain and nausea, removing the EEG monitors, eating for the first time in days, having a neurological assessment, and receiving the new plan for anti-rejection medication. The main concerns at that point were making sure the pain and nausea were kept at bay as well as the fact that Faith had slowly begun to lose feeling and mobility in her body throughout the day, mainly her legs. After the assessment, the neurology team assured us that nothing was too concerning, that her body had been through an awful lot and simply needed to go through a reconditioning process. Her transplant team was also optimistic about the new anti-rejection medicine they had decided upon, called Belatacept (primarily used after kidney transplants), which would be introduced the following day via IV infusion. It was a different class than Tacrolimus and Cyclosporine so it wasn't expected to exacerbate the PRES.

The following day, I received a sweet message from Lauren, the director/owner of Faith's first competition dance studio. It was such an amazing message from God, prompting the following post,

"NUGGETS FROM GOD — These last few weeks have definitely stretched our faith many times and in many ways. As Faith faced the hardest fight of her life, and things seemed at their darkest, at times we felt forgotten and alone. At times we cried out in anger and desperation to God. At times it was a whisper of pleading. I lost count of how many times I watched Faith hold her head as if trying to keep it from ripping apart, eyes tightly shut as the pain steadily increased to levels never before felt, whispering 'please! please!' under her breath. It was terrifying as the number of doctors also steadily increased as each new team tried to come up with anything—ANYTHING—that would give her relief! Pulmonology, Neurology, Infectious Disease, Psychology, An-

esthesia / Pain Management, Physical Therapy, Ophthalmology, Nephrology—a virtual ARMY! I whispered desperate pleas of my own as I helplessly watched another 'army' tend to her when she had seizures, just as I had many times throughout these past weeks watching her battle incomparable pain. But through it all, God sent nuggets when we needed it most—reminders that although we couldn't always see or feel Him, He was always there, still watching over us and still in control.

"*I received one such nugget Wednesday from a sweet friend . . . in the form of a song by Lauren Daigle that, from first verse to last, seemed to be written just for us.—'You are not hidden / There's never been a moment you were forgotten / You are not hopeless / Though you have been broken . . . I hear you whisper underneath your breath / I hear your SOS . . .' Then as the chorus began—'I will send out an army to find you / In the middle of the darkest night / It's true, I will rescue you.'[7]—I couldn't help but think of the army of nurses and doctors coming to her aid, as well as the huge army of prayer warriors standing daily in the gap for us! The rest of the song is no less poignant or right on point and I pray that you will be as blessed by it as we were.*

"*Faith's been doing much better yesterday and today, with minimal pain. It's been a relief to see her blood pressure returning to normal after watching it spike as high as 193/104. The feeling in her limbs has returned and she was even allowed to leave the floor with me yesterday to attend one of the transplant classes! Her vision is still somewhat 'off,' most likely due to the PRES still healing. They began her new anti-rejection medication, which she seems to be tolerating well. If all goes as planned over the next few days, she should be able to be discharged sometime on Monday! Thank you all for being part of the army God sent to surround us in His care. Please keep the prayers and support going, as both are continually needed.*"

By February 20th, Faith was showing considerable improvement. She made four laps around the unit and was beginning her fifth when the nausea set in.

On the 25th of February, we were finally given the exciting news that Faith was once again being discharged. They believed they had pain management under control, seizures under control, and with the new anti-rejection medication, she could hopefully get on with living her life with her new lungs! She was ecstatic and with much thanksgiving posted,

"*Discharge dayyyy! (Again) Finally, after weeks of pain and some of the most terrifying moments of my life, I'm back out of the hospital! I can now once again start living the new life that was gifted to me. Still dealing with mild headaches while the PRES continues to run its course, but just hoping for smooth sailing from now on! Thank you to everyone for all of the support, encouragement and prayers through such a hard time! I wouldn't have been able to get through it without my friends, family, and most importantly my amazing God! . . ."*

Bumps in the Road

March 1, 2019

13

Road to Recovery
(Life in Chapel Hill)

The next several months would prove to be some of the best months in Faith's life. She experienced victory after victory and was able to breathe in deeply without the need for oxygen or feeling like she was breathing through a straw. We settled nicely into life in Chapel Hill, taking many walks around our community, going to movies, and eating at Al's Burger Shack, our favorite local burger joint. I continued working remotely while Faith diligently did her online school. We had frequent visits to the transplant clinic for follow-ups, blood tests, X-rays, transplant classes, and Belatacept and IVIG infusions. Life was good, and Faith was more than ready to start living . . .and her fighting spirit began to kick up a notch!

Now that she was able to foresee a future, she was ready for that future to unfold and did not want to put anything off, such as going to prom, spending time with friends, dancing, going to Snowbird that summer with the church youth group, and visiting family. But above all, she was itching for the day we could move back home to Charlotte! She was not content to wait to live her new life. She wanted to enjoy it now. And she wanted to enjoy it at home. She understood the need to remain in Chapel Hill while certain issues were being resolved, yet began pushing her transplant doctors and coordinator to loosen the reins a bit and let her start living her new life. She was ready for her future to begin, much to the consternation of her transplant team, who wanted her to slow down a bit and focus on the medical side of things. She was very feisty, and I honestly don't think her transplant team quite knew what to do with her at times. They even made several calls to Doctor D, her former pediatric pulmonologist, for advice on how to deal with her spitfire attitude.

March 1st, 2019, was Faith's first clinic appointment since being discharged after the episodes from PRES, and for the most part, it went really well. She had gained weight, her lab levels were good, and the PRES appeared to be progressing in the right direction. The only downside to the appointment  was that her lung function was not as high as the doctors were expecting but was still way higher than pre-transplant. They performed a CT scan of her lungs that day and scheduled a bronchoscopy for after the weekend, just to make sure there was no rejection or infection brewing. Sitting in the waiting room that following Monday, waiting to be called back for the bronchoscopy, Faith would continue working on her online school as I continued to work.

Because the bronchoscopy and CT scans did not show any complications and Faith was doing so well, she received permission from the transplant team to travel to Raleigh on March 9th to see her dance team perform at their first competition. It was a beautiful and heart-warming reunion as all the girls screamed upon seeing Faith, and many hugs were shared all around. But one of the greatest victories came after the competition when we went to dinner with a couple of the girls and their moms—we *walked* two miles to the restaurant without Faith needing any oxygen, getting winded, or being reduced to wracking coughs. It was phenomenal. Faith would later post,

"I don't know where I'd be without my amazing dance family. Even though I haven't seen these girls for a couple months, it feels like we haven't spent any time apart. Love y'all and can't wait to get back to competing together!"

On March 14th, for her two-month "lungaversary," I was overjoyed to post,

"HAPPY TWO MONTH LUNG-AVERSARY! — Two months ago today, Faith and her new lungs formed a beautiful new union together. The road leading up to transplant and the journey that's followed has been a path of many hills and valleys, discouraging setbacks and exciting victories -- but through God's strength and the powerful prayers and loving support of so very many near and far, Faith has persevered through every challenge on this journey with a courage, grace and determination well beyond her years!!

"Please continue to keep her lifted in prayer for the days and months ahead, as her journey is far from over and will no doubt be filled with many more hills and valleys . . . Thanks to all for your love, prayers and support, and Congratulations to Faith on her two month lung-aversary!"

And Faith would post,

"Wow. I cannot believe it's been two months since transplant. What better way to spend my 2 month "lungaversary" than being able to walk around on such a nice day WITHOUT getting out of breath or going into coughing fits! I still have a long journey ahead but days like these give me so much hope and encouragement. Thanks to everyone who continues to support me through all of this! . . ."

A few days later, we went to see the movie, *Five Feet Apart*, which is a movie about several teenagers with cystic fibrosis. The movie focused on their struggles with the disease, their camaraderie with one another, and their desire to "take back" one foot of the required six-foot distance they were supposed to keep from one another. We were somewhat apprehensive about seeing the movie, as we did not know how accurate a picture it would paint, and if it would cause a warped view of cystic fibrosis. This was Faith's "review" . . .

"Yesterday, my mom and I went to see the movie Five Feet Apart. There's been a lot of controversy over this movie within the CF community because some feel it brings awareness and that's awesome, but others are concerned it's going to give false information. For those of you who may not know, it's a movie/book mainly about two CF'ers who are struggling with keeping to the CF guidelines of staying 6 feet apart so they don't catch each other's

bacteria. Because CF has stolen so much from them, they decide to steal one foot back. I don't want to say anything more that will spoil the movie. But I will say that as far as explaining the captivity CF'ers always feel, the struggles of coughing and dealing with tons of treatments and tons of medicines multiple times a day, it hit home. It showed losses we face, whether that be people, things we want to do but can't because of hospital stays, doctor visits, or simply because our lungs can't breathe enough, and normal childhood or teenage experiences. Both my mom and I did enjoy the movie, but bawled our eyes out because it so closely captured so many things we've experienced. It did have its moments and details that weren't exactly accurate, which was slightly frustrating. (Like who actually gets to stay in a hospital that nice and with that much freedom) But that's Hollywood, and even with that, it is still bringing awareness to a disease so many people aren't aware of and opening up conversations. And THAT is definitely a good thing!"

Faith would also continue her physical therapy to help condition her new lungs. She would have to pass specific benchmarks with her physical therapy before she would be allowed to go home, and as with everything else in her recovery process, she surpassed them and "graduated" early, putting us one step closer to returning home to Charlotte! It was an exciting day on March 20th when I was privileged to post,

"Who would've ever thought that aching muscles would be a blessing? But then who would've ever thought that Faith would be able to do THIS!?! Jogging—uphill—no need for oxygen to recover afterwards—and not followed by uncontrollable coughing fits! Faith has done so remarkably well with physical therapy that, after only 7 sessions, she already far exceeded the goals they have in place for post-transplant patients. So today she officially 'graduated' from physical therapy, which is typically a several month process and which is ONE of the steps required in order to be released back to Charlotte! So although there still may be several hurdles to yet jump through, this got us one step closer to home!!!

"Please keep her lifted in prayer as she continues to push on through the recovery process and overcome the numerous obstacles that pop up along the path of her amazing journey."

While at physical therapy one day, I noticed a mom and son who looked very familiar sitting across the room. Being so far from home, I was trying to pinpoint how I could possibly know them. And then it hit me. Earlier in the year, a page called "Running With Danny" began following our Lungs4Faith page. Out of curiosity, I navigated to their page to see who they were and discovered it was for a teenage boy from Florida named Danny who also had CF. I began following their page in return. We followed each other's journeys closely for several months. So when I saw them in the physical therapy waiting room, I leaned over to Faith and said, "I think that's Running With Danny!" To confirm my suspicion, I walked across the room and asked the mom, "Running With Danny?" When she nodded, I pointed to myself and Faith still sitting across the room, and said, "Lungs4Faith!!" Even though we had never met before that moment, it felt like two old friends running into each other after a long time. We did get to know each other fairly well over the next several months as we attended many of the same transplant classes, and it was wonderful to have this sense of camaraderie with a fellow CFer and caregiver. Due to contact precautions and the "six-feet-apart" rule for CFers, Faith and Danny were not able to interact much, but I felt like I got to know his mother, Mari, pretty well.

Transplant classes were another requirement for lung transplant patients to attend. They were filled with people in all stages of the transplant process . . . those waiting to be listed, those listed but still waiting for lungs, and those, like Faith, who had already had their transplant. The classes had various topics such as the surgery, post-transplant nutrition requirements, rejection, etc. They also had Q&A sessions with patient panels or caregiver panels to answer questions posed by other class members. Faith sat on the patient panel once, and I was on the caregiver panel once. Even though the majority of patients in our classes were there for reasons other than CF, it was still another source of camaraderie that made us feel not quite so alone in the process.

By the end of March, Faith was, for the most, doing pretty well on the medical front but still needed to overcome a few hurdles before any talks about a release date to Charlotte could be held. After a full day of clinic on the 28th, complete with a CT scan, chest X-rays, lab work, PFTs, and a bronchoscopy, they found her PFTs to be down from the previous week, and the CT scan to be a little cloudy. The team said this could indicate infection, rejection, or a form of lymphoma common with post-transplant patients. Because Faith wasn't feeling sick—in fact, Doctor L of her transplant team said at this time she looked great!—Doctor L said infection and rejection were less likely. He assured us that if it was lymphoma, it was not the "scary" kind and was very treatable. He also said he could see from the bronchoscopy that her lungs were still beautiful. It would take a few days for biopsy results to come in. They also began talking about setting her up for surgery to correct acid reflux issues which they feared might be causing injury to her lungs, resulting in the low PFT numbers.

Faith's hard work and diligence were not just captured on the medical front. Faith was doing a phenomenal job catching up on schoolwork through NCVPS (North Carolina Virtual Public School). Even though she had not been able to start the spring semester until March, by the end of that month, she was already ahead of the class in one subject and caught up in two others. She loved to do her schoolwork sitting at Starbucks drinking her favorite caramel iced coffee with cream or sitting in an eno (a type of hammock) at the park. We registered her for the SATs and ACTs, and serious discussions about colleges were in their beginning stages. Looking toward the future with great anticipation and excitement became the norm.

Faith also received a wonderful visit from some friends from Charlotte. They, their moms, and I had a fantastic time catching up, eating at Al's Burger Shack, and spending some time being silly and just having fun—something Faith hadn't been able to do in such a very long time.

At the beginning of April, Faith was able to experience some additional victories. On the 3rd, during a visit from my dad, he bought her a bicycle in celebration of her new lungs. She was so excited to be able to enjoy riding a bike again, something she had not been able to do in years. And then on the 6th, Faith got to do something she had longed to do for months and months

– she got to dance! Oxygen free! We found a local dance studio in Durham that welcomed the chance to give her some private lessons to get her back up to dance form in preparation for her senior year on the competition team in Charlotte. Not only was it an extremely exciting time for her, but it also gave her the added benefit of additional physical therapy to keep conditioning her beautiful new lungs. The instructor, Elliott, agreed to give her lessons, and even let her "audit" a few classes, saying she could do so until the time we were given the green light to go home.

Faith, in her desire to fully *live* with her new lungs, continued to push for the things that she deeply wanted to do – one of which was to return to Charlotte for a weekend and attend her junior prom. Having received the required permission from the transplant team, Faith returned to Charlotte for the weekend of April 12th and enjoyed a beautiful night with her friends at prom on the 13th. It was an amazing way to celebrate her three-month lungaversary.

At Faith's next clinic appointment, upon returning to Chapel Hill after a phenomenal weekend, the chest X-rays showed something a little concerning, which combined with her low PFTs, prompted another bronchoscopy. The results showed a small section of rejection, which they said could be handled with a three-day burst of high-dose steroids. This would, of course, require a hospital stay. At this time, they also determined that Belatacept, the current anti-rejection medicine, was not the optimal one for lung transplant patients, and they wanted to slowly reintroduce Cyclosporine, the second one they had previously tried right before her seizures. They thought while she was already in the hospital for the steroids would be a good time to try this, so she could be closely monitored should any complications arise.

April 24th was discharge day for what we hoped would be her final hospital stay for our time in Chapel Hill, which we also hoped and prayed was soon drawing to a close. The three-day burst of steroids seemed to help bring down the inflammation, and Faith's lung function showed dramatic improvement. The reintroduction of Cyclosporine was also going well, as they began the tedious task of slowly increasing the dose every few days. All of our nerves were shattered during this time as we anxiously awaited to see if she would be able to tolerate the medication without migraines, increased swelling in her brain, seizures, or a stroke! All I could think was that it was well past time for the path on this journey to propel her forward to truly enjoy life with her beautiful new lungs, instead of continually boomeranging her back to the hospital. Also, at this point, this was the *only* thing holding us back from returning to

Charlotte, as they wanted her close in case any more PRES symptoms started to happen.

The following Saturday was gorgeous and sunny, and Faith was feeling great. We sat out by the pool (she was unfortunately not allowed to go *in* a pool for the first year following the transplant), and we took some pictures of her scars from the transplant surgery, of which there were many. She then posted,

"I've always wanted to hide my CF, run away from it. But I've learned to embrace it and my scars because it only shows what I was able to overcome, and that I won, and I am still winning."

With her appetite dramatically increased since the transplant, combined with our many trips to Al's Burger Shack, we also attempted some new recipes at the apartment. One of the things Faith wanted to try was making broccoli cheddar soup in the Instant Pot. I was still very unfamiliar with using the Instant Pot but thought it would be fun to try together. So we got all the ingredients, including a can of cheddar cheese soup. I placed the broccoli in the pot, followed by the soup, turned the steam nozzle to "seal" and started the pot. After the allotted time, I turned the steam nozzle to "release" and, instead of steam coming out of the nozzle, cheddar cheese began spewing everywhere! It was all over the counters, all over the cabinets, and all over the floor. At first, we panicked, but then we simply laughed and laughed at ourselves as we cleaned up the mess and decided googling some instructions might have been the better course of action. We then went to Al's.

A couple of days later, following Easter Sunday, we received a very sweet visit from Pastor Mike and Pastor Richard, the senior adult pastor. They arrived with two huge Easter baskets that had been put together by members of our church for me and Faith.

I continued to enjoy watching Faith dance several times a week at the local studio and posted in early May 2019,

"Can't WAIT to again be able to watch this girl pour out her heart and soul on the stage! And this time we'll no longer need to have oxygen tanks waiting on each side of the stage for recovery after she finishes a dance!!!"

I think of this often now and so wish I would have been able to see her dance at least at *one* competition without the need for oxygen.

On May 14th, Faith's four-month lungaversary and the day before her eighteenth birthday, I had arranged for Pastor Aaron, along with Faith's dear friends Kyle and Glenn, to decorate our Charlotte home. I wanted the house to be cheerful and celebratory when we returned for a long weekend for her birthday. When we arrived, I let her go in first . . . there were balloons and decorations everywhere! It was truly amazing and very special.

But not as special as getting to celebrate her eighteenth birthday in the first place—a birthday that toward the end of 2018, we were not even sure she was ever going to see. But if anyone had ever fought for and earned a birthday like none other, it was Faith! She had been through more than any young lady should ever have to endure. But as always, her beauty and strength continued to outshine the struggles and hurdles. She exemplified courage, and to many people was the definition of a warrior. I was beyond proud

of how she had traveled her journey and was excited for the beautiful plan God had in store for her in the years ahead.

We were also very excited to be able to celebrate this birthday back home in Charlotte, along with family and friends, instead of stuck in Chapel Hill or worse yet, the hospital. A few days after her birthday, Faith would post,

"A few days late but I'm officially an adult! At the beginning of this year, I didn't know if I'd make it to this birthday. But I did and I got to celebrate it with the most amazing people the whole week"

Another exciting, joyous, and victorious weekend came around Memorial Day, in which we got to spend another long weekend at home in Charlotte. On June 1st, we went to Carowinds Amusement Park as a family to enjoy the rides and to "cash in" on our free tickets to see *for KING & COUNTRY*, which included entrance into the park. It was a gorgeous day filled with beautiful moments and memories, and happened to be during a time when Faith was feeling

at her best since the transplant. Before the concert, we were invited to join the "Meet & Greet" with Joel & Luke from *for KING & COUNTRY*, and they were so excited to see Faith, especially given the last time they had seen her she was sitting in the hospital on 24/7 oxygen. They filmed a short video then had their broth-er, Josh, take us all over to the merchandise booth and told us to get anything we wanted—on them!

The concert, as we expected, was amazing! The most special moment came during one of their songs, "It's Not Over Yet," where they have about a ten-second pause in the song. Joel was making his way up the aisle singing the song and suddenly jumped up on top of an empty seat . . . right in front of Faith! He had no idea, at first, that Faith was right in front of him. When he saw it was her, at the very moment of the song's pause, he jumped off the seat, waved the band to hold on a moment, and said, "I have to take a picture with a very special young lady just to commemorate this moment." They took a selfie together, and

he gave her a huge hug before proceeding up the aisle continuing the song. Following the concert, we were all invited backstage to talk with Joel and Luke again, and Joel still could not believe he had ended up directly in front of Faith at just the right moment in the song. We talked and laughed and got some more pictures of Joel, Luke, and Faith. It was truly a magical night! Faith shared her excitement and appreciation for the band with the following post,

"Words cannot express how amazing and perfect this day was. Getting to see for King & Country once again and hearing them say how much they've

been thinking of and praying for me means so much. They are the most genuine people I've ever met. Their music, their faith, and God have gotten me through some of the toughest times in my life and I couldn't have asked for more. Thank you guys so much!"

It was an amazing way to close out a fabulous day, and our whole family was so grateful to *for KING & COUNTRY* for making it possible. Faith thoroughly enjoyed reconnecting with them before and after the concert. It was amazing to reflect on the fact that the first time they met Faith, they were hugging her in a hospital room where she was struggling to breathe, and exactly six months later, they were hugging her at a concert as we celebrated her new life with her new lungs!

The following day, Faith was able to spend a phenomenal day hanging out with friends, something that was in very short supply for her these days.

HISRadio also once again ran a segment about Faith and *for KING & COUNTRY*, highlighting that special moment in the middle of the concert. The heading for this His Morning Crew segment was *"for KING & COUNTRY Pauses Concert for a Special Reason."*

ALISON STORM: *"There are fans, and then there are super fans. And I want to tell you about someone who loves for KING & COUNTRY. Her name is Faith Shaw, and at the end of last year she wanted so badly to attend the for KING & COUNTRY concert, but she was in the hospital waiting for a lung transplant. So Joel & Luke Smallbone from the band actually gave her a private concert there in her hospital room (they then played a small portion of a video from for KING & COUNTRY's Instagram page from December 2018 when they visited Faith in the hospital and sang some of "Little Drummer Boy"). . . . Faith got her new lungs January 14th, and she's still been in and out of the hospital as her body heals, but overall, she's doing really well. So when for KING & COUNTRY came to Rock the Park this weekend in Charlotte, she knew she had to be there. And then the most amazing thing happened during the concert. As Joel walked out into the crowd singing, he saw Faith and stopped everything."*

She then mentioned our GoFundMe page, along with the exorbitant medical expenses we were still facing, such as my co-pay for Faith's prescriptions, which were around $350 per month.

After such a magical and fun-filled, exciting weekend, it was so hard on both of us returning to Chapel Hill, but more so on Faith as she would, once again, be bound for the hospital.

On the morning of June 4th, 2019, Faith woke up with excruciating pain in her belly. After consulting with the transplant coordinator, we were instructed to take her immediately to the ER, where we found ourselves in what I was calling a God thing! Not only had Faith enjoyed the previous four weekends at home before further complications arose, but we also found ourselves in one of those situations where something that was not too terribly serious but painful enough to bring us to the ER resulted in finding something that had not yet presented symptoms, but could have become a lot more serious if not jumped on early.

From a CT scan, they were able to determine the initial issue that brought Faith to the ER was relatively common and easily remedied. However, the CT scan also showed that Faith was dealing with either pneumonia or rejection in her left lung. She was admitted—again—to the hospital, and they arranged for a bronchoscopy the following day to determine the issue at hand and the course of action they needed to take. She had originally been scheduled for a routine five-month, post-transplant follow-up bronchoscopy the following week, but that would have afforded the infection or rejection many additional days to take hold and get worse. So we found ourselves very thankful for the intense pain that had brought her to the ER. Not that we were ever thankful she was in the hospital or in any kind of pain, but things could have been worse. The issue ended up being rejection, so she was able to again receive the three-day high-dose steroid regimen and be discharged. Having already passed the original hoped-for release date of May 3rd, we were praying this was the final resolution needed to get the path toward home to Charlotte back on track.

Unfortunately, the hits that month did not stop. Only a week later, on her five-month lungaversary, Faith began experiencing severe abdominal pain resonating to her back and ribs, nausea, and a low-grade fever. The transplant coordinator instructed us to once again make yet another trip to the ER to get her started on fluids and IV medication. They scheduled her for another CT scan and set her up for admission for at least the weekend to address whatever the cause was. The one praise I could see was in the timing. After having spent the previous four weekends at home for her birthday, Memorial Day, the *for KING & COUNTRY* concert/Carowinds, and to take her ACT exam, this particular weekend was one in which we had already planned on staying in Chapel Hill. Certainly not in the hospital, of course, but I do not believe it was a coincidence that her current issue had not interfered with her having been able to enjoy those moments back home. We were hoping and praying hard that this would be another short hospital visit.

Four days later, on June 18th, 2019, I sadly made the following post:

"ROLLERCOASTERS ARE SUPPOSED TO BE FUN . . . Unfortunately, the rollercoaster of transplant recovery doesn't always fall into that 'fun' category. Thinking Faith would be discharged from the hospital yesterday or today on an oral antibiotic regimen, a tougher-to-treat bug reared its ugly head in the cultures from Saturday's [bronchoscopy], changing the course of the treatment plan. Tomorrow—which also happens to mark SIX MONTHS that we've been in Chapel Hill—Faith will be having a PICC line (long-term IV line) put in for hopefully just a couple weeks of IV meds, but potentially longer. Not only does this delay the hospital discharge by a few days, the IV schedule is typically brutal, the PICC line can be uncomfortable and gets in the way of daily tasks, but this also puts the release home to Charlotte back to 'up in the air.'

"Six months away from friends, away from our church family, away from our home, and away from our support network—along with six months of paying double rent & utilities—is taking a heavy toll on both of us. Though we certainly don't want to return home until she is medically ready, we so desperately long for that time to come quickly. And although we know God has already traveled this path ahead of us and prepared the way—in His perfect timing—we long for that timing to be SOON!

"So, my friends, please join us once again in prayer that the current IV plan will be swift and 100% effective in destroying the infection, and that this is simply God's springboard to get her home in the healthiest condition with the absolute best outcome for years and years and years of a wonderful and blessed life. To receive new lungs and a new life has been nothing less than a miracle! Please pray we cling to that and to the gentle Hand that has brought us through every hurdle, every circumstance good and bad, has never left our side, and never will!"

That same day, Faith would also post,

"Alright, these past 5 days have been really rough. I went to the ER

Friday for some really bad stomach pains, got admitted that day, and Saturday they took a look at the lungs and found an infection and some bacteria that I've struggled with before many times, even before transplant. Then we had to wait for some more results over the weekend (which, a lot of the time is one of the most anxiety provoking parts). We at first were told most likely I could go home yesterday or today on some oral antibiotics but this morning they found more bacteria growing and these bugs can be hard to treat. So they want to be aggressive and do -hopefully- just a couple weeks of IV antibiotics. I'll admit I'm angry and frustrated because it seems like things just keep popping up, but after some time of reflection and thinking I know this is probably the best thing and it's all a part of the plan. All I ask for is thoughts and prayers while my family and I try to get past this next hurdle and that it hopefully goes away quickly and easily!"

A couple of days later, in a surprising yet extremely exciting and welcome turn of events, even given Faith's continuing situation with pneumonia, the transplant team told us that all else was good, and we were free to return to Charlotte following her IV antibiotics treatment—for *good*! This was the moment we had long been waiting for and provided no other complications arose within the next week, we were now on track to return home to Charlotte somewhere between June 28th and July 1st—home to *stay*! At long last! There would still be frequent follow-up visits to Chapel Hill, but we would finally be at *home* home.

In a post on social media, after announcing the news that we were coming home, I expressed my intense gratitude to our amazing support network:

"Two days ago marked SIX MONTHS that we've been in Chapel Hill, and I can't thank each of you enough for your undying support, love, encouragement, and prayers! This has been the most difficult time in our lives, and the support from our friends, family, co-workers, my company, our church, people near and far that we've never even met—everybody—has made the burden that much easier to carry.

"But please don't stop praying! Just because we're returning home doesn't mean the fight is over. I continue to fight insurance on several fronts; our monthly co-pay for her lifelong medications is around $350-$400 (that's a car payment—for a nice car!); Faith could experience rejection at any time; and because she is so immunosuppressed to try and keep her body from rejecting the lungs, she is also less 'armed' to fight off even the most mild of viruses

and bacteria—in fact, this latest hospitalization and bout with pneumonia is because somewhere she came in contact with someone who had the rhinovirus—i.e. the common cold! So the battle will continue on some level for the rest of her life. The key to that, though, is that she is here to face that battle!!! There was a time at the beginning of this whole process that we weren't sure she would be."

I also immediately—and secretly—began reaching out to as many of Faith's friends from school, church, work, and dance as I could to set up a surprise "Welcome Home" party for her. I delegated certain tasks to a few people since I was two and a half hours away, and they quickly got to work. Pastor Mike's wife, Susan, was the go-to for RSVPs, as well as making a large banner saying, "Welcome Home, Faith." Faith's supervisors from work, along with some of her friends, provided food and drinks. Susan even reached out to some news outlets to see if they wanted to cover the story. We also had a "grand" excuse for getting Faith to the church instead of the house when we returned to Charlotte—we had to meet Pastor Mike there to pick up some chairs that Faith's sister, Kelsey, was going to borrow. Everything was very quickly being pulled together and put into place for this wonderful surprise—that almost did not take place.

At the Thursday clinic appointment, the day before we were to head home, her transplant doctor was disappointed with some of the lab test results and PFTs, so wanted Faith to continue the IV antibiotics for another week and for us to remain in Chapel Hill for a little while longer. I pulled Doctor K aside and told her about the surprise party. She shook her head and said, "I wish you guys wouldn't do things like this. You know that going home is always up in the air." To which I replied, *"You* told us it was time! *You* gave us the go-ahead. Why would we *not* make plans for going home?!?" She reluctantly agreed to let us continue with our plans to go home, as long as we waited for Faith's final week of IV antibiotics to be delivered to the Chapel Hill apartment.

The following day, both of our cars were loaded with things from the apartment that we were taking back home, but Faith was still not allowed to drive, due to the seizures she'd had in February. So her sister, Jenni, and Jenni's husband came from Raleigh to help us get both our vehicles back to Charlotte. We were quickly approaching the time we had to leave to make it for the surprise party, yet her IV medications had not yet arrived. I called the pharmacy to get an ETA. Unfortunately, they were going to be about another hour, so with the excuse that Pastor Farley couldn't wait too much past a particular time, I told Jenni, James, and Faith to go on ahead while I stayed behind and waited for the medication delivery.

I was very sad to miss the surprise part of the party, but from video footage, and even one channel's news coverage, it went extremely well. She was sufficiently surprised and deeply touched! I arrived about an hour late and was shown the videos of her arrival and later that evening got to see the news coverage:

NEWSCASTER: "[A Concord teen] is finally home, six months after a dou-ble-lung transplant. This evening the family and friends of 18-year-old Faith Shaw joined together to give her a big surprise Welcome Home party. Shaw has cystic fibrosis, and she spent the last six months in Chapel Hill to be close to the hospital."

PASTOR MIKE FARLEY: "And she's really been an example too, not just the young people here at the church, but to me, to everybody. She's just—we think of her as a hero, her and her mother especially, both of them. Her mother's a single mother and just the sacrifice and the amount of care that she's given her daughter, it's just an amazing story."

NEWSCASTER: "Faith's loved ones surprised her at West Concord Baptist Church. They are so happy to have her back home. And she looks pretty happy to be home."

It was another magical and victorious moment that would, sadly, once again be short-lived. The following morning, Faith spiked a 102.3 fever and was feeling worse than she had before the two weeks of IV antibiotics began. She had no energy and was feeling very run-down. I called the transplant co-ordinator on call, who instructed us to head back to Chapel Hill for her to be admitted to the hospital. In the meantime, Kelsey had planned a six-and-a-half birthday party for her son, Gabriel. She had not been able to throw him a sixth birthday party due to Faith being in the hospital and all of us with her through the evaluations and Christmas. When I told Faith that they wanted her back in Chapel Hill for hospital admission, she just sat there sobbing and sobbing. She then decided she was not about to miss this special day for Gabriel, as she had already missed so very much. So she told the coordinator that she was going to spend a couple of hours with her nephew and *then* would come to Chapel Hill. As much as she looked forward to that day with Gabriel, it was still a very difficult day for Faith since she was feeling so horrible. She felt horrible more than just physically, however. On the way back to Chapel Hill, through another round of tears, she talked about how the "Welcome Home" party the previous evening had all been for naught. I assured her that we were still considered "home," and this would hopefully be very short. I was, however, thankful to still have the apartment, the lease for which was not up until mid-September, so I did not have to get a hotel room.

A couple of days after being re-admitted to the hospital, Faith was slightly cheered up by a post made by *for KING & COUNTRY* referencing the June 1st concert at Carowinds —

"Remember Faith? We certainly do—8 months ago we met her in the hospital as she was awaiting a double lung transplant—she had planned to join us in concert but had taken a turn for the worse—But [recently], thanks to the miracle of modern medicine and after a double lung transplant she joined us in person! She's a heroine."

Shortly after that, I again shared a post of tremendous gratitude for all the support and prayers we had received from so very many people:

"In addition to the uplifting, gracious support by for KING & COUN-TRY for Faith during this most difficult journey of her life, another source of tremendous strength has been—and continues to be—the rock solid steady support of amazing family & friends, and our phenomenal church!

"Never wavering in their love, assistance, and powerful prayers, they've lifted us up to the Lord daily . . . sometimes hourly . . . giving us the peace, comfort, and strength to keep fighting!

"From occasional visits by family and friends to huuuge Valentine's wishes from church arriving just when needed most—the timing of which was unquestionably providential—to critical, crisis moments when Pastor Michael Farley and Youth Pastor Aaron Thomas dropped everything late in the evening, drove 2-1/2 hours to be by my side & pray with me before driving 2-1/2 hours back, saying they'd do it again the next day if I needed them to! From my brother, Tim, who also dropped everything multiple times pre- and post-transplant, traveling back and forth (from Maine!) to offer any assistance he could, to my mom, my dad, and many others who were standing READY to drop everything if the need arose! And, of course, Faith's sisters, Jenni & Kelsey, who along with their husbands have made many sacrifices to care for and minister to both Faith AND me!

We are profoundly blessed by this support network, and no words can express the depth of my gratitude and love for each of you! We appreciate continued prayers as Faith's battle continues and she still faces many difficult challenges. Thanks so much, and God bless!!!"

My next post would be July 3rd, when Faith was discharged again and allowed to return home to Charlotte—just in time for the 4th of July festivities she was hoping to get to enjoy.

"THE LONG ROAD HOME – So last Friday, June 28th, Faith was released to come home—as in MOVE home—back to Charlotte home! With the help of some fabulous "Home-Coming Elves," we successfully pulled off a wonderful surprise Welcome Home Party for her that even had some local news coverage!

"I never got a chance to share the excitement from this occasion before we, unfortunately, had to take a slight "detour" back to Chapel Hill the very next day for her to be re-admitted to the hospital to try and determine why she had a 102.3 fever and was feeling worse after two weeks of IV antibiotics. Five additional days in the hospital later, following multiple tests and a change-up in the IV medication plan, the team believes they have a clear handle on the issue and that their new treatment plan will get her back on the right track. They felt confident enough with the positive progress she was already making in just that short amount of time, they decided she could continue her IV medication therapy on an outpatient basis—and from Charlotte!!!

"So, my friends, I am extremely excited to share that WE ARE HOME! Home home! Charlotte home! We'll go back to Chapel Hill here and there for follow-up appointments and lab work, but those are expected to be simply day trips. Please keep lifting her up in prayer that this current therapy does what it's supposed to do and that no other complications arise! Please pray that when we go back in a couple weeks, she will have improved enough that she can discontinue the IV medication and have the PICC line removed. Please pray that this is just the beginning of a long, happy, healthy life with her new lungs and that future complications will be minimal and easily resolved. The world of organ transplant is tricky and unpredictable. But we can rest in the knowledge that God has already traveled the road before her and has prepared the path she'll travel.

"Thanks, as always, for your continued support, love, encouragement and prayers!"

But, as seemed to be the new norm, our excitement would once again be cut way too short.

July 2019

14

Beginning of the End

Faith was tolerating the reintroduction of her anti-rejection medicine, Cyclosporine, very well, with no migraines, seizures, vision difficulties, etc., and she was finally up to proper therapeutic levels giving her proper coverage. What none of us realized, however, was that the months she had spent not getting proper coverage had already caused her T cells to awaken and recognize the lungs as foreign. Masked by all the infections she kept getting, her body had already slowly begun rejecting the lungs undetected by the medical team.

Less than ten days after again returning to Charlotte, complications continued to rear their ugly head and spoil one plan after another for Faith's return to "normal" life and truly get to enjoy the beautiful new lungs with which she had been gifted—enjoy them someplace other than in the hospital! On the morning of July 12th, she awoke with a high fever, increased cough, and shortness of breath. Upon calling the transplant coordinator in Chapel Hill, we were instructed to head to the ER at CMC Main in Charlotte for labs and X-rays. Her O2 saturation had dropped into the eighties, and the X-rays showed her pneumonia to have progressed even after nearly a month on IV antibiotics. Our emotional state suffered another huge blow, as they decided to transport her back to the hospital in Chapel Hill to get yet another antibiotic regimen in place. Faith was extremely upset and angry, and I couldn't shake the feeling that I was going to lose her.

Now two days before her six-month lungaversary, I watched Faith being loaded into an ambulance for transport from CMC Main to the local airport where she would be transported to Chapel Hill via small plane. As I helplessly watched, I recalled the last time I had witnessed this scene on December 19th, 2018, as they transferred her from Levine Children's Hospital to UNC Chapel Hill to begin the transplant evaluation. We were hoping and praying

this hospital stay would turn out to be much shorter than the one that began in December. We pleaded with God that the issues could be resolved quickly and effectively so she could once and for all get on with living! Senior year was just around the corner, she wanted to participate in cheer tryouts, and it was going to be her final year of competition dance. She had so many goals and dreams we were praying would come to fruition.

On her six-month lungaversary, as she lay quietly resting in her hospital bed following a bout of tears, I posted a message to her on social media:

"My dear, sweet Faith—I know this wasn't the where and the how you—or any of us—hoped and expected you to be 'celebrating' this tremendously momentous occasion. It has without a doubt been a rollercoaster ride to end all rollercoaster rides, and I know the number of setbacks and hurdles you've had to endure has been overwhelming and unfair. But there have also been many victories and joyous moments you wouldn't have otherwise been able to enjoy or be a part of, and I believe those are only the beginning! I believe God has some great things ahead for you, and we need to somehow reach up through the murk and the muck of our frustration, discouragement, disappointment, and fear, grab hold of His hand, and let Him lead us through to the other side. I'm hoping and praying that together – along with the prayerful support of family and friends – we can lean on each other and on our Lord for encouragement, strength, and peace and try to focus on those beautiful positive moments. Pulling from yet another for KING & COUNTRY song, we need to '. . . CHOOSE joy!' I love you with all my heart and am so proud of you! You are an amazing young lady who deserves an amazing life, and it is coming! You WILL get through this!!"

But to Kelsey and Jenni, I expressed my sheer frustration and confusion with everything, as I texted, "I don't understand at all what God is doing and why. I know I obviously can't see the big picture . . . but I don't live in the big picture. I live in the here and now and that's from where my emotions are fed . . . my prayers don't seem to be getting past the ceiling."

On July 15th, as they prepared to do a bronchoscopy, Faith's oxygen needs became too great for her to tolerate the procedure without additional

help. In order to keep her oxygen levels up during the procedure, it was necessary to move her to ICU so they could put her on a ventilator. I was sick to my
stomach. I walked into her ICU room just as they were putting in the ventilator,
and it completely freaked me out. Other
than on TV shows, I had never seen the
procedure before, and it looked for all the
world to me like something had gone terribly wrong. I later found out that someone
at the nurse's station was supposed to keep
me from going to Faith's room until after
the procedure was done so I *wouldn't* witness the process. But that never happened.

Fortunately, Faith came off the
ventilator quickly afterward, but it caused
a small collapse in the upper part of her
lungs. The doctors were not overly concerned with the collapse, stating that
it looked stable and would expand back to normal over time. But it was very
painful for Faith. She was also now on eight liters of oxygen, which, of course,
was very discouraging given the fact that she was supposed to be enjoying new
lungs oxygen-free. It felt like pre-transplant all over again.

Preliminary results from the bronchoscopy showed no signs of infection, but there was still inflammation, leading the doctors to believe that her
lungs were dealing with one of three issues: immunologic injury, restrictive
Allograft Syndrome (a form of chronic rejection), or some other kind of injury. The available options for treating any of the three were limited. Doctor K
told Faith that she basically had a 50/50 chance of getting better. Faith's initial
response was that if a second transplant was her only chance of getting better,
she would rather die. She was, to say the least, frightened as we awaited further
results from the bronchoscopy and lab work, which could take several days.
The resulting news was devastating.

When the final test and lab results were received, it turned out that Faith
was, after all, facing a complex form of chronic rejection that up to this point
had gone undetected. The rejection was severe, and there appeared to be very
little hope for turning things around. While Faith slept, Doctor K and I stepped
out of her ICU room to discuss the prognosis. When I asked her if the team
felt the lungs would heal and Faith would get past this, the reply was, "I don't
know, to be completely honest, and we are very concerned." She discussed with
me the very limited options available and was not very optimistic about those
options being able to, at a minimum, stop the rejection process. When I asked

her what it would mean if they did not work, she gave me the grim news that it would probably give Faith no more than another six months. Much of what was said after that is lost in a fog of emotion. I merely remember many, many tears and a very heavy conversation with Doctor D—who had by this time become a dear friend to our whole family—about what was going on.

After waking up, Faith was very clearly and understandably distraught with many questions going through her mind. However, the only things she said to me all day were, "Why is this happening? I just want to be back to how it was . . . I want to do cheer, I want to dance, I want to hang out with my friends." This would be followed later by, "Can I get two grilled cheese sandwiches from the cafeteria?" Other than that, she spent the majority of her time sleeping, on her phone, or just staring.

Uncle Tim returned to Chapel Hill that evening (July 17th) primarily to offer *me* support this time. On July 19th, Pastors Mike and Aaron also drove to Chapel Hill again to pray with me, cry with me, and listen to my fears. Faith was also battling an ever-increasing depression and was "sure" that nothing was going to work to help her lungs because nothing seemed to be working for her. The team also did not seem very confident.

On July 20th, with Jenni's help, we posted an update about all that was currently happening:

"Trying to catch our breath after a long, hard week. Determining what is causing Faith's lungs to not function properly and how to help them heal has been many things: draining, frustrating, terrifying, and much more. While we have ruled out infection, it seems we are dealing with some complex form of rejection. Because we experienced so many issues getting Faith on the correct class and dose of anti-rejection medication, her body began to recognize and fight back against the new lungs. This went unnoticed as Faith was continuously dealing with new infections back to back, and by the time all the infections were finally clear, the extent of the injury and damage from the improper anti-rejection coverage revealed itself. Faith's oxygen needs have remained between 6-8 liters of oxygen this past week, and the doctors took several days determining the best course of action as they had to balance effective treatment while ensuring no more harm was done. Ultimately they landed on a plasma exchange (PLEX) procedure. Summarized simply, this involves a machine simultaneously removing Faith's blood, cleaning out harmful antibodies, and putting "clean" blood/plasma back.

"Her first PLEX session was yesterday and will continue every other

day (minus weekends) for 5 sessions, with Faith receiving an intense IV regimen on the off days. We ask everyone to specifically pray that PLEX will do what the doctors hope it will, as this is one of the only options we currently have to heal Faith's lungs. We are greatly encouraged and praise God that Faith's oxygen has already been reduced to 3-4 liters this afternoon! It is too early to definitively say whether this is a result of the PLEX or the high-dose steroids she was given earlier in the week, but we pray that this progress continues, that X-rays will show improvement over the course of the coming week, and that these hopeful lungs will breathe big breaths of air again very soon."

A few days later, round three of PLEX began much like the previous two rounds. However, about an hour into the process, Faith's blood pressure began to tank, her heart rate became extremely elevated, and her oxygen levels dropped dramatically. They bumped her oxygen up to eight liters, immediately aborted PLEX, and began infusing fluids to try and get her stabilized. Faith was understandably terrified as she struggled just to take in a breath. Over time, her numbers leveled out, and she was able to tell us that she had started to feel like she was drowning. The transplant team decided to discontinue future rounds of PLEX and try the only other treatment available. Although this treatment held promise, it also came with higher risks as it would kill off the white blood cells in her lungs – in essence wiping out her immune system.

Wanting to get started on the new treatment as soon as possible, they gave her the first dose that afternoon. As the evening progressed, Faith began to feel somewhat better but was still too anxious to allow them to reduce her oxygen, not wanting to feel even remotely close to what she had felt earlier that day.

The following day, July 25th, Faith showed definite improvement. Doctor L was amazed and extremely pleased with how much better Faith looked compared to the previous day and how much better her lungs sounded, especially her left lung. They began the second of five doses, each running for six to eight hours, as Faith continued making steady progress, including a substantial decrease in her oxygen needs. We began to risk feeling hopeful about this new treatment. She was told, however, that it was unlikely she would be well enough for rapidly approaching life events and activities, including starting her senior year of high school. Dance and cheerleading were also now completely out of the picture—devastating news to Faith.

The next morning, Doctor L was again ecstatic with how much improvement was happening so quickly, and he had not at ALL expected her to be doing so well, especially so soon. He even said, making NO promises and saying it very, very cautiously, that if Faith continued improving at this rate, she might—MIGHT—even get to her senior year. He then listened to her lungs and said, "We're definitely making progress."

Even with the positive movement, however, the process was taking a heavy toll on Faith's emotional state and that evening hit an all-time low in her level of discouragement and depression. She said she was tired of fighting and didn't feel like doing it anymore. She didn't know where God was. She was trying to turn to Him but wasn't feeling any comfort or peace or that He was even anywhere around. She didn't want to lose her new lungs or her life (not just in terms of life vs. death, but *life*—doing the things that brought her joy and meaning), but she just didn't feel like she could keep on fighting. She kept going back to the fact that she had fought so hard for so long to get to new lungs so she wouldn't have to fight so hard anymore. And now she was having to fight even harder than she had pre-transplant. She just didn't want to do it anymore.

The next day, once Faith stabilized and Uncle Tim sadly returned to Maine, she was cheered up with some of the best "medicine" she could get—a visit from four of her closest friends from home. They had a wonderful time catching up, and their support and encouragement were exactly what she needed to help her keep pressing on.

As Faith continued pressing on medically, she was also still trying to work on a couple of summer classes to make sure she was ready for senior year. I recall wheeling her around inside and outside the hospital in a wheelchair the next day with her camera so she could take various pictures to complete her photography assignment. It amazed me that, even given the huge hurdles she continued to face and the devastating news she had received throughout the last few weeks, she kept going—kept pushing forward—kept working towards living the best life she possibly could and preparing for her future.

That future, however, was very unclear and uncertain. On July 27th, Doctor L—always the most positive of the three doctors on the transplant team—spoke with me privately about a second transplant being a very real possibility if neither of these treatments worked. As if that wasn't bad enough, he did not believe the whole transplant team was on board with listing her again, in which case, he would try to link us up with the transplant team at Duke. However, on July 31st, Doctor C recommended beginning the evaluation process for a second transplant to get it out of the way in case things became worse. That day began very badly for Faith, with her blood sugar dropping to 51, nauseated, shaky, unable to catch her breath, and she was on high levels of oxygen. It took a while to get her stabilized. These complications prompted the re-transplant discussion. Doctor C informed Faith she would be lower on the list this time since her oxygen requirements were not as high as they had been in December, so her wait would be longer. And being a second transplant, which had potentially greater complications, they would require us to remain in Chapel Hill for a *minimum* of one year following the transplant. Faith's fragile emotions were not yet ready to broach this subject, and she shut down once again, refusing to talk with any of us about it.

In early August, with the completion of the treatments administered to kill off her white blood cells to try and turn things back around, the waiting game began. All we could do at that point was wait—wait to see if the hoped-for benefit would be achieved. It was confirmed that the process had success-fully halted Faith's system from attacking the new lungs. What we *didn't* know was how much improvement she would have, or the amount of lung function she would be able to regain, if any at all.

She did show enough improvement that the transplant team believed her to have stabilized enough to at least play the waiting game out of the hos-pital. They discharged her and released us back to our Chapel Hill apartment where we would be required to stay for two to four weeks while waiting to see if her lung function continued to improve. She remained on oxygen full-time, which we hoped to see decrease over the next several weeks, until eliminated altogether. We also began trying to get insurance approval to set her up with pulmonary rehab to exercise her lungs and recondition her muscles.

Over the next few weeks, if there was no improvement or even small improvement but it plateaued, the plan was to begin talking about re-listing her for another transplant and discuss whether that was a path Faith even wanted to go down again. Depending on how long the anticipated wait for new lungs might be this time, the team hoped to send us home to Charlotte to wait for the call. However, should Faith's lungs show improvement that was definitively trending upward, they would release her back to Charlotte to move forward with life's plans and simply monitor her progress with frequent clinic visits to Chapel Hill. The whole situation continued to take a very heavy toll on our whole family—physically, emotionally, financially, and spiritually. As both Faith and I, not surprisingly, ended up on anti-depressants, I called out to all my prayer warriors to pray for healing, strength, peace, support, and wisdom in all areas, and that we would be able to press on firmly supported by the love and grace of Christ.

When Faith was discharged on August 8th, after a long, frustrating four weeks, we headed back to the apartment hoping and praying that getting some real rest at night in her own bed, along with real activity during the day not trapped in a small hospital room, would be just what was needed to ramp up the healing process and quickly allow her to wean off the oxygen. The next few weeks were going to be critical in determining how effective the treatment was that killed off the T cells attacking her lungs, and how much healing her lungs would be able to do as a result. In the meantime, pulmonary rehab was set up three times a week to try and help with the healing and strengthening process.

A couple of days after Faith was discharged, she received an amazing surprise batch of *for KING & COUNTRY* cookies, as they wanted to do something to try and cheer her up. She was deeply touched and posted,

"Nothing like some for KING & COUNTRY cookies to brighten your day!"

Joel Smallbone from *for KING & COUNTRY* commented on Faith's post,

"We love you and are believing for your healing and JOY. Our dear friend @thewildflour created these with love and prayer. Keep fighting, dear. Love, @moriahsmallbone and me."

To this day, their humble spirits, generosity, support, prayers, and encouragement for Faith on her most difficult journey never cease to amaze me! They are not only a great band, but a great group of Godly individuals.

On August 20th, we received the exciting news that, although the wait continued, we would get to have a change in location. Faith had her first clinic visit after having been discharged from the hospital. The visit included chest X-rays and PFTs to determine what kind of progress had been made from the treatments she had received while in the hospital. The determination was that there was as of yet no clear determination. Her X-rays were unchanged—no better, but no worse. There was a significant decline in her lung function compared to her last PFT in June, which was no surprise to anyone given everything she had been through, but she had also experienced a decrease in oxygen needs and was overall feeling better since leaving the hospital.

Physical therapy had proven to be very beneficial, as after only the first week, Faith's oxygen needs during exertion dropped from eight liters to four. And while at rest, she was on anywhere from two liters to even some periods on room air.

Therefore, given the fact that she was feeling better, and we were simply waiting to see if there was an increase in lung function—which *could* take several months—they decided the wait could at least be done from Charlotte. AND they gave her the green light to go back to school—just in time for the first day that following Monday, the 26th! While this was extremely exciting news, it was still going to present her with quite a challenge as she navigated going to school while toting around oxygen tanks. So, we headed back home to Charlotte with the next Chapel Hill visit scheduled for three weeks later.

As we sat in the living room that weekend preparing Faith's book bag for the start of school, figuring out how many oxygen tanks she would need, and trying to figure out how to get them all to school on Monday, she was questioning why she was having to go through what she was going through. Why was she having to deal with all of this all over again after having received apparently such beautiful lungs? Why was God allowing this to happen? Having already been struggling with a nagging feeling for several days, I shared with her that I could not get over the feeling that God was protecting her from something. This did not sit well with her, and she very angrily replied as she emphatically held up the oxygen tube, "This! *This* is what He should be protecting me from!"

As I looked back on this conversation a few months after she died, while the country was being locked down due to Covid, I began to think about Faith having been so immune-suppressed and potentially having to deal with the Covid era. I honestly cannot say this is what He was trying to protect her from, yet I couldn't help but envision her surviving a double-lung transplant only to get Covid due to her severely compromised immune system. And then I thought about her being hospitalized with Covid, about what would have happened if she had died from that—alone—not getting to say goodbye to everyone and not having the chance to die on her own terms like she would end up doing. As much as I desperately miss her and will for the rest of my life, I do find myself very thankful that she did not have to deal with the effects of the pandemic.

First day of Senior year, August 26, 2019

15

Senior Year

Although not exactly the way we had envisioned or hoped for Faith's first day of senior year to begin, it was still a tremendous victory on this path of struggles and discouragement. A month prior, we did not think she was even going to be able to make this first day, so although challenging, it was still a blessing!

And though it got off to a bumpy start, as the school had not yet received the paperwork authorizing Faith to use oxygen on school property, that was far outweighed by the tremendously sweet surprise message her friends had waiting for her!! As she awaited the authorization papers to be faxed or emailed to the school, Faith drove around to the front of the property where she discovered the spirit rock had been painted with a purple background, a pair of lungs, and "Welcome Home Faith" painted in large letters. This heartwarming gesture touched her deeply and certainly made up for the rocky start to her day.

Once the school received the official papers and was allowed to let Faith into the building, they worked with her in amazing ways. Every morning, someone would help her bring extra oxygen tanks inside to store in the nurse's office, they let her leave classes slightly before the bell rang so she could begin the walk to her next class, and every afternoon, someone would help her bring the used oxygen tanks to her car.

On top of having allowed me to work remotely during our time in Chapel Hill, avoiding the need for a leave of absence, my company also worked really well with me during this transition time of Faith going back to school. I was allowed to come in late to help her get all the necessary oxygen tanks into her car, and I was allowed to leave early to help her remove the empty tanks from the car when she returned home from school and to assist her with any other needs.

Another blessing was Faith's wonderful group of friends. Not only did they visit her in Chapel Hill on more than one occasion when she was in the hospital, but one time, a small group of them also went with her to Chapel Hill when she had to go for some tests and blood work. Whenever Faith would go to the clinic or hospital, she always had to wear a mask due to her immune suppression, so on that day, her group of friends all wore masks in solidarity with her. It was very sweet. This group of friends supported her, encouraged her, and helped her in whatever ways they possibly could.

But being on oxygen full-time began to take a heavy toll. Not only was it becoming increasingly difficult to walk from class to class pulling an oxygen tank behind her, it was affecting other things most people probably took for granted. Faith came home from a football game at halftime one Friday night visibly distraught. When I asked her what was wrong, since she had been so incredibly excited to go, she said that because of her oxygen needs, she couldn't even jump up and down and cheer when their team played well and scored. When she saw someone at a different location in the stands that she wanted to go say hi to, she couldn't because she was chained to the "stupid oxygen tank" and it was too difficult to try and roll through the crowds of students. She felt completely defeated.

All the while, talks were underway with Chapel Hill about the possibility of listing her for a second transplant, and if that was what Faith even wanted to do, then she would need to go through the evaluation process again.

On September 25th, 2019, as I was scrolling through Facebook while an exhausted Faith napped, I came across the devastating news that Danny from "Running With Danny" had passed away while waiting for new lungs. Heartbroken, I posted a tribute that night in remembrance of him.

"Remembering Danny . . . Danny Quesada was an inspirational 18-year-old young man from Florida who, like Faith, spent his life battling Cystic Fibrosis. Although we first 'met' Danny by our social media pages simply following each other's stories, we had the pleasure of meeting him and his mom, Mari, when we happened to run into them at physical therapy in Chapel Hill. They had moved there as Danny continued working towards getting on

the transplant list. We enjoyed getting to know them a little better as we shared transplant classes together, and we rejoiced when he was officially listed. Some of the bravest, strongest, most courageous, and perseverant people you will ever meet in your life are those that fight this unforgiving and horrible disease. It is true of Faith, and it was true of Danny, who sadly lost his fight early this afternoon while waiting for new lungs. Please remember this precious family in your prayers. Mike and Mari, my heart grieves alongside yours, and I pray for God's comfort to overwhelm you during this time. All my love to you and your family and friends! Go rest high on that mountain, Danny, and breathe deeply in the presence of Almighty God."

The following day, with the news of Danny still weighing very heavy on our hearts, I discovered just how hard his death had affected Faith. I walked into her room to see how she was coming with packing for our trip to Chapel Hill, and she was just sitting there sobbing. I held her for a long time as we cried together and mourned his loss.

After regaining our composure, she continued packing, and I looked for something to distract me. I realized I hadn't given an update on Faith in a while, so I made the following post,

"Not really sure where to begin, with a month having passed since the last update on Faith. As exciting as it was to move back home to Charlotte and return to normal life, it has been nothing shy of a challenge trying to adjust to the new schedule with Faith returning to school, me returning to the office, and trying to navigate 'normal' life with oxygen tanks and a general decline in the medical situation.

"After seeing small initial improvements shortly before coming back to Charlotte, we were certainly hoping and praying for better news by the time a month went by. But unfortunately, things have not gone as hoped. She has been finding it more and more difficult to walk around school, especially while lugging her oxygen tank around with her, her oxygen needs have not decreased any further, with some days even requiring higher amounts, and at her last clinic visit a couple weeks ago, her lung function was only 19%. This is certainly not

the outcome any of us had envisioned following a double lung transplant, and it has taken a very heavy emotional toll on all of us.

"Our Friday will be a long, full day of labs, procedures, and meeting with each member of the transplant team individually to discuss the process of getting her back on the transplant list once again and prepared for a second transplant. This has been the most difficult road we've ever been down, and the thought of going down it again – especially so soon – is overwhelming to say the very least.

"We ask again for you to please join us in prayer for wisdom and strength throughout this process, that all goes smoothly and that the path before us is made clear. Pray the Lord provides the grace necessary to face whatever comes our way with peace and confidence in His plan. As always, thank you for your continued support, prayers, and love!"

Faith's appointment the following day, September 27th, 2019, would end up being a very tough day with a very tough confirmation. Given the obvious decline in Faith's lung function and other symptoms stemming from her body's silent attack on her new lungs, the transplant team decided it was indeed time to actively and aggressively work toward getting her re-listed for a second transplant. However, Faith first had to decide if this was something she even wanted to pursue.

Talking with Doctor L, through tears, Faith officially made the decision that she wanted to proceed with a second transplant, as she shared in her post following the visit:

"A lot of you know what's been happening recently because of our Lungs4Faith post, but I felt I needed to post something myself. My lung function has been slowly declining and we're now entering the re-evaluation process for a redo transplant. My lung function number today was 17%, when before transplant, the lowest I ever saw was 23%. However, even with this, as well as being on oxygen 24/7, the "mock allocation score" (basically determining where I would be on the list) was pretty low. This means even if I were to be listed soon,

it's still going to be a long, very difficult wait because there are people who are worse, needing lungs sooner. At my appointment today my doctor also made it clear 'You're going to get worse before you get a transplant' and to be honest, that really sucks. This has definitely been a hard blow, physically, emotionally and spiritually. We thought last time was horrible timing, but then we thought maybe not, maybe it was perfect timing because I was breathing easy, ready for senior year of high school, & I had the quality of life I've always longed for. But then, it seems like it's all just been taken away, and all so sudden, like a wave pulling me under. People keep saying how strong I am. How inspiring or encouraging I've been. But at some point, those just end up being words, and they end up reminding me that I am so incredibly tired of having to be strong, of having to be an inspiration or an encouragement. I'm going to be very honest in saying I questioned whether or not a redo transplant was something I even wanted. If I really wanted to endure more physically and emotionally draining procedures and tests and everything else that will come with a redo transplant. But I've also come to realize that my story isn't over. I've seen people who haven't had a second chance like I did, and I'm so lucky to even be getting a third chance if I get this redo. Someone told me recently that life isn't determined by your situation and circumstances, it's determined by how you respond to those things and you choose to live your life based upon them. I've decided I want to fight, I want to live. #continue"

Our hope was that they had learned a lot from her previous complications potentially resulting in fewer setbacks the next time around. The downside, however, was since she was currently out of the hospital and not requiring nearly as much oxygen as she had in December of 2018, she would be quite a bit lower on the list, making her wait time potentially long and hard. As devastating as this news was, she was a fighter and a warrior and was determined to face the battle head-on. The decision was not without its own feelings of tremendous loss and grief, though, and we knew it would come with a multitude of mini-battles along the way.

I honestly can't say that our faith had not been seriously shaken during this time, nor that we did not question the sense of it all. It just wasn't fair. But I *can* say that God never promises life will be fair. In fact, He promises quite the opposite so that we can arm ourselves to be prepared and put our trust in *Him* for peace, not the world around us or our circumstances. As Jesus tells us:

"I have told you these things, so that in Me you may have peace. In this world you will have trouble. But take heart! I have overcome the world."

John 16:33 (NIV)

"Take heart" . . . I was trying. Faith was trying. Kelsey and Jenni were trying. And although there were days in which the doubt and despair were overwhelming, I tried to believe that He had a greater and more beautiful purpose and plan – even through the pain. I again reached out to my community on social media to continue standing in the gap for Faith, her medical team, and all of us with fervent prayers for wisdom, peace, strength, grace, and healing as we embarked on this long, difficult journey once again.

This holds true today, as we struggle through the grief and pain of losing Faith. I'm still trying—Faith's sisters are still trying. And God is no less alive and in control. We still question and doubt sometimes, but we also rejoice in the knowledge that Faith is whole and healed, breathing deeply without pain, complication, or limitation. And when reliving memories that come up, some of which are so very hard, I have learned that they are no less important in remembering the life of a loved one lost. As much as it hurts to revisit the pain and discouragement of the direction things had taken at this time, it also reminds me of what a fighter and amazing inspiration Faith was to me and so many others! And that helps me to press on.

On September 30th, 2019, Faith realized it was becoming just too difficult to walk around the school with her declining lung function and increasing oxygen needs, especially while pulling an oxygen tank behind her. But she was bound and determined to do whatever it took to graduate with her class and even told one of her doctors she'd graduate via FaceTime if she had to! So after much prayer and discussion, she decided the best course of action to ensure she still graduated on time would be to switch back to online school through NCVPS. We received confirmation that this would not affect her status as a Hickory Ridge student, that she would still be able to graduate with her class, remain a member of the Student Council, and any other things related to her being a student at the high school.

Along with the changes in her high school setting, the other activity adversely affected by her declining lung function and increasing oxygen needs was dance. On October 1st, 2019, Faith and I visited her dance studio so she could say goodbye to her team, since she was obviously unable to return and it would have been her final year. As her team sat on the floor in the dance room, Faith sat in front of them, cross-legged, explaining everything that was going on, where she was in the potential re-transplant process, and thanked them all for being a part of her "family," offering her so much support and love and encouragement. After many hugs and tears, Faith later wrote a now-ominous, almost foreshadowing, post that read,

"*'Goodbyes are not forever. Goodbyes are not the end. They simply mean I'll miss you until we meet again.'*

"*With everything going on regarding the need for another transplant, I'm unable to dance once again, and sadly, with it being my senior year, that means I won't be coming back to dance at Miss Donna's. I want to thank them though for giving me a family, for always supporting me, and always having my back at competitions, recitals, etc. Thank you especially to Jana and Haley for pushing me and helping me grow in the time that I was there. I'll miss you all so much! But it isn't goodbye forever! I'll see you at the competitions! (and y'all better kick some butt out there on stage!)*"

Reading these words again makes me think about how life is so fragile, and you never know when your last goodbye will truly be your last goodbye. It is so important to make every moment count! We certainly did not envision that a mere six weeks after this post, we would be saying goodbye to Faith for the last time this side of heaven.

During the fall at school—before Faith returned to NCVPS—votes were tallied for members of the Homecoming Court. Faith came home from school one day simply ecstatic as she had been selected for the Court and was in the running to be Homecoming Queen. This was simply more evidence of what an inspiration Faith was to so many people, and how her entire school community rallied around her with love and support. So we set out on the Homecoming dress shopping spree.

Due to having a follow-up appointment in Chapel Hill, we decided to do the dress shopping in the Chapel Hill/Durham area so Jenni could join us from Raleigh. Searching for a dress proved to be exhausting, with her lung function so compromised, and her oxygen needs seeming to be only on the rise. However, Faith found two beautiful dresses that she could not decide between. In an effort to cheer her up, as she was feeling very discouraged with how much the simple act of shopping had taken out of her, I decided to purchase both dresses, thinking that whichever one she decided not to wear for Homecoming, she would have an opportunity to wear it at another formal event in the future. Sadly, she would never have a chance to wear the second dress.

Homecoming arrived on October 4th, and my best friend's daughter, Lisa, a professional photographer, offered to take Faith's pictures both before and during Homecoming at no charge. We went to a local park before the Homecoming game and got some absolutely beautiful pictures. We then proceeded to the high school. Again, as a way of working with Faith in her difficult circumstances, the school had placed a cone in front of one of the handicap spots by the football stadium, saving it for us to ensure Faith would not have to walk too far with her compromised lungs and her oxygen tank. We had also been informed earlier that day that someone had anonymously purchased our tickets to enter the game.

When we arrived at the stadium, Dr. Poole, the principal of the school, had a golf cart waiting to drive Faith down to the field to await half-time. Upon seeing her, the student section exploded in cheers! Twenty-five youth and oth-

ers from church also came to show their support and cheer Faith on. It was such an amazing and heartwarming sight to see and get to experience with her.

When half-time arrived and it was time for the Court to be introduced, they drove Faith in the cart to the other side of the football field, where everyone would walk on the field. They offered to drive her onto the field as well, but she was bound and determined to walk onto the field under her own power. So with me carrying her oxygen tank, she and I walked across the field and took our spot near the 50-yard line to wait for the Homecoming Queen to be announced

(the Homecoming King had already been announced earlier that day at a pep rally).

They introduced the Court, who accompanied them, then began with the runners-up. As it got down to the Homecoming Queen, I was sure the whole stadium could feel and hear the beating of my heart and knew that if my heart was beating like that, I could only imagine what Faith's heart was doing. And then it came . . . they called out "Faith Shaw" as the Hickory Ridge High School 2019/2020 Homecoming Queen! The stands again went wild. After Faith was crowned, there were tears and hugs all around while the football team prepared to take the field for the second half. The rest of the night was simply magical. She was so excited, and everyone was so excited for her. And to top it off, we got to watch the football team win an amazing game 50-0! Following the game, after getting many more pictures and many more hugs, we met up with some of her friends at Sonic to celebrate with chili cheese dogs.

A couple of days later the photographer, Lisa, made a beautiful post:

"Every once in a while, I meet someone so special that they touch my heart in ways I couldn't have imagined. Meet Faith.

"Faith is a senior in high school, has Cystic Fibrosis, and has fought to live the life of a normal teenage girl. She has endured a double lung transplant, many hospital stays, and needs the assistance of an oxygen tank. They are also actively working to have her re-listed for a 2nd transplant . . .

"Faith is a warrior.

"I had the ultimate pleasure of going to photograph her, all dressed up before her high school homecoming game, as she had been nominated for homecoming court. Not only was she kind, and beautiful, but she was a complete natural in front of the camera!

"And spoiler alert, she WON!! And the entire stadium went nuts!"

On October 10th, Faith received a really neat message that added to her joy and excitement. Someone who followed Faith's story on Instagram attended a *for KING & COUNTRY* concert in Atlanta and saw a very familiar face on their Meet & Greet banner! It was a picture of Joel, Luke, and Faith from their time together at Carowinds earlier that summer. She was ecstatic! Following Faith's passing, *for KING & COUNTRY* sent me the banner, signed by Joel & Luke with a sweet message that

said, "Sending our love!" Between that and Homecoming, Faith was still walking on cloud nine when we reported to Chapel Hill for further meetings and evaluation tests.

We spent four days in Chapel Hill, October 15th-18th, 2019, with Faith undergoing multiple tests, procedures, meetings, etc. to evaluate her eligibility once again for the transplant list. All the tests and procedures, though not comfortable or fun, went smoothly. All we had to do now was wait for the insurance approval as well as for the team to let us know whether they were willing to even go down that road again with Faith, given her propensity to push back on certain things.

In her desire to actually live her life with her new lungs, Faith continued to make it abundantly clear that there were certain things she wanted to do, and she fought hard for them—prom, trips home for specific events and activities, walking across the stage at graduation—monumental occasions she did not want to have to miss since she had already given up so much. She also had a way of fighting against certain things that she did not want to do, although she would always do them in the end because she recognized they were necessary for her recovery process—she was just very good at expressing her displeasure. Because of this, the team expressed some concern over whether or not she was still a good candidate for re-listing and was still toying with the idea of referring her to the Duke transplant team. Fearing they might decide to deem her not a good candidate, I wrote them a heartfelt letter with some things to consider as they met together to discuss whether or not to re-list her . . .

"Dear Team,

"As you discuss Faith and her future, it was important to me to share my heart since our time was cut shorter than we wanted or needed on Friday due to the ECHO running over.

"When Faith was a little girl growing up, as I'm sure will come as no surprise, she was a very strong-willed child. I used to tell my mom that I dare not break that will because she was going to need to draw on it throughout her life as she

dealt with this horrible, unforgiving disease . . .

"And as she has grown, that strong will has without a doubt been extremely beneficial to her! It is her FIGHTING SPIRIT!

"It is this fighting spirit that got her as far in life as she got.

"It is this fighting spirit that enabled her to live for four years on 32% lung function while pushing through and living life to the fullest, including her competition dance, which has been her place of passion and joy.

"It is this fighting spirit that got her through early December last year when it was apparent her lungs were failing and she had to enter a new chapter, getting plunged into the adult world with no warning and no type of 'transition' period.

"It is this fighting spirit that got her through surgery and recovery, including insurmountable pain and trauma of PRES—that has undoubtedly been at the root of what's now brought her to this current point.

"It is this fighting spirit that has gotten her through each and every hurdle and obstacle she has faced in this process, yet still pushes on without giving up, even when she begged the Lord to just take her home.

"It is this fighting spirit that pulled her up from this latest bout of depression just enough for her to realize SHE WANTS TO LIVE AND SHE WANTS TO KEEP FIGHTING!

"And it is this fighting spirit that will propel her through the next surgery and recovery process.

"She is a fighter. Yes, she is headstrong, strong-willed, stubborn, pig-headed, whatever name you wish to give it, but it all boils down to the fact that SHE. IS. A. FIGHTER! What you see as 'push back' or rebellion or defiance is her fighting spirit which we can't allow to be broken!

"We've heard so many, many times throughout these past 9 months that the transplant process is a rollercoaster with no guarantees. Well, with a rollercoaster of circumstances, there is also obviously going to be a rollercoaster of emotions, especially for one who is still so young and who has only just barely

begun to have real dreams and build real goals—only to have them stripped away. And what has made it so much worse was having a 'tease' for a few months of what she thought was going to give her that opportunity.

"Not only should Faith (and me, for that matter), be allowed to express those feelings, disappointments, discouragements, and just plain anger at really sucky situations, but if there's anyone she needs to be able to be completely honest and transparent with, isn't it her medical team?! And in her anger, despair, and intense grief over losses she's experienced, she's going to draw from that fighting spirit. Sometimes it's all she has that gives her a sense of control in a situation completely out of everyone's control.

"I say all this because I walked out of Friday's meetings feeling like the team was considering not re-listing her because there was a concern about compliance. But I sincerely hope that you as a team recognize that even when she says she doesn't want to do something—even when she outright says she won't—she always does! As I told Laurie in our meeting on Friday, not once did Faith not do what was required or asked of her. She may have kicked and screamed the whole way sometimes . . . but she still always complied!

"And please also recognize and acknowledge that her losses and her grief are very real and very valid. Take dance, for instance – I'm not sure you realize that this was it. This was her final year of competition dance because she ages out after this year. And after missing last year, she was so excited to get to 'go out with a bang.' Dance has been a very large part of her life and her identity. But that is now completely out of the picture, which is a HUGE loss, and for which we are both deeply grieving! As mom, I would ask for you to please not minimize or discount that and her other current losses. Even with a chance at an amazing future, the loss of today is still immensely painful and hard to see slip away.

"So she fights. Because she is not only fighting for her life, she's fighting for life—for truly living! . . .

"She has fought so hard for so long, and she's not ready to give up now! And I am asking the team to also not give up on her. Please fight for her as hard as she has fought for—and continues to fight for—herself!

"Thank you!"

As we waited for an answer, which we hoped would come the following week, we at least had the pleasure of closing out that long, exhausting, and tough week in Chapel Hill getting refreshed and renewed at the Extraordinary Women Ministries' conference held at Concord's Cabarrus Arena & Events Center. It seemed an appropriate conference to attend, as Faith truly was an extraordinary woman in her own right! All week, we looked forward to worshiping with Natalie Grant and Michael O'Brien, laughing with Tim Hawkins, and sharing the hearts of some wonderful speakers such as Ainsley Earhardt, Sheila Walsh, and Angela Thomas Pharr to name a few. The first night of the two-day conference was an awesome experience. Unfortunately, Faith was unable to make the second day, still feeling completely wiped out and exhausted from the week in Chapel Hill.

While she had been going through all the tests and meetings in Chapel Hill, her school community once again displayed their overwhelming love and support for her through a surprise video put together by the Leadership class. The beginning of the video was from a previous recording of Faith introducing herself and giving a brief explanation of cystic fibrosis and what she was going through. As a surprise, this was followed by wonderful messages of encouragement and love from her friends and classmates and posted on YouTube. It was a very special gift following a truly difficult week in Chapel Hill.

As we waited for the final answer from both the insurance and the transplant team, Faith had several more phone meetings with the team as questions or information came up. We found out they were leaning toward a yes, but there were a few more things they wanted to work out first and have one more face-to-face meeting with Faith, which we scheduled for October 31st, 2019.

And through all the uncertainty, disappointments, and increasing exhaustion, Faith, having transitioned back to online school, would continue to diligently press on with her NCVPS classes as best she could. But even that would not be easy.

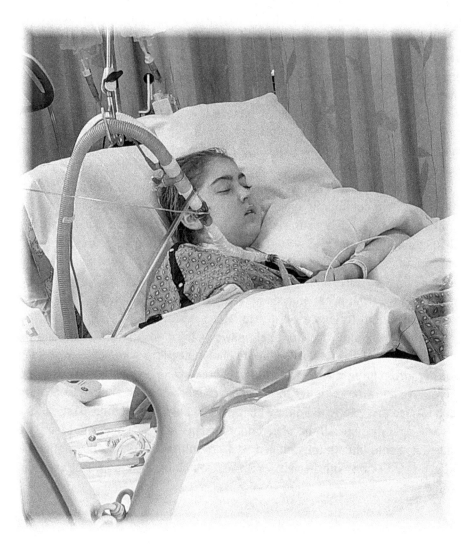

Early November 2019

16

Final Days

Around mid-to late-October 2019, Faith began to feel extreme fatigue and exhaustion and had trouble concentrating. The symptoms were such that on October 25th when our carbon monoxide alarm started chirping, I was certain that she had carbon monoxide poisoning. We immediately left the house and I dialed 911. When the fire department arrived, they did a thorough check and found no traces of carbon monoxide but said our alarm was extremely old and probably just needed to be replaced. We were still very concerned about her symptoms and the fact that her oxygen needs seemed to be increasing, but we were only a few days away from our transplant meeting with the team in Chapel Hill, so we decided to bring it up with them then.

On October 31st, we traveled back to Chapel Hill for the final re-listing meeting, fully expecting and planning to return home that evening to watch "Stranger Things" while handing out candy to the neighborhood children. By this time, the exhaustion and fatigue were so great that Faith could not bring herself to walk through the hospital to the various "stations" (blood work, X-rays, PFTs, and the transplant conference room), so I transported her to each location in a wheelchair I had recently purchased.

At the meeting, Faith was very subdued and quite exhausted, not really having a lot to say. This meeting was to be the final "interview" to determine whether or not the team was going to re-list her for a second transplant, and there were several more details and potential hurdles to discuss. The most discouraging part of the meeting was when they had Faith sign a "contract" stating that she would do everything they asked her to do, without question and without putting up a fight. This contract was something new, and it was evidently put in place because of the spit-fire attitude Faith had during her recovery from the first transplant. She pushed back many times and let her feelings be known on a number of occasions, but one of the things that made this contract so infuriating was that, even with the push-back, Faith had never failed to do exactly what she was supposed to do! I could see in Faith's eyes that she was very angry, but she was simply too fatigued to say anything about it. The only question she voiced to them was when would she know it was time for her to go back to the hospital? When would she know it was time to seek a second transplant? I think she was mainly asking this question because she felt it might already be that time, but for the first time in a very long time, she was unsure what her body was telling her.

After all parties were done signing the contract, the team finally agreed, pending insurance approval, to go ahead with seeking re-listing for a second transplant. But before we headed home, they wanted her to have one more blood test they had forgotten to order with her blood work that morning—her blood-oxygen level (CO2). We were asked to wait until those results came in, and it turned out she had extremely high levels of carbon dioxide in her blood, which explained the symptoms resembling carbon monoxide poisoning. It was *vital* to bring this down so it did not adversely affect her other organs, such as her heart and her brain.

So once again, she was admitted to the Emergency Department to await a room and to begin the process of getting her CO2 levels down to more normal numbers. I sent out a text alert to the family that said, "Don't panic! Faith's being admitted. I'll fill in more details later once we're a little more settled in." I should probably have panicked.

After more than twenty hours in the Emergency Department, now on high-flow oxygen and attempting to lower her CO2 levels using a BiPap, they moved her to ICU, admitting her into the hospital for what would be the last time in her life. She would never go home again.

All measures at getting her CO2 levels down, however, proved to be unsuccessful, and the very day that insurance approved her for a second transplant, we were dealt a devastating blow.

Friday, November 1st, 2019, would begin a weekend that was definitely one for the record books as one of the most difficult, heartbreaking times of Faith's journey. When all three doctors on the transplant team walked into the room together, I knew that we were either about to be given extremely good news or extremely bad news. Unfortunately, it proved to be the latter. Although we had very quickly gotten the insurance approval for Faith's re-listing, the team also realized her health decline had reached a point in which she was currently too sick and her body too weak to be eligible. They said that even if lungs were to be available that day, she more than likely would not survive the surgery. We found ourselves at a true crossroads of life and death as Faith was faced with having to make a decision no eighteen-year-old should ever have to make. She had two choices, and the decision was ultimately hers alone.

One path entailed being ventilated via tracheotomy to give Faith the oxygen she needed while eliminating the high levels of CO_2, along with putting in a G-tube again to give her the nutrition needed to bring her weight back up to healthy levels. At the same time, she would be required to do physical therapy to try and restore her strength—all in order to *hopefully* get her stable and strong enough to be eligible for the transplant list. This path would be painful and hard with no guarantees that it would work.

The other path, if she decided she could just not bear the thought of going through what the first path would require of her, would be to simply allow them to keep her comfortable until the Lord took her home—which was her initial decision.

After the team left, both Faith and I began sobbing as she exclaimed through her tears that she just could not fight anymore. It was too hard, and she was just so very tired. She told me that she was not giving up – she just felt her fight was over. She did not want me to be sad. She knew where she was going. She told me she wanted me to be sure and surround myself with my friends, especially my best friend, Janet, and for me to get a dog so I would not be lonely. After many tears, lots of prayer, and lots of thinking through it some more, she was not really sure which path she wanted to take and felt we should discuss it as a family.

On Saturday, November 2nd, 2019, Faith's sisters and their husbands came to the hospital so we could share the information with them face-to-face and talk everything through. We, as a family, assured her that we loved her deeply and would support whatever decision she came to, although we, of course, had our preference! After lots of discussion, tears, paging the team for answers to questions that came up, and more tears, Faith came to the decision that she wanted to keep fighting! One of the things that changed her mind was thinking about her niece and nephew. She came to the realization that she really wanted to watch them grow up and be a part of their lives. Another determining factor in her decision to keep fighting was her Uncle Tim. She said she still needed to be here for him to help him come to know Christ and it wouldn't be fair to him if she decided to let go of this life. We paged the transplant team with her decision, and they said she would be scheduled for the trach and tube to be done within the next couple of days. Following the very difficult discussion and to try and end the day on a "happy" note, we played some games to lighten the mood.

On Sunday, November 3rd, the youth pastor's wife, Jenna, along with some other ladies from church, came to Chapel Hill to visit Faith and pray with her before her surgery. And on Monday, November 4th, 2019, the trach and tube were put in. As I waited for Faith to be brought back from surgery, I received a very sweet text from my best friend, Janet, who offered to let me and Faith stay with her for as long as needed so I could get out from under the rent, utilities, and yard work of my house, yet still have a "home base" whenever we returned to Charlotte.

The surgery went extremely well with no issues or complications. In the next days and weeks, Faith would be faced with many challenges while getting used to how this new chapter in her journey played out as she worked toward the goal of getting her body and strength back up to transplant eligibility.

The first day after the surgery Faith was doing very well, and things looked promising and hopeful. Because of the trach, she was not able to talk, so she communicated with us using a writing tablet called a Boogie Board. She shared with us that she actually found it easier to breathe with the trach and ventilator. She said she'd slept better that first night than she had in a *very* long time, and she was feeling optimistic. She was awake, alert, as positive as one could expect under the circumstances, and even walked a lap around the entire unit. She was doing better than the team thought she would, and all things considered, she was in pretty good spirits. We continued to ask for prayers that Christ's strength would course through her and help ease some of the burdens she had to bear. We also asked for prayers for me and the family as we cared for and supported her, and for wisdom to best meet her needs.

But the blows would not stop coming, and we could not keep up with how quickly things would change. Two days following the surgery, Faith spiked a fever, needed dramatic increases in her oxygen, and was just all around feeling crummy. At 5:00 in the morning, I received a text message from Faith saying, "So I have a slight fever, I have a lot of secretions apparently which is making the ventilator feel like it's not working as well, my [oxygen] sats aren't as great, and my heart rate has been pretty high for a while. They're going to try some Ativan since it's early, and maybe it can help me rest a little and chill because I am feeling pretty anxious. But I don't know if you or Jenni could maybe go ahead and come?" I immediately got dressed and headed to the hospital.

Following chest X-rays, they determined that she had developed bad pneumonia in her right lung, one of the risks of the surgery and which now meant getting re-listed for transplant was currently off the table completely.

They started her on a regimen of four different IV antibiotics to try and knock out the infection so we could again get back to working on getting her strong enough for re-listing. At that point, Faith was beginning to see the end was near and asked me on her tablet, "Am I dying?" In an effort to keep her (and myself!) encouraged, I tried to assure her that they would get this infection taken care of and we would get her back on the list! She then wrote, "Even if I don't ever get re-listed, I'm at peace & know I will be comfortable." When I shared this with Doctor K and Jenni outside her room, Doctor K replied, "Well, yes, she *is* dying." Not at all what I needed to hear at that point in time. I was terrified enough. But the next forty-eight hours were going to be crucial in determining whether the antibiotics were going to be effective and what direction things would go.

Over those next couple of days, Faith's health continued to decline rapidly, as did her energy and strength. She was very groggy most of the time, and even her messages on the Boogie Board did not always make a lot of sense. There was also talk about potentially sedating her if she needed more oxygen support than she could comfortably tolerate awake. It was very heartbreaking and discouraging. Uncle Tim flew back into Chapel Hill, and I was told by Pastor Aaron that the church had held an intentional time of prayer for Faith.

Early in the morning on November 7th, I was awakened by a text from Faith shortly after 3:00 am asking where Jenni and I had gone. I replied that she had fallen asleep, so we went back to the hotel to get some sleep. I didn't hear another reply, so I went back to sleep. At 4:20 am, her grogginess and anxiety came through in her text when she tried to ask if we were on our way, as it came through text as, "argus you on yourbwayb." Unfortunately, Jenni and I both slept through this text alert. When I awoke at 5:40 and saw her message, I texted her asking if she was okay. She replied, "Yeah please come as soon as possible." Jenni headed straight over while I quickly showered.

Later that day when some of the anxiety had eased, during a moment when Faith was feeling a little more alert and was even able to do some bedside physical therapy, I shared with her the song titled "Faith" that her friend, Sara, had written in her honor. When I played it for her, tears flowed down her cheeks. This would end up being the last time I ever saw her cry. Not only were the words and music beautiful, but the message of strength and support was sorely needed for *all* of us in that season of strife.

Hey, Faith, your strength can't be tamed
They say time's runnin' short, but you were born for more
And I don't care what statistics show,
Your heart's gonna get you through this road

And hey, Faith, don't you ever give up
Even when the waves get rough
You've got an army to pull you up
And hey, Faith, don't you ever think twice
It's all gonna be alright
Your breath will be worth the fight
Cause God's holding you in His hands
That's just the truth
It ain't your lungs that's supporting you

Hey Faith, we'll never walk away from your name
I know you've heard it enough, but in our love you may trust
And I don't care what the chances are
They don't apply to your heart

And hey, Faith, don't you ever give up
Even when the waves get rough
You've got an army to pull you up
And hey, Faith, don't you ever think twice
It's all gonna be alright
Your breath will be worth the fight
Cause God's holding you in his hands
That's just the truth
Yeah God's holding you in His hands
That's just the truth
It ain't your lungs that's supporting you
It ain't your lungs that's supporting you.

On Friday, November 8th, 2019, she knew before any of us that continuing to fight was only prolonging the inevitable, that there was nothing left to fight for, and that she felt it was time to call in the family. Not willing to accept this, I told her to please think and pray about it some more, get as good a night's sleep as she could, and we would talk more about it in the morning. I did not want her to be making such a monumental decision from a place of discouragement, so I went back to my room at the SECU house and prayed and prayed and prayed that God would give her the clarity she needed, thinking of course that this "clarity" would be her realizing she needed to keep on fighting.

The next morning, Saturday, November 9th, I walked into Faith's hospital room to see her sitting up, bright and alert with a cute, peaceful little smile on her face. I was so excited knowing that God had answered my prayers and given her the clarity I had asked for! He had certainly given her clarity, but not with the answer I had wanted so desperately to hear. She knew she had fought the fight she was supposed to fight for as long as she was supposed to fight it, and now her time to go "Home" was here. She had such a deep faith and love for Christ and knew that her final destination would be more awesome and beautiful than one could even imagine. She said she was not giving up or quitting—it was just time. And she was at peace.

Her sisters, Uncle Tim, and I paged Doctor L to talk with him and see if he could convince Faith she could still win this fight. We spent some time with him in a conference room explaining what was going on, her mood, and our desire to help her keep fighting. After listening to each of us say our piece, he said that he knew Faith was a fighter and would see what he could do. But when he walked into her room and looked at the machines with all her numbers, he knew that she was correct and was making the right decision. He told her how deeply, deeply sorry he was things had not turned out differently and he was very proud of her. She was at peace with her decision, which I could see written all over her face. It was as if a huge weight had been lifted from her shoulders and she was actually feeling relieved.

Faith desperately wanted to see her niece and nephew again, then aged three and six. After receiving permission from the hospital to have them come so she could visit them one last time and tell them goodbye, Kelsey asked her mother-in-law to bring the kids to see Faith the next day. Faith and I then decided that Monday would be "friend day," where we would get as many of her friends as possible to come and say their goodbyes, Tuesday would be "family day," and then we would let her go on Wednesday. After figuring out the timing of things and discussing the decision in full with the medical team, I left Faith with her sisters and proceeded to make the most difficult set of phone calls I would ever in my life have to make. I took the task of calling in the friends, while Uncle Tim called in the family.

When Faith's niece and nephew came in the next day, I was so happy that she was still very alert and lucid and got to spend a good afternoon with them before telling them goodbye for the very last time. After the kids left, and only me, her sisters, and Uncle Tim remained in the room with her, Faith's nurse from that day came in to say goodbye since her shift was over. She told Faith how proud of her she was for making the decision she did with such grace and maturity. The nurse then asked if she could pray with her before leaving to which Faith wholeheartedly agreed. After an amazingly beautiful and moving prayer and the nurse had left the room, Faith had an incredible look of awe on her face. She quickly grabbed her Boogie Board and wrote, "She must've been an angel! I FELT God!"

I also began to realize that we were being selfish by making Faith wait until Wednesday, and after discussing it further with Kelsey and Jenni, we decided to let her go on Tuesday after making her good-byes with the family. When we shared this change with her, she looked at us with sheer relief on her face and mouthed, "Thank you!"

After discussing the plan with Pastor Mike, I texted Faith, "Pastor Farley wanted you to know he loves you so much and admires you tremendously and will be working on getting here Tuesday. In the meantime, he also wanted to know if he should send out this news to the church or hold off until later." Faith replied, "Probably say something about things are not going well, but hold off until later about the final decision. And tell him I appreciate that very much and I love him too."

We knew people were anxiously awaiting updates on Faith, but we were not yet prepared to make the decision public until Faith had the chance to tell specific people goodbye. So on November 10th, as she spent quality time with her niece and nephew, our simple post would read,

"We don't have more details we can provide right now, but we are still facing a rough road. It may be a few days before we have more information to share. Please continue to pray for comfort, peace, and healing for Faith and our whole family."

Also on that day, I received a text message from Lauren, the director/owner of Faith's previous dance studio, that shattered my heart. Lauren told me that the following weekend was their in-house convention and some of Faith's favorite dance instructors from Showstoppers were going to be there. They were staying through Monday the 18th and she wanted to know if Faith would like a visit from all of them. Knowing the decision to let Faith go on the 12th but her not yet wanting to make it public, all I could do was say, "That'd be great. Thank you!"

On Monday, November 11th, several groups of Faith's friends from school and church came in to say their goodbyes. Faith was a little groggier that day, but she still had a wonderful time conversing with them on her tablet and praying with them. We brought in the groups a few at a time so as not to completely overwhelm and further exhaust her. The time they all shared together was precious and sweet, heartwarming and heartbreaking. I lost count of how many people I hugged as they each said their goodbyes, the tears flowing freely for all of us.

On this day, I also received word that Faith's class ring had been delivered to my post office box back in Charlotte. Faith was very sad that she would not have a chance to see her ring, which she had been anxiously waiting on for several months. I contacted Pastors Mike and Aaron to see if they could go by the post office before coming to Chapel Hill the next day, explain Faith's circumstances, and ask if they would be allowed to pick up the ring so Faith could see it before she died. After they spoke with the supervisor on duty, she called to verify I was authorizing them to pick up the box. And the ring was retrieved!

On Tuesday, November 12th, we brought in the rest of the family—Faith's grandma and grandpa, Nana and grandpa Toby, Uncle Tim, and Uncle David—the pastoral staff, and a few others from our church family to say their goodbyes. Pastor Aaron delivered Faith's class ring and she put it on her finger with a sweet smile on her face. I sat with her for a few moments while she admired the ring, I then asked her permission to have it resized to fit my finger so I could wear it in her honor. She said she would love that.

The time Faith spent with each of those present was precious and sweet, especially as she continued witnessing to her Uncle Tim almost right up to the very end. They carried on an entirely private, intimate conversation on the Boogie Board while the room was filled with other people. Faith was then able to write a personal message to everyone as she said her goodbyes. She had wanted to say so much more to so many of them, but the fatigue and weariness had become too great. She was so ready to let go and go Home.

God looked around His garden
And found an empty place.
He then looked down upon the earth
And saw your tired face.
He put His arms around you
And lifted you to rest.
God's garden must be beautiful
He always takes the best.
He saw the road was getting rough
And the hills were hard to climb,
So He closed your weary eyelids
And whispered, "Peace be thine."
It broke our hearts to lose you
But you didn't go alone,
For part of us went with you
The day God called you home.
~ Author unknown.

17

Dancing With Jesus

Following the final goodbyes by the family and the church pastoral staff, everyone left the room except for me, Kelsey, and Jenni. We turned off the lights, turned on music by *for KING & COUNTRY* and *Michael O'Brien's* album "Be Still My Soul," and gathered around Faith on her bed, holding her hands. The doctor came in and started the morphine drip to make her comfortable and help her sleep.

At one point, she opened her eyes, and with that sweet, peaceful smile, glanced at me and then each of her sisters and closed her eyes again. Shortly after that, she opened her mouth and moved a little bit as if she were reaching for a straw. She opened her eyes again and silently laughed, mouthing, "I thought I was drinking lemonade." That would be the very last thing she would ever "say." When she was soundly asleep and comfortable, the doctor came in and removed the trach.

At 3:34 in the afternoon on Tuesday, November 12th, 2019, surrounded by me and her sisters with *Michael O'Brien's* song, "The Lord's Prayer," playing quietly in the background, Faith Mackenzie Shaw took her final breath, and she received her glorious new lungs, breathing in deeply the sweet aroma of heaven, dancing freely hand in hand with Jesus. She faced death as courageously and gracefully as she lived her life and was at complete peace with letting go. She knew where she was going, was excited about her new Home, and had told so many of us to be happy *for* her.

After Faith had taken her final breath, the doctor came in to officially pronounce her time of death. He took his stethoscope and listened for the lack of a heartbeat, looked up at me with sorrow in his eyes, and very gently said, "She's gone." He then left the room so her sisters and I could spend our final moments with her. Having previously removed all our personal items so we would not have to do so after the fact, the only thing left to do was to say our goodbyes one final time. Through my tears and sobs, I pulled the blankets up to cover the hole in her neck left by the tracheotomy, and gently laid her braids and one of her arms outside the blankets making it look like she was simply peacefully sleeping. When I stroked her cheek, I was taken aback by how her skin was already cold and her lips were already blue. I kissed her forehead one last time, and her sisters and I walked out of UNC Chapel Hill Medical Center for the final time. We then joined the rest of the family for a somber dinner.

A very large piece of my heart danced its way through the gates of Heaven on that day, and a large part of me died along with her. But I also rejoice in the knowledge that she is fully and completely healed, breathing in deeply without restriction, discomfort, or pain. Faith had told me a couple of weeks prior that she did not want to spend another Christmas in the hospital. What a joy, blessing, and comfort it was to know that she was now going to get to celebrate the Savior's birth in the presence of the Savior Himself!

Faith blessed and enriched our lives over her short eighteen years in ways beyond description. The strength, determination, perseverance, and grace she showed to get her through the many battles she fought head-on was going to be something we would draw upon to get us through the coming days as we learned how to face a future without her.

The day after Faith died, one of her best friends from school texted me a picture of the spirit rock from the front of the school. It had been re-painted with a white background, gold wings beneath a gold halo, and the words "Fly High Faith" painted across it in large letters. She also told me that students and teachers were wearing purple – the cystic fibrosis color – in Faith's honor, and that the school had made an announcement about her passing. We were so deeply touched, moved, and grateful for the outpouring of support and love for Faith and the family. Although her presence was taken from us way too soon, it became evident that her memory, spirit, and heart would live strong in all of us for years to come. I knew that she had been an inspiration and touched many lives but I had not realized until she died just to what extent. Even amid the overwhelming pain and grief, it filled my heart with joy.

Kelsey returned home on the 13th where she and Jarrett celebrated Faith by having a dinner with some of her favorite foods. Jenni, Uncle Tim, and I remained in Chapel Hill over the next couple of days as we began making arrangements for what the next steps would be and closing out any loose ends before leaving Chapel Hill for the final time. It felt very strange to be leaving Chapel Hill without Faith, as the funeral home and hospital would work together to have her body transported back to Charlotte.

On Thursday morning, November 14th, 2019, Tim returned to Maine, and Jenni and I returned to the Charlotte area. One of our first stops was Hickory Ridge High School to talk with the principal, Dr. Poole. Through some emails back and forth, he had shared that several students had approached him with ideas for honoring Faith, and he wanted to discuss those ideas with me to make sure I was okay with them. Dr. Poole was gracious and compassionate when we met with him and very eager to do whatever he could to honor Faith and support our family.

One of those ideas, which had already been agreed upon via email, was a candlelight vigil to be held Friday evening, November 15th, at the spirit rock. It was completely student-arranged and organized. Several hundred people came, the majority of whom were dressed in purple t-shirts that read "Faith is Bigger than Fear/In loving memory of Faith Shaw." We played music from Faith's Apple music playlist, her friend Sara sang a new song she had written about Faith called "A Heaven Away" (which I would ask her to sing at Faith's Celebration of Life service), and a couple of her friends spoke. It was even covered by a couple of local news outlets, including Spectrum and Fox Charlotte (now known as Queen City News). The Spectrum news headline read, "Hundreds gather at vigil to honor high school homecoming queen who died from cystic fibrosis." That night was many things: beautiful, sad, poignant, devastating, comforting, healing, and heartbreaking.

These are the words from her two dear friends that spoke:

RACHEL: *"First I want to say how absolutely proud I am to have been Faith's friend. How much she changed how I see others and how I see God sprinkled all around. She was so funny, kind, and undeniably brave. Not only in her constant CF battles but how she approached life as well. One of my favorite memories of her involved a plan that Paige, Faith, and I created over the summer* to eventually have Faith and the guy she liked kiss. Now when I tell you we had this planned, I mean we had this thing down to a science. Movie nights where they 'just happened' to sit next to each other, group dinners where everyone 'just happened' to be a couple, car rides where Faith 'just happened' to be the only one available to take him home. A two-week endeavor all led to one truth or dare game where Paige and I had scripted dares to all lead to one: a kiss. She had been so nervous, but more than that she was undaunted by possible disappointment. Along with all-nighter sleepovers, group hospital visits (where we took advantage of Faith's meal service), and wasting days away in an Eno, Faith gave me a record-book summer and most importantly taught me how to take chances. When I got a call Sunday night [November 10th, 2019] from Mama Shaw to tell us we needed to drive to Chapel Hill to say goodbye to Faith, I was heartbroken. I couldn't believe I was going to have to say goodbye to someone I cared so deeply about. I couldn't believe how even though God allowed her to have a new pair of lungs, that she was now lying in a bed, unable to talk. But when we spent the first five minutes crowded around her hospital bed trying to decipher what she was trying to write, only to find out she was trying to ask us to "spill the tea," I knew Faith was going to be okay. God gave her new lungs so she could be with us just a little bit longer. She embodied strength and took everything with a smile. I can only imagine how much bigger her smile is now."

PAIGE: *Faith Mackenzie Shaw. One of the first words that comes to mind is inspiration. She has not only touched my life and changed my view on life, she has done it with so many others as well. I hadn't been super close with Faith until June [2019]. On the last day of school, some of us had a cookout and eno'd [a type of hammock] which later became a summer ritual. Rachel invited Faith, and I immediately knew I had made an amazing friend. On July 3rd, Rachel, Faith, and I decided to go to Sonic to eat some chili cheese dogs. There was a problem with the idea, though. At the time, I worked at Sonic, and employees weren't allowed to take off for July 4th because of the amount of people that came. Lucky for me, I had been in Pennsylvania the week prior, so I just said I was still up there so I could do something with friends to celebrate. To avoid one of my coworkers seeing me, I had to hide in Faith's trunk to ensure I wouldn't be seen. After that day, we had chili cheese dogs for the next three days and we had countless others together after that. A few days later, Rachel, Sam, and I went with Faith up to Chapel Hill so that she could get some blood work done. On the ride back, I was in shotgun and we started listening to oldies. When the song playing was almost over, we'd decide on what the next song* *would be. I remember having the windows down and music blasting, and for the whole drive, we were singing. Not many people listen to the music I like, so having someone to sing with in the car was an amazing feeling. Out of the many songs we listened to, Whitney Houston's 'I Wanna Dance With Somebody' sticks out to me, which was Faith's choice. I know that Faith is dancing up in heaven right now. Rachel sent me a post from Instagram that said, 'There will always be a reason why you meet people. Either you need them to change your life or you're the one who changes theirs.' Without a doubt in my mind, I can say that Faith changed my life for the better. She taught me to accept people and that life is a beautiful gift. I am truly honored to have been able to be Faith's friend. She was the most beautiful, kind, loving, and brave person I have ever met. I am going to miss you so much Faith, but I know that you'll always be with me. Through my whole life, I know I'll see things and think to myself, 'That's Faith with me.' I can't wait to see you again, but until I get to heaven, I will always remember you. Fly high buddy. I love you so much.*

The vigil was concluded by another one of Faith's dear friends, Noelle, closing in prayer:

"Thank you all for coming to honor the beautiful life of Faith Mackenzie Shaw. Please feel free to stay and fellowship after, but please bow your heads and close your eyes as I close us out in prayer. Dear Lord, thank you for allowing the community to gather here and celebrate the life of Faith Shaw. We know that she is gracefully dancing in Your arms and watching over us all every day. Although our hearts are heavy, please allow us to be graceful and trusting in You. I pray for the family of Faith Shaw. Please help them have peace and strength as they go through this time of grieving. Please allow the rest of the community to remember Faith Shaw in all the best ways possible. We know that You have a plan for all of us and that her story's not over yet. I want to thank You for allowing Faith to feel peace and comfort and allowing her to breathe with her new lungs by Your side. She impacted every single person standing here today, and we know that we will see her again one day. But until that day comes, please allow her story to continue to inspire others. I pray all of this in Your name. Amen."

Prior to leaving the vigil, Courtney Davis with Spectrum News interviewed me and a few of Faith's friends.

COURTNEY DAVIS: *With songs and memorable stories, the Hickory Ridge*

High School community came together Friday to remember their Queen, Faith Shaw.

ANNA: She always had a smile on her face. She just walks into a room and lights it up.

COURTNEY DAVIS: For eighteen years, the shining star battled with cystic fibrosis. But those who knew her well said she never let her illness define who she was.

ME: [She] just never let it stop her . . . never let it get in the way of living the life that she wanted to live.

COURTNEY DAVIS: A life full of dancing, fun adventures, and journeys with her family and classmates along for the ride.

NOELLE: It's really amazing to see someone go through so many struggles and still be uplifting because you would expect her to be sad and angry, but she wasn't.

COURTNEY DAVIS: Strength and passion her friends say was fueled by her namesake.

ABBY: She stayed true to herself and the Gospel and was very driven in her walk with the Lord.

COURTNEY DAVIS: And even when times got tough, such as right after her lung transplant last year, her friends say they could always rely on Faith to turn things around.

MEGHAN: She knew we didn't know what to say to her about it, but she helped us be more comfortable and make jokes about the silly things that she had to do.

COURTNEY DAVIS: And while her mother admits the loss is devastating for their family . . .

ME: We're definitely going to have moments where it's not easy at all but seeing the impact that she's had on other people's lives has really helped make that burden a little easier to bear.

COURTNEY DAVIS: *She knows Faith's story is bigger than her daughter.*

ME: *Just her passion for life . . . and just to always fight. One of the hashtags that we have on all of her posts was "fight on fighter." And that's what she did.*

COURTNEY DAVIS: *And by sharing Faith's story, they hope to continue her fight to find a cure for cystic fibrosis.*

ME: *And that's what she wants to keep going . . . she wants that story of perseverance and strength and passion and love just to keep going.*

Following the vigil, we met up at Pastor Aaron and Jenna's house with a large group of youth and college students from the church to pray together, eat Taco Bell, and share stories about Faith. It was a sweet time of fellowship and support—and utterly heartbreaking.

Jenni and Kelsey (who had returned to town with her husband for the vigil) spent that weekend with me, so I would not be alone in the house. On Saturday, November 16th, we sat down in Faith's room and began going through her personal items together so I would not have to do it by myself. Many items were split between the three of us, many items were slated to be given away, and some things that held sentimental value were kept, such as her dance costumes, dance awards, art projects, journals, etc.

HISRadio's morning crew aired one more segment about *for KING & COUNTRY* and their connection with Faith. They first talked about the previous night's CMA awards and what a special night it was for the guys with *for KING & COUNTRY* who got to sing their hit song, "God Only Knows" with none other than Dolly Parton, sharing God's hope at the CMAs in front of the world on television. They then proceeded to give such a sweet tribute to Faith and her beautiful journey with *for KING & COUNTRY*.

ROB DEMPSEY: *"And these guys, I don't know if you have ever followed them on Instagram or Facebook, but they are the real deal. We've known for KING & COUNTRY ever since they've been little guys because their sister is an artist* *that used to be around in the 90's, her name is Rebecca St. James, and they grew up in this. And so, they could be jaded, they could, you know, be 'well we're big artists and we sing music . . .' They really love people. And you may remember last year during this time, near Christmas time, that for KING & COUNTRY was on a Christmas tour, they were coming through the Raleigh-Durham area, and there was this young lady that was in the hospital at the time, a teenager who loves for KING & COUNTRY. Her name is Faith, and she had to live with cystic fibrosis. As a matter of fact, it was getting so bad that she needed a double-lung transplant, and she was in the hospital waiting for that in Charlotte and she couldn't go to the concert. But you know what the guys from for KING & COUNTRY did? They went to her hospital room and did this before the concert started (played footage again of for KING & COUNTRY singing "Little Drummer Boy" for Faith and all of us in her hospital room). That's the guys who sang on the CMA's last night with Dolly Parton . . . for KING & COUNTRY . . . they are the real deal. Let me tell you, since then Faith finally had her double-lung transplant. That was back in January. She was able to go to high school and go through what a high school student should go through and did her studies and everything. She got out and for KING & COUNTRY . . . I don't know if you knew this, but they were in concert at Carowinds over the summer at Rock the Park. You know who was at that concert finally? Faith was at the concert . . . she was behind the scenes . . . she got her picture with them . . . I mean it was absolutely phenomenal. The smile on her face . . . she didn't have to have oxygen in her nose anymore . . . she wasn't in a hospital room . . . she was at Rock the Park. Well, sadly, in the past recent months, Faith, after this double-lung transplant, after she was Homecoming Queen for 2019 at her school, things started to get a little bit worse with her condition, and we just learned a couple of days ago that she passed away. She's with Jesus, now, completely healed in Heaven. And for KING & COUNTRY has been a part of her journey and made life just a little bit more joyful for her during a very trying time for the family. And the family will never forget for KING & COUNTRY, the same guys that were at the CMA's last night, who'd go out of their way to help others just like Faith. . . . "*

Obituary

CONCORD – Faith Mackenzie Shaw, age 18, died on November 12, 2019, in Chapel Hill, NC, due to complications from Cystic Fibrosis and a double-lung transplant. Faith is survived by her mother, Susan Shaw; sisters, Kelsey Biggers (Jarrett) and Jennifer Wilson (James); nephew Gabriel Biggers; niece, Kyla Biggers; grandparents Donald & Shirley Tobin and Michael & Ann Brooks; uncles, David Brooks (Tateyana) and Timothy Brooks (Fiona); cousins, Michael Brooks, Charlotte Brooks, and Hannah Brooks; along with many other family and friends that she deeply loved. Faith was born on May 15, 2001, in Concord, to mother Susan Shaw. Faith was a senior at Hickory Ridge High School in Harrisburg and was preparing for graduation with the Class of 2020. She was very active in her church, West Concord Baptist, and had a deep-rooted faith in her Lord and Savior, Jesus Christ. The trust in her faith as she faced the daily struggles of Cystic Fibrosis head on was inspiring to all who had the pleasure to know her or follow her story. Faith embodied strength, perseverance, determination, grace, and passion for living life to the fullest. She never let cystic fibrosis define her and chose to live life on her terms to the best of her ability in spite of the many challenges her illness threw at her. She taught those around her what it was to truly live, to truly love, and to find victory in whatever fight life requires of you. She had many passions, particularly in dance, art, and photography. Faith danced competitively for 6 years, performing group, duo and solo performances at local, national and world competitions. She danced with an unmatched determination, pursuing it even when her disease made it difficult and required her to recover with oxygen after rehearsals and performances. One year, she even performed a solo, complete with her oxygen tank, to a song titled "Breathe" in order to tell her story with Cystic Fibrosis through a medium for which she found so much joy. Faith also had a deep love for her family and friends. Even as a child, she had a natural way of drawing people to her, and her family would say that she walked the red carpet wherever she went. This tendency continued all through her life, and she developed many close relationships through school, church, and family who loved and supported her on the journey of her fight for life. A service to celebrate Faith's life is scheduled for 2:00 pm on Saturday, December 7 at West Concord Baptist Church, with a reception to follow at the same location. Rev. Aaron Thomas will officiate. All are welcome and encouraged to attend and celebrate her life together as a community. The family would like to thank the many family, friends, and prayer warriors near and far for their continuous prayers and encouragement throughout Faith's journey with Cystic Fibrosis and her fight to live life large. They would also like to thank the donor who provided Faith with new lungs on January 14, 2019, without which they would not have been blessed with these past 10 months of Faith's life, joys and experiences. In lieu of flowers, donations can be made to the Cystic Fibrosis Foundation in Faith's name. Or donations can be made towards the Shaw family's expenses via the Lungs4Faith GoFundMe campaign or mailed directly to West Concord Baptist Church, 225 Warren C. Coleman Blvd, Concord, NC, 28027. Online condolences may be left at wilkinsonfuneralhome.com. www.gofundme.com/lungs4faith.

Dancing With Jesus

PART THREE

Faith's Story Continues

December 7, 2019

18

Celebration of Life

The day before Faith's Celebration of Life service, a group of her friends met up with me at the church to help decorate the Fellowship Hall for the reception that would follow. As incredibly sad as the circumstances were, it was a joy to witness through our conversations the impact Faith had on each of their lives.

At her Celebration of Life service, December 7th, 2019, the legacy Faith left behind continued to be evident by the number of people in attendance, the spoken tributes shared, and the messages given. Lowes Foods, where she had worked, donated food for the reception following the service, as did many of the church family and various friends. The owner of the house we were renting at the time also owned a printing company, and they printed all of the bulletins for the service at no charge. We asked everyone to wear purple in memory of Faith, and it was such an amazing sight to witness a sea of purple filling the sanctuary. Our hearts, though *deeply* broken, were incredibly touched by the outpouring of support and love for the family and obviously for Faith. At the front of the room, along with pictures of Faith, sixty-five roses stood beautifully behind her urn representing the "65 Roses" campaign of Cystic Fibrosis, and eighteen yellow roses laid across the table representing the eighteen years of sunshine Faith brought into the world.

Following a slide show of Faith and her life, set to the song "Weep With Me" by *Rend Collective*, the service opened with a personal video message from Joel and Luke Smallbone of *for KING & COUNTRY* expressing their condolences to me and the family.

JOEL: "To our dear friend, Susan, and to all of Faith's family, Joel and Luke here with *for KING & COUNTRY*, and we've been following along obviously for the last . . . what . . . "

LUKE: ". . . year"

JOEL: ". . . year, and particularly over the last few weeks. So we just wanted to take a moment to share and also send our condolences to you all."

LUKE: "Yeah, absolutely. And I do want to just say this, we got to see Faith last December and then we got this beautiful gift of seeing her when she came to see us in Charlotte for . . . at Six Flags [i.e. Carowinds], and just to have that moment together I will . . . I will cherish as a beautiful memory . . . "

JOEL: "Yeah . . . I mean what was so cool was, we have this moment in one of the songs, 'It's Not Over Yet,' where we kinda pause in the show for about ten seconds, and I had no idea . . . there was probably 7-8,000 people there that night, no idea where you all were sitting, but it just so . . . I mean I was as shocked as I think Faith was, but it just so happened that we walked all the way back and we got to pause right at that moment and there we were, together, and . . . so many rich moments, not to mention coming to the hospital at the end of 2018 where we all got to meet for the first time and Moriah was there, my wife was there—so it was a rich journey."

LUKE: "In that short time so many rich moments. And we're celebrating this beautiful life, and also Faith will always be our favorite Homecoming Queen, so hope to see you guys all sometime very soon."

JOEL: "Most certainly. Bless you all."

This was followed by a video clip of the special moment at the concert Joel had mentioned where he encountered Faith in the middle of their song followed by another slide show I had put together, featuring for KING & COUNTRY'S song, 'Hold Her,' of her moments with for KING & COUNTRY and her life growing up.

PASTOR MIKE: "Dear friends and family, we are gathered here today to celebrate the life of Faith Mackenzie Shaw. I'll never forget when I first encountered Faith. She was about eight or nine years old, her family had just joined the church, and she was having a hard time taking her breathing treatments – she didn't want to do it. So her mother brought her into my office and thought,

'Well, Pastor, maybe you can talk her into it.' So Faith came into my office and sat on the couch and proceeded to fold her arms, sat ramrod straight, looked at me with a defiant look on her face, and said, 'I know what my mother wants me to do, and I don't need to do it.' And I thought, 'Okay – we have a firecracker here.' And I think we got her talked into it a little bit later on. But Faith was a firecracker. She had a wonderful tenacity about her. And that's what I will always remember. It was that same tenacity that we all observed that held Faith … held her up and pushed her along in her very difficult journey. So much so, that whenever I hear now and later someone call for a tenacious faith, I will always think of Faith Shaw. Faith Shaw stubbornly fighting. Even when buffeted and tempted by the difficulties she was experiencing, even when she was tempted to let go of God, she hung on, until she fell into the arms of God. Finally winning in the end. That is the tenacious Faith that we celebrate today. And that is the tenacious faith we need today. A faith that will win in the end. We're struggling with emotions today; we're struggling with grief because a dear sweet young lady has been taken from our presence. She had such an impact on everyone here – her wonderful family, those of you who were her friends, those of us here at West Concord and other churches, we will miss her terribly. But today we rejoice as well. Because as I said, Faith won in the end. She fell into the arms of Almighty God, and she is living life in a way we can't imagine right now. And she is dancing on golden streets—breathing in celestial air and holding the nail-scarred hand of Jesus Christ her Savior. And so we celebrate that, and we celebrate the life that she lived. So that we might navigate through these difficult emotions, I'd like to read Psalm 23, the Shepherding Psalm. For as we seek God's face today, we need to see Him to shepherd us through this. It says,

"The LORD is my shepherd; I shall not want. He makes me to lie down in green pastures; He leads me beside the still waters. He restores my soul; He leads me in the paths of righteousness for His name's sake. Yea, though I walk through the valley of the shadow of death, I will fear no evil; For You are with me; Your rod and Your staff, they comfort me. You prepare a table before me in the presence of my enemies; You anoint my head with oil; My cup runs over. Surely goodness and mercy shall follow me all the days of my life; And I will dwell in the house of the LORD forever.
Psalm 23:1-6 (NKJV)

"Would you bow with me in prayer – Our Heavenly Father, we've gathered today to celebrate Faith Shaw. Father, we thank You for her tenacity, her stubborn will, her strength. We also thank You for her joy and infectious smile. We thank You for giving her the ability to dance and to celebrate life as she lived it. And, Father, we thank You most importantly that we were privileged to have her as part of our lives. And, Father, I know that I will never forget her. And it is because she has impacted us so much, Father, we're grieving right now because *we will miss her*. And, Lord, we don't understand everything that has happened and why it has happened, and our grief is difficult. But, Father, we don't grieve for Faith, we celebrate for Faith because, Lord, she is with You. Enjoying splendors and wonders and amazing things that we cannot imagine. And she is okay. And, Father, we rejoice that through Jesus Christ and faith in Him, one day, Lord, we can stand with her and spend eternity with her, enjoying Heaven in Your presence. But until then, Father, we're here. You are the Shepherd of our souls, Lord. Shepherd us through these emotions. As we grieve and as we celebrate, carry us along. May we be encouraged by the music played, the songs sung, the word that will be spoken; and, Father, may we always cherish Faith in our hearts, and may we have faith that through Christ one day this is not good-bye but 'til we meet again. Bless us we pray in Jesus' name. Amen."

Faith's friend, Sara, then played a beautiful song that she had written following Faith's death, called "A Heaven Away."

I can't imagine what you're doing right now
Breathing in the air or dancin' on the clouds
I can't imagine that smile on your face
When you see the Lord, when you feel His embrace

Yeah, your heart's finally at peace
And your breath is at ease

So walk the streets of gold
With no worry in your soul
Sing with all the angels
And praise the Lord you're home
And we know you're in a good place, not too far
You're just a heaven away.

I can't imagine the joy in your heart
You're guarded from pain, and safe from harm
And I can't imagine what you're thinking
But you can fill me in when we meet again

You're heart's finally at peace
And your breath is at ease

So walk the streets of gold
With no worry in your soul
Sing with all the angels
And praise the Lord you're home
And you'll hear from us when we pray like you're still here
You're just a heaven away

Don't fear when you see our tears
They're just praising your life
And time will raise our cheers
Here's to an angel flyin' high

Walk the streets of gold
With no worry in your soul
Sing with all the angels
And praise the Lord you're home
And we'll always remember your name
'Cause you're not gone
No you're not gone
You're just a heaven away
Oh, Faith, you're just a heaven away.

GLENN: "Hi everyone. My name is Glenn. Faith and I met when we were both pretty young. I got the chance to grow up with her in the church, and I knew her for about ten years. In that time, me and her became pretty close friends, from trips to youth camp called Snowbird and late-night trips to go get food, which if you knew her, you know was probably Taco Bell. One thing remained the same. She really enjoyed making fun of me. She was always catching me saying something stupid or doing something dumb or messing up a word, and which she would follow by mocking me. She was probably one of the most sarcastic and sassy people I ever met. I still hope she was joking about some of the things she said. I'm sad because I won't get to see her again on this earth, but Faith wanted us to know she's okay and she's happy and healthy with Jesus right now. Every dumb thing we laughed at, every time she made fun of me for doing something stupid, I will be forever grateful for. But I'm much more thankful for the way she pointed me to the Lord. She fought her entire life, and, although she lost her life in the end, she ultimately won. And although we're confused, angry, and sad, we should celebrate her life today, and remember and be grateful for the years we had her here."

KYLE: "Hey guys. For those of you that don't know me, I'm Kyle. Faith and I have been friends for longer than I can even remember. Like, I can't remember a time we weren't friends. I have tried, and I couldn't. We met in youth group here a long time ago and ended up going to high school together as well, and Faith and I always had this sibling-like relationship. When we were in middle school, we actually used to call each other bro and sis, and I can't help but laugh and smile at how ridiculous that is, but also sweet. And I was always amazed at how Faith was both the sweetest and sassiest person, like Glenn said, I've ever met together. I actually think she called me 'loser' more than she did 'Kyle.' But that was entirely out of love—and truth—But Faith truly was the sweetest and most selfless person I've ever known and will ever know. And through everything she went through and struggled with her entire life, she never complained. Instead, she used everything she experienced to minister to others. I know she did for me, and when I was sick and going through things in my life, she was there pushing me through, constantly checking on me, telling me she knows what things are like, and constantly being a light. Though I am, like Glenn said, very sad that Faith's no longer here with us physically, I'm able to rejoice because she is with Jesus right now. And I know I'll see her again. And she smiled at me and asked me to be happy for her. So that's what I'm going to do. And I hope everyone here can as well."

JENNI: "To anyone that might not know, I'm Jenni. And I'm probably going to look at this paper the whole time because I can't look at you guys. But I'm one of Faith's older sisters. And there's just too much to say about Faith and what she meant to all of us and how much we loved her and every memory we have of her is cherished. But I want to talk specifically just about how much this past year with her meant to me, even though it was incredibly hard. So with Faith staying in Chapel Hill, it allowed us to be in each other's lives in a way that we hadn't gotten to experience since I moved to college. She came over to mine and James' house in Raleigh pretty frequently to visit and spend the night. We would watch movies or binge TV shows, make Target runs or book runs – basically find any excuse to be in the car and jam out to throwback songs. She was the most frequent visitor to stay in our guest room, so much so that in my head I basically thought of it as her room. And, of course, James and I were also able to visit her and my mom frequently in Chapel Hill, also, whether that involved a trip to Al's, our favorite burger shack, or seeing the *Avenger's End Game* premier together. But we were able to share many wonderful memories while during the hardest year of our lives, and I'm very thankful for every single one. When any young person dies, especially one as incredible and dearly loved as Faith, we all feel the deep sorrow of what they've missed. We all ache because, to us, they've just started to live their life. While Faith's passing will always be strongly felt, the truth is she started living her life to the fullest a really long time ago. There are many things those of us left on earth lament that we'll never get to see her do. We wanted to see her go to college and to get married and to move to a beach town or a ritzy urban apartment. All of the things that she had planned for herself. But in reality, there were so many things Faith *did* get to do, in spite of her CF because of her strength and persistence. She was able to go on trips to Hawaii, and to New York, and to Washington, DC. She got to be a Girl Scout, a member of the youth group, Student Council, and Leadership. She was able to attend prom twice and become Homecoming Queen. She was my make-up artist and my maid of honor in my wedding. She was able to explore and express her passions, become very talented in art, photography, and dance. She got to be a friend to so many, as well as a sister, a daughter, and an aunt in our family. And in each of those relationships, she got to feel and give so much love. And at the end, she was fortunate to be able to tell all those people she loved so much goodbye. And not everyone gets those moments. As much as they rock me to my core, I will always feel blessed that we had a few days to prepare for what was coming, spend meaningful time individually with her and together as a family, say goodbye and then hold her in those very last moments. Her life may not have been long, not nearly long enough, but no one can deny that her life was full, it was complete, and it was whole. I would be lying if I said that I didn't feel betrayed by God. When we knew that Faith wasn't going to make it, the only thing that I could say in my prayers was, 'How could You?' But what I have clung to since her passing is the overwhelming peace that she had in those last few days. Amidst my still present anger, that peace helps me continue trusting God to carry my family through this and to use her legacy in ways we can't imagine. It brings me comfort and hope and it emboldens me to believe and live confidently and gracefully like she did. I hope we can all find this comfort, hope, and security as we grieve and move forward and, like Faith did, give it all to the Father who loves us and who is taking care of her until we get to see her again."

KELSEY: "I'm Kelsey, I'm the oldest sister. Unlike Jennifer, when I went to college, I stopped seeing Faith as often because I went the opposite direction.

When she went to Chapel Hill, she actually moved farther, so it was hard for me to see her; but we were . . . we had periods . . . we were both very outgoing, stubborn people. So there were times where we would fight like none other. But at the same time, we were . . . we were very close. I remember when she was a little girl and I was obsessed with 'A Series of Unfortunate Events,' and they have the main female, Violet, the older one, and then the baby which was Sonny, and Faith would always pretend to be Sonny and I'd be Violet and I'd put Faith in a rolling book bag that had like a flat bottom and I'd put it up on my back and I'd walk around with her. And I would take her to school and do things to the point where people thought she was my daughter even though she's only eight years younger. But even though I wasn't able to see her as much this past year it was amazing seeing the person she grew into after being that little girl. Unlike everyone else, as her family, as her sisters, we saw the complaints, we saw the anger, the anger at God, the times where she was losing faith and she was struggling. But to me that almost makes . . . in the last few days those last moments she was completely at peace with everything, and she was . . . she felt joy, you could see it in her face. I have never felt . . . I've never seen her just lit by the Holy Spirit the way she was. She was just absolutely at peace and excited about where she was going. And knowing that just a few months before then how dark of a place she was in, that gives us hope for the rest of us because I know we're all in dark places too. And I'm angry. And I miss her. And I've . . . the fact that I will not be creating any more memories with her on this earth kills me. But I've . . . the week after, I spent time at home by myself . . . I kept the kids in school, or . . . they were with my mother-in-law . . . I can't remember . . . they were somewhere . . . (mother-in-law: 'they were with me.') okay . . . and I just stayed home and didn't do anything. I listened to music a lot. I would listen . . . there were things on YouTube called 'Time Alone with God,' and it was just instrumentals and there was verses, and even though I was angry, there was just some kind of comfort you found there. And I found a song, and it's not, I don't believe, a Christian song, it's not written in the point of view that I'm taking it as and so I will probably change tenses just a little bit; but, I remember being angry and asking God, 'If we had just done this, if we had just done that, could there have not been a way?' And I heard this song come on the radio, and to me what it made me think of was it was the moment Faith opened her eyes and was face to face with God for the first time. And this is God speaking to her, it says,

"'Hello. I've been waiting for you. I didn't know if you'd recognize My voice, because I've been whispering your name again and again. I've been imagining this day and I'll never be the same. Welcome home, welcome home. It's so

good to see your face. Welcome home. You danced and sometimes only fell. You sang even when there were no words. And love lifted you up again and again. And though you lost your way, now let Me be the first to say, welcome home, welcome home, it's so good to see your face. Welcome home. Come inside from the cold and rest your weary soul. You belong, you are loved, you are wanted, you're not alone. I've missed you so. Welcome home. Without you here, it's not the same, and I've been waiting here, welcome home.'" [8]

SUSAN: "I think probably most of you know who I am, I'm Faith's mom, also known to most as Mama Shaw. And, of course, those who knew Faith well also knew her as (holding up Faith's license plate) Baby Shaw. Over this past year, and most especially the past several weeks, our family has been completely overwhelmed by the number of people that Faith obviously touched and the lives that she impacted. The messages, the tributes, all the posts—and of course looking at all of you here today . . . it's evidence of her impact. As many of you know, she lived large and so it's only fitting that she is honored large—and from the depths of my heart, I just appreciate all of the words, the encouragement, the love that you've given her . . . that you showed her . . . that you've showed us. And as you can imagine, the grief at losing Faith is deep and intense—but seeing the love that she engendered has helped somewhat to ease that grief, and I'm very, very grateful.

"In the last few days of Faith's life, when we knew that her time to fight had reached its . . . it's completion, she began sharing with people final words, final thoughts, things she wanted and needed to tell them. I at first thought it was . . . was cruel that she had had to put a . . . had a trach put in and so she couldn't speak. But then I realized that because her only way of communicating was in writing, that there was a beauty in that because it was a very focused, intimate form of communication with each person she needed to speak to, and they could have this moment, even when there were a whole bunch of other people in the room, and it was . . . it was just very, very special and I realized that that, too, was a part of God's working.

"Whereas several of her final thoughts with me were personal, there are three distinct final wishes that she had that I'm able to share. First, as some of you may have heard, she wants me to get a dog, I'm perfectly willing to comply with that when the time is right. The second was she wanted us to spread her ashes in Hawaii, which I'm also more than happy to comply with! When she was nine years old, we went to Hawaii on her Make-A-Wish trip and she always wanted to go back because she . . . she couldn't remember it very well. And so she said the one thing she could remember was the water there was just so clear and so beautiful, and so that's where she wants her ashes spread.

"But most importantly, the third wish that she had was to make sure that her story kept going. She was not afraid to die—she knew where she was going, and she, like her sisters said, was actually excited to get there—but she WAS afraid of her story dying along with her. She made her sisters and I promise that we would keep her story alive and continue trying to raise awareness for cystic fibrosis and the fight against . . . that she had against this unforgiving, horrible disease.

"I was recently asked what were some of the aspects of her story that I found the most important—that she found the most important. And, of course, her strength is, I think, foremost . . . everybody sees that . . . everybody saw that, especially over the last year. She was one of the strongest people . . . I think everybody could agree, one of the strongest people that we know. But it did start at a very young age—I think Pastor Farley alluded to that.

"She never did go through the 'terrible twos'—but when the threes hit, she made up for lost time—and then some. Some of the words you might've heard us use to describe her throughout those years were pig-headed, stubborn, hard-headed, strong-willed. I remember calling my mom on a number of occasions just completely exasperated, and just how hard it was. But I also told her I dare not break that will because I knew she was going to need to rely on that as she went through life with this disease.—but boy was it hard to parent!

"But she was also incredibly sweet! So sweet, in fact, that a lot of people didn't believe me when I told them about her temper. I remember one time taking her to Sunday school at a former church and warning them that she was . . . she had a 'devil' side. And they didn't believe me, they just said she was . . . she was too sweet. Then there was one day I was walking to the Sunday school room to get her, and as I turned the corner, her Sunday school teacher was halfway up the hall coming to meet me, with Faith in tow, with a very exasperated look on her face that I recognized all too well. She handed Faith over to me and said, 'Okay . . . I believe you now,' and turned around and walked away. She didn't want to talk about it at that point – we did eventually, and we did get it worked out. But . . . but as she grew and matured, there was still definitely a stubbornness and a pig-headed streak – but most of it progressed and transformed into the strength, determination, perseverance, and fight that most of you knew her for.

"For instance, she spent much of her life in and out of the hospital as she would get lung infections from her CF. And five years ago, she ended up with an infection that was so bad, it . . . she had permanent lung damage. She left a month . . . after a month in the hospital . . . left on oxygen 24/7 with 32% lung function. The doctors told her . . . as you know dance is a big passion of hers . . . the doctors told her that she would not be up to competition level that year. And she refused to accept that. So she and her physical therapist worked very, very hard with specific goals in mind over the next several months—and she was cleared to dance one week before the first performance. It was so exciting . . . By the end of a couple more months, she no longer needed the oxygen during the day, only at night to sleep and after exertion. And she spent the next four years in competition dance with 32% lung function. She would go out on the stage, and she would lay it all out there on the stage, and then immediately get off, put her oxygen on and recover.

"She was also a very passionate person—obviously passionate about dance, the beauty of art and photography, dogs, and other cute fluffy animals—and she had a deep love for her friends and her family. She always made it very clear to the people that were important to her that they *were* important to her and that they meant the world to her. She had an intense passion for LIFE! Once during the past year, she told me that she faced death so many times, that it didn't really phase her. What it did do was give her an amazing appreciation for life. And not just being alive but LIVING—truly LIVING. And she fought HARD to live, and she fought hard to live a life that she felt was worthwhile. She wanted to experience life TODAY, even when others were telling her she needed to not put so much focus on today but look towards the future that they were trying to help her get to. But she knew. She knew the importance of living for NOW and fought very hard for that.

"A few months ago, as she was trying so hard to get her medical team to understand her desire to not let 'today' slip away while she waited for 'tomorrow,' Faith shared a post by Claire Wineland, who was a fellow CF-er who lost her fight last year because it so precisely explained what she was feeling at that point and what she was trying to get them to understand. Claire wrote, *'I've spent the past year just barely holding myself above ground—juggling between being sick with the deep incessant need in me to do something of value with my time. I've been exhausted just keeping myself alive and have nothing left to give to the world around me. That has always been my biggest fear in life, that I would spend everything I had fighting my illness and have nothing to offer – and for me, living without being able to give something of yourself to the world, living without adding value to the world, is not a life I want—I can sense how fragile this life is, how fragile our futures are. How easy it is to let yourself be swept into a version of your life that you despise. It's far too easy to let your life become something you resent. Everyone was scolding me for wanting to stay living on my own, for wanting to move to a different side of town and find a home while being on the transplant list. 'Why not just wait until after the surgery to try and start your life?' they would say. But you can't put your life on hold until your 'better' life begins. You have to fight—to make sure that the life reflected back at you right now is one you want to be living. I'm not going to let myself live a life I'm resentful of. Not if I live for another three months and not if I live for another 30 years.'*

"Sadly, like Faith, Claire didn't get to experience the life that everyone was wanting her to wait for—nor did Danny, another eighteen-year-old with CF that we met in Chapel Hill who died in September while waiting for new lungs. All of these drive home the point that Faith fought so hard to make—the importance of fighting for living the life you want today. Sure, plan for tomorrow but LIVE for today!

"And LOVE for today. Tomorrow isn't promised to any of us – we're all living on borrowed time. And like Jenni was talking about, we were lucky enough to have that chance to say our goodbyes. And we spent the last few days with each other just saying 'I love you' over and over and over again. But that's not always the case. I urge anybody here that if you are holding grudges, or if you're walking in disharmony or anger with somebody, or walking in unforgiveness, make it right because you don't know what tomorrow's going to hold! Make sure the people that you love KNOW that you love them—that you love them today!

"And, finally, another extremely important part of Faith's story that made her who she was, was her belief in and deep love for the Lord. Even when she was angry at Him and not understanding why He was allowing her to continue going through such struggles after a few great months following transplant, she still knew that He loved her and could see Him working through her pain. She was able to make peace with Him and restore that relationship several weeks before her passing, and she seemed to see things so very clearly. It was so obvious the clear connection that she had with God.

"I'll never forget the day she let us know that it was time to call in the family. Her nurse from that day came in to say goodbye at the end of her shift and she wanted to tell Faith how proud she was of her making that decision and being so mature about it. And she asked if she could pray with her. As she walked out of the room following a beautiful and very moving prayer, there was an uncanny look of awe on Faith's face. She quickly grabbed the board that she would use to write to us and said, 'She must have been an angel. I FELT God!'

"Another evidence of her connection with God, as has been discussed, was her profound peace. She had fought and struggled and pushed for so long, I didn't realize how much of that struggle she wore on her face until I saw her at true peace. After she made the decision to stop fighting for something that was no longer attainable, I saw a peace in her that I had never seen before. One thing her sisters and I noticed and have wondered together about several times since her passing was that in the last three or four days of her life, she never cried. Even with all of us blubbering around her, she didn't cry. We basically attributed that to the ultimate peace she was experiencing—but an additional possible revelation came to me last Sunday as I was getting ready for church. The Bible gives us a beautiful glimpse of Heaven in Revelation 21:4 (NKJV):

'And God will wipe away every tear from their eyes; there shall be no more death, nor sorrow, nor crying. There shall be no more pain, for the former things have passed away.'

"I believe that, just like she felt God when the nurse prayed with her, at this point, Faith's connection with God was so close and so real that I think she was already feeling Heaven. It also says in Romans 8:18 (NKJV):

"'For I consider that the sufferings of this present time are not worthy to be compared with the glory which shall be revealed in us.'

"Faith was there. She KNEW the glory she was about to enter very soon, and the sufferings were no longer of import. Therefore, certainly no need for any more tears. She wasn't afraid to die because she knew without a doubt where she was going. And she knew before any of us that she had reached the end of her race. She had fought the fight she was supposed to fight for as long as she was supposed to fight it and because of that, her fight was won! On the back of the bulletin and on the urn, you'll notice reference to some more Scripture that basically describes her life. 2 Timothy 4:7-8 (NIV) . . . and I thank Jennifer for reminding me of this one . . . says,

> "'I have fought the good fight, I have finished the race, I have kept
> the faith. Now there is in store for me the crown of righteousness,
> which the Lord, the righteous Judge, will award to me on that day –
> and not only to me, but also to all who have longed for His appearing.'

"About six weeks before Faith passed, she went to Miss Donna's to tell her team she wouldn't be able to return to dance, after which she posted, 'Goodbyes are not forever. Goodbyes are not the end. They simply mean I'll miss you until we meet again.' So until we meet her again, please join me in honoring her wishes to keep her story alive!"

SONG: "To The End" by *Mack Brock*

YOUTH PASTOR, AARON: "My name is . . . my name is Aaron, and I've had the privilege of being Faith's youth pastor for six years. She had a huge impact on so many different people, as you've heard testimony of and as you've likely experienced yourself. And as Susan mentioned, one of her last wishes was for us to keep her story going, and so I want to spend a little bit more time talking about Faith's story. Because Faith's story is Jesus' story. Faith's story is God's story. Faith's story, in part, is your story. It's a story of creation and brokenness and redemption.

"When God made Faith, He made her with purpose, intentionally and intimately crafting her into the person that she was. Faith Mackenzie Shaw was a daughter, a sister, a niece, a granddaughter, a friend. She was kind, and loving, and witty; she was a dancer, a proficient eye roller, she was a voracious eater, a lover of fine cuisine—at Taco Bell and chili dogs; she was a skilled nap taker, she was surprisingly competitive, and she was a secret athlete. One of my favorite things to do when Faith showed up at church, whenever I would see her, I'd say, 'Faith, heads up!' and then I would grab something that was close to me and I'd throw it at her. And it didn't matter what it was. And most of the time she'd say, 'No don't! I can't catch!' And then she would quickly snatch whatever it was out of the air. Always—'No don't!! I can't catch!' *snag* Hey . . . I don't . . . the girl had reflexes. It was awesome.

"And we miss her, and we mourn her loss, and we celebrate the life that she lived. Friends and family have already shared stories about who she was and how she lived, and I want to say, Susan and Jenni and Kelsey, you guys did such a good job helping her live a life that wasn't defined by cystic fibrosis. Though she was constantly aware of her illness, she did not wield it as a defense or a crutch.

"And while . . . while Faith was a lot of things to a lot of people, the most important thing about her was that she was a child of the One true King. She was a daughter of the living God. Faith was a Christian. She wasn't a Christian because her mom or her sisters are Christian, Faith was a Christian because she believed that she was sinful and in need of a Savior. Unable to save herself, Faith trusted that Jesus was the Son of God who came to live a sinless life in her place, died the death that she deserved for her own rebellion against God, and that He rose from the grave, conquering death, and giving her the promise of eternal life with her God and King. The God who she loved was the God who made her. He's the God who made each of us. And He's holding all things together right now.

"He knew that this day would come before Faith even took her first breath. He knew that she had CF before the doctors diagnosed her at seven months old. He knew all of her days. And He knows all of your days. Before you even knew her name, He knew that you would be sitting here today, celebrating her life, and mourning her loss. And He cares about the pain that you're feeling because He designed that pain to do something in you.

"He gave Faith her sense of humor, her love of junk food, her ability to dance, those big eyes that she rolled so well, and her cat-like reflexes. And also, for reasons that we don't understand, He allowed her to suffer with cystic fibrosis for her entire life.

"And I want to be clear, this was not a punishment given to her, or her mother, or anyone else. This was the result of living in a world broken and corrupted by sin. And each of us feels and experiences the effects of sin in different ways.

"Faith drew each breath that she took with difficulty. It was a constant reminder to her that things were not the way that they are supposed to be. God created her, but He did not create her for suffering. He did not make you for suffering. The pain that we've experienced at this loss of life is an indicator in us that things aren't the way they're supposed to be. Don't numb out to those feelings. I want you to lean into those feelings. God gave you those feelings . . . gave us those feelings . . . so they'd remind you that He did not make us for this. In the beginning, He made all things perfect. In Genesis 1:31 (ESV),

"'And God saw everything that He had made, and behold, it was very good.'

"After He made all things, after He made people, He looked at them and He said, 'this is very good.' And He gave us life and meant for us to live in a relationship with Him forever. But we rejected His authority, and we rejected His rule. And the result of that was sin entering the world. Our relationship with Him, with each other, and as Faith experienced so intimately, our relationship with creation was broken.

"Broken relationships, natural disasters, illness, disease, are all a result of sin entering the world, and it is not supposed to be this way. We all find ways to cope and deal with this brokenness, but I want to submit to you that the only healthy way to do that . . . the only truly effective way to do that is to do what Faith did and put your trust and your hope in Jesus.

"Though we hoped for a cure, the brokenness remained. Though we hoped that breathing treatments would help and that medications and procedures and everything else, we hoped that it would help, the brokenness still remained. And these things we were putting our hope in could not hold or sustain the weight of our hope. Though we hoped that the transplant would increase Faith's quality of life, the brokenness remained. Medicine and healthcare can't hold all of our hope because they can't fully address our greatest need.

"We need Someone who can save us from the effects of sin. Save us from the brokenness. Save us from ourselves as we so quickly reject our Maker. We need Someone who can heal our broken hearts, the ones that have been . . . have separated us from God because we've been rejecting Him. We need Someone who can heal all of the brokenness in the world and that Someone has a name, and it's a set-apart and holy and powerful name. It's Jesus.

"Believing this does not make everything magically okay, as Faith knew very well. You're still going to suffer, and it's still going to hurt, and when the pain hits, you're going to wrestle even more with this truth, as Faith wrestled with it. I and others had very difficult conversations with her about what was going on with her where she would ask questions, 'Why is God allowing this? Why won't He heal me?' And I wished that I knew the mind of God so that I could give her that answer.

"But watching Faith struggle with those questions, what she came to realize was that ultimately she didn't just need functioning lungs, she needed a new heart. She needed a heart that would allow her to love God instead of rebelling against Him. I want to say to you that each of us needs that new heart. And God provided that heart transplant through the Gospel of Jesus Christ. The Son of God, Jesus, whose birth we celebrate this month. He lived a perfectly sinless life so that He could die as a substitute in our place for our sin. And He died the death that we deserve.

"But He didn't stay dead, He rose from the grave to give us life, and He rose in victory over sin and death, and He ascended into Heaven and sat down at the right hand of God, and He is waiting to come back and make all wrongs right. Forever. He's crying out to us in our pain saying, 'I'm coming back.' It's not supposed to be this way, and it won't be like this forever, and this . . . that is where Faith's hope rested. Nothing else can sustain your hope. That's how she was able to remain so positive while dragging around an oxygen tank with her everywhere she went. After weeks long, months-long hospital stays over and over again and after suffering setback after setback after surgery, after she suffered so much, she was still able to think of others. Because her hope was ultimately not in her own healing, but it was in the God who made her and saved her through Jesus.

"Though she desired . . . though she desired her healing and so did we, the full weight of her hope was not in that healing, it was in the eternal promise that God is making all things new through Jesus. And as Susan already quoted from Revelation 21, Revelation was written by one of Jesus' disciples, John, and God allowed John to see the end of the story. And he said,

> "'And I heard a loud voice from the throne saying, 'Behold, the dwelling place of God is with man. He will dwell with them, and they will be His people, and God Himself will be with them as their God. He will wipe away every tear from their eyes, and death shall be no more, neither shall there be mourning, nor crying, nor pain anymore, for the former things have passed away.' And He who was seated on the throne said, 'Behold, I am making all things new.'* Revelation 21:3-5a (ESV)

"The brokenness is still here. But Jesus is going to take it all away. And Faith saw that and believed that. She saw life as it is meant to be seen – broken and fleeting. Life offers us healing and hope that it's ultimately unable to fill, and she experienced the brokenness of this creation in a way that the majority of us will not – every day of her life. And in her suffering, she saw life for what it was – broken and temporary.

"May we see life this way, so that we too will put our hope in something eternal. Jesus . . . believe that He came for you, as well as Faith. Believe that He died in your place because you need rescue from your own rebellion against God. Believe that He rose from the grave to give you abundant life here and eternal life with Him. That … that is Faith's story. A story of creation, and brokenness and redemption through Jesus. Those of us who believe are heartbroken at her passing still, but we do not mourn without hope.

"Mama Shaw, because of Jesus, you will see your baby girl again. Jenni and Kelsey, you will too. Not because you are good, but because Jesus is. And she'll probably roll her eyes at your jokes on the New Earth. She is whole, now, in a way that she never could've been here. She is in the presence of her God and King and everyone who believes the Gospel is true will one day join her in His presence. Let that be you.

"There's no greater way to keep Faith's story going than to enter the story that God has authored from the beginning. He will require much from you, but it's totally worth it. You will suffer and, like Faith, you should suffer well. Suffer with hope, not in this life, but in the one to come, so that at the end of your life, you can look at your friends, look at their face, look in their eyes, like she did us, and say, 'I want you to be happy for me' because you know that you're going to be with your God and King.

"Remember Faith. This life is short. Believe in the Gospel and cling to Jesus. He is our sure and only hope. And I'm grateful to Faith for helping me see that more clearly. The brokenness remains, but not forever because Jesus is making all things new. Let's pray.

"Father God we . . . we love You, and because of what You did through Jesus, we know that You love us. And You've told us in Your word that You are near to the brokenhearted, which means You are near in this place because our hearts are broken because we miss . . . we miss Faith Shaw. And we mourn her loss, and God we ask that You help us to mourn with hope, mourn with the hope that we have in Jesus that we will . . . we will see her again, and we will live in Your presence forever with her. God, we thank You for who You are, and we ask that You comfort this family, comfort the people in this room, comfort . . . comfort us. Help us to see our pain as a reminder that things aren't supposed to be this way, and God, we praise You and we thank You that they're not going to be this way forever. And we love You still, and I pray this in Jesus' name. Amen."

SONG: "I Am Loved" by Mack Brock

As the family and I were dismissed to the Fellowship Hall to receive those in attendance for a reception in Faith's honor, Pastor Mike gave the closing remarks and closing prayer.

PASTOR MIKE: "Would you please stand with me? At this time we're going to excuse the family. They will be heading back to the shelter, just behind this building, the picnic area, where there will be a reception that has been put together for all of you who have come today. And on behalf of Susan and the family, thank you so much for being here and celebrating Faith's life with them. We invite you to join them and to continue to share your memories and share time with them. You can head straight back to the back after we close the service. There are some refreshments back there, some wonderful snacks and food lovingly prepared by the West Concord Baptist Church family, and by the Harrisburg Lowes Foods, where Faith worked for quite some time. And so we appreciate you being here. Susan's looking forward to seeing you, and again I thank you for being here. Let's bow together in prayer.

"Our heavenly Father, we again, thank you for the life of Faith Shaw. For, Lord, in her brief time with us, she has taught us so much. She has taught us that in spite of adversity beyond what many of us can imagine, you can still find joy and happiness in life. Yes, indeed, she did struggle, and Father, a great unfairness occurred, that she was taken from us because of the cystic fibrosis. But Father, we thank You that Jesus Christ endured a great unfairness by bearing our sin on the cross of Calvary. Our sin, and the sin of Faith, and all of us gathered. And Father, we thank You that Faith knew and now knows Jesus as her Savior. And so, Father, we can celebrate the fact that she is with You now. And it is my prayer that everyone in the sound of my voice knows Christ as his or her Savior so that one day we can gather again around Christ and around Faith, with Faith, and celebrate Heaven. Father, wrap Your arms around Susan and the family.

Father, a great void has been left, fill it and we'll praise You. But help us as we leave this afternoon to know that through Jesus Christ this is not goodbye but till we meet again. And we thank You in Jesus' name. Amen.

"Please join us in the back for a wonderful time of fellowship."

As all the guests poured out of the church building and headed toward the picnic shelter, a long, seemingly never-ending line formed to hug me, Kelsey, and Jenni. I have never hugged so many people in one setting in my entire life! It was exhausting and beautiful all in one. But my heart remained deeply moved by the number of people who came to join us in celebrating Faith's beautiful life. It was a beautiful, truly celebratory service and reception that I believe genuinely honored her and her life.

The Fellowship Hall was decorated with photographs, Faith's artwork, dance attire, awards, medals, *for KING & COUNTRY* memorabilia, and many other memories. The walls were filled with notes of encouragement she had received from her high school while she was still in the hospital in those final

days, and another wall held the banner the football team had displayed at their playoff game which read "Through it all we have Faith."

The day after the service, Faith's friend, Glenn, helped me clean up the Fellowship Hall and take her things to my car. It was a sweet time of remembrance as we discussed many things about Faith and her and Glenn's long-time friendship.

A few days after her service, I would find the strength to send out a thank you post:

"Thank you so very much to all who joined us Saturday—in person, in spirit, via live-feed (and apparently even Face-Time!)—to celebrate the beautiful life of one of the most beautiful, strong and courageous souls! Faith's sisters and I remain deeply moved by the show of

love for Faith that completely filled the sanctuary and beyond, and the loving support for us as we journey thru the grief process & figure out this new way of life. I honestly don't recall ever having hugged so many people in one setting. And yet, as I later looked thru all the names in the guest book, there were also so many of you who came that I never had the opportunity to see or hug!

"I'm also so grateful to the many others who worked to make this tribute to Faith such a beautiful and fitting honor to her, the fight she fought, the life she lived, and the love she shared!—To the musicians, to those who spoke—to God for helping ME hold it together long enough to speak!—Those who brought food, those who helped set up and serve the food—all those who worked behind the scenes setting up the many chairs, decorating, running sound, lighting, video, etc.—those who helped direct guests where to park, where to sit, & undoubtedly many other tasks I don't even know about that resulted in everything going so smoothly and—again—beautifully!

"I wish with all my heart and everything within me that we hadn't needed to have this celebration and don't think I'll ever understand this side of Heaven why God chose to share her with us for only such a brief time. But what a blessing it was to see how brightly the sunlight she brought to us all still shines. It helped to warm this mama's grieving and broken heart. God bless you, and please continue to keep our family in prayer for strength and grace to face the days ahead."

19

Letters from Heaven

For Mother's Day 2019 (May 12th), Faith gave me an amazing little booklet called "Letters to My Mom." Inside the booklet was a series of prompts Faith used to write me letters. She then decided what date I was to open each letter and wrote it on the envelope. As of the writing of this book, I still have one remaining letter to be opened, dated for Mother's Day 2024 (also May 12th). I admit to being somewhat apprehensive about opening this final letter, as we were both expecting, hoping, and praying for her to still be here for a good long time after receiving what we were told were such beautiful lungs. At the same time, I feel as though I'll be receiving a letter from Heaven, much like I felt when I opened the letters dated January 28th, 2020 and June 15th, 2020. As much as reading them breaks my heart, I am also filled with inexplicable joy at the tremendous blessing of having all these special letters that I can treasure for the rest of my life. They give me a tangible piece of her heart to hold forever close to mine!

Date Opened: *05/12/2019*
Prompt: A Special Memory I have of you is . . .

"The luau in Hawaii & you held me in your arms while we danced. I remember laying my head on your shoulder & you singing along to the music gently. I don't remember much about Hawaii sadly (guess that means we just have to go back!) but that is one thing I'll never forget about that trip.

You are such a caring, loving, warm-hearted, and gentle mother. And with this memory, those are all I can think about, those characteristics. I hope we make it to Hawaii again some day & are able to create even more special memories like this one. I love you mommy!

~Faithy <3"

Date Opened: 05/12/2019
Prompt: I always wanted to tell you . . .

"I was terrified that I was going to die before I got my transplant. But I was also so ready to be done. Ready for there to be no more pain or suffering. No more anxieties, or 'what ifs,' or fear of what would happen next & if it would be too much for me to handle, finally the thing that made me break. I was to the point that dying, going to Heaven, seemed like the easiest option, the most certain choice with no question of what would happen next, & the least painful – physically & emotionally.

But there was one thing that made all of that worse than the fear of transplant or pain. And that was knowing how much pain you would be in. How much pain my sisters & their families, & grandparents, aunts/uncles, friends would be in. But most of all you.

I couldn't let that happen. I couldn't do that to you. YOU KEPT ME FIGHTING. YOU KEPT ME STRONG WHEN I THOUGHT IT WAS ALL OVER & NOTHING WAS WORTH IT ANYMORE. You're why I wanted to keep living.

P.S.　I'm not crying, you're crying . . ."

Date Opened: 05/12/2019
Prompt: In the future I hope we . . .

"Never grow apart, never lose the incredible bond we've formed, & keep making as many wonderful memories as possible.

You will always be my mom & nothing can change that.

I hope we get to travel to more places we've never been to together.

I hope you get to see me continue dancing & continue living my life to the fullest.

And lastly, I hope we always remember the special memories we've made & cherish the love we have for each other, & the fact that we will have each other with us always, even if it's just in our hearts.

I hope we both live long happy futures. I love you so much, words can't even express it.

Love, Faithy <3"

Date Opened: 05/15/2019 (Faith's birthday)
Prompt: I always think of you when . . .

"When I'm feeling down & I know you always know what to say.

Or when I'm away for a long time (like Snowbird) & I miss hanging out with you, & laughing with you, & just talking in general.

I think of you any time someone mentions another person caring so deeply & loving so much, & being there for someone they love.

You will always be in my thoughts & in my heart. I could never forget you or the things you've done for me & my sisters.

It's going to be so, so, so hard going to college & not seeing you every day. But I promise we won't lose our close-ness! We will talk every day & I'll be visiting a lot! Don't worry :) (You might actually get sick of me!)

I love you! And I won't ever stop!

Love, Faith <3"

Date Opened: 05/17/2019 -- "when with everyone"
Prompt: I love that our family is . . .

"I love how close we are & how that will never change!

From when we were little, - playing games on family games nights, having movie nights, going on vacations, to now – all grown yet still making time for game nights, movie or show nights, & so much more (& with more family to enjoy it with now too!)

I love that we're the type of family that enjoys each other's company even if we're all doing completely different things.

I love that we always say sorry & forgive each other after fights, instead of letting these things fester.

And lastly, I love that we are always there for each other through some of the toughest times in our lives. We have/would drop everything to be there for one another. We make so many sacrifices for each other.

So many families aren't like ours. I am so lucky & so grateful to be a part of this one.

Love, Faithy

P.S. Don't forget, you all still push my buttons a lot! But I love you anyway. :)"

Date Opened: 06/01/2019 -- "at night" (the day we saw for KING & COUN-TRY at Carowinds)
Prompt: From you, I learned the importance of . . .

"Well, so many things actually . . .
I learned the importance of family, love, being strong in my faith, being brave & courageous, being humble, & so much more!
I know you may not always feel like it, but all of these have been shown through you as I grew up.
I also learned the importance of not giving up & most importantly not giving up on God. You have taught me & reminded me constantly of the importance in trusting in God & letting Him lead the way with complete control, even if it seems terrifying.
You are one of the strongest people I know when it comes to your faith & your beliefs.
Thank you so much for being such an amazing role model, & truly, one of my heroes.

I love you!
~Faithy <3

P.S. I HOPE 'ROCK THE PARK' TODAY WAS JUST AS AMAZING AS WE THOUGHT IT WOULD BE!"

Date Opened: 07/07/2019
Prompt: One thing I'm glad we share is . . .

"My dance life. I found my passion for dance with you & we have shared so many fun, silly & amazing experiences at competitions, different studios, conventions & so much more. You always cheer me on (sometimes to the point of bruising! LOL!) You are my biggest supporter & I'm so lucky!

I don't think I would love my dance life & all of the experiences it's brought me without you in it.

I'm sad it's almost over, but I will continue with dancing, so this special thing we share will never die. It will always be a part of our lives.

Love you!
Faith <3"

Date Opened: *08/01/2019*
Prompt: One thing I admire about you is . . .

"Your strength, determination, & love for your kids.

I know that's not one thing, but I felt like you deserved more.

You play both mom & dad, which takes so much out of you & you sacrifice so much but you push on & don't let anything stop you.

You make sure that my sisters & I are safe, loved, & cared for. You want the best for us & always do everything you can possible to make that happen.

I don't think we thank you for it.

I love you so much!
~Faith"

Date Opened: *08/07/2019*
Prompt: The best adventure we've had together was . . .

"Going to New York for World's & Myrtle Beach for Nationals in summer 2018! Walking all around New York City with you, seeing the Statue of Liberty & the Empire State Building, & all the other things we did there was the cherry on top of winning World Champs! I'm so happy I was the one able to go with you on your first (real) trip to New York! I can't wait to go again next summer!

This past Nationals was so fun & unlike any of the others. I loved exploring Myrtle Beach more, shopping, playing mini golf, & going to that little amusement park! That week is one I will cherish forever!

Both of these trips are ones I could never forget. There are so many special memories with each one & so many things/moments I can't wait to experience again! (And this time with new lungs!) There's also no one I would rather have these special memories with.

I can't wait to see what our next adventure will be/hold.

I love you so, so much!
Love, Faithy!"

Date Opened: *01/28/2020 (my birthday, and two-and-a-half months after Faith died)*
Prompt: None

"I wanted this message to be a celebration of making it another year! Well, just about, haha! You and I have been through a lot the past 8-ish months. But we have grown so much from it & learned so much.

I hope that at this point in time we're doing amazingly! I hope you are celebrating another birthday, that I'm still dancing & in my senior year of high school (with the beautiful lungs!), & that we're happy.

I hope that whatever is going on in our lives at this point in time, that this message brings a little joy to our day.

Love you!
~Faith

Also, Happy Birthday!"

Date Opened: 06/15/2020 (seven months after Faith died)
Prompt: Thank you for . . .

"Always being there for me, through my whining, arguing, attitudes, self-doubt & more.

Thank you for all the sacrifices that you have made to get me to this point now.

Thank you for the support & encouragement through school, dance, transplant, etc.

And thank you for loving me unconditionally. I will never be able to repay you for everything you have done for me throughout my life.

You are the best mom anyone could ask for. Don't you ever forget that or think differently. I love you so very much.

Your favorite, Faith <3

P.S. Wow, can you believe I've graduated! Couldn't have done it without you. :)"

After reading the last letter, I was struck with the idea of a song called "Letters From Heaven." I reached out to Faith's friend, Sara, and asked her if she would write another song entitled "Letters From Heaven." Once again, she did not disappoint.

The sun was shining bright on the world today
And I knew you must've been close by
When Jesus sent down His rays
Never seen it shine that way
And I know it's you
Reaching to help me through

You're in the clouds, in the rain
In the sun I see your face
You're in the stars in the window pane
When I close my eyes I feel your embrace
And what a blessing to have you here too
How kind of heaven to share you

The birds were singing out to your favorite song
And it was the prettiest sound
I swear I heard you singing along
I could listen to it all day long
And I know it's you
Reaching down to help me through.

You're in the clouds, in the rain
In the sun I see your face
You're in the stars in the window pane
When I close my eyes I feel your embrace
And what a blessing to have you here too
How kind of heaven
And what a blessing to know it's true
How kind of Jesus to share you.

Letters from Heaven

Sister Kelsey, mom, and sister Jenni (left to right), November 12, 2021

20

Final Wishes Fulfilled

As described in the Celebration of Life service, Faith gave me three main final wishes before she died—get a dog so I wouldn't be lonely, spread her ashes in Hawaii, and do not let her story die along with her.

When I asked Faith what kind of dog she wanted me to get, she told me to just look for the one in which I could see her, and that I would know when that was. I asked her what she wanted me to name the dog, and she told me Scarlett for a girl and Billy for a boy. I was currently still living in a rental home that did not allow pets but began looking at various rescue sites and the dogs they had available, just to get some ideas. After moving into my new house in March of 2020, I started looking a little more seriously, but still was not sure if it was quite time for me to get a dog. I had started following a couple of the rescue sites on social media and saw many, many puppy pictures cross my screen. They were all incredibly cute, but none of them jumped out at me. And then it happened—I discovered that Faith was completely right about my knowing when I saw a dog in which I could see her. I don't know how I knew, but on June 18, 2020, the moment I saw this sweet little  puppy online, I knew she or he was "the one." I immediately reached out to the rescue to inquire about the puppy I had seen, ask about the adoption process, and hopefully get a chance to meet her. It was a little girl about eight weeks old that they called "Chloe." They believed her to be a lab/boxer mix, and she was currently being fostered with one of her sisters. At one point, it looked like the foster mom might adopt her along with her sister, which made me very sad because I just could not get past the feeling that she was the puppy I was supposed to have.

Four days later, I was informed that the foster mom would only be keeping the other pup, so the one I was interested in was available! The "meet-and-greet" was set up for July 2nd, when "Chloe" was about ten weeks old. Several of Faith's friends accompanied me to the "meet-and-greet" so they could be a part of the process in Faith's honor. Once I met her, I was completely smitten, and there was absolutely no doubt in my heart that she was my puppy. I took her home that very day and renamed her "Scarlett Chloe Faith Shaw." Her foster mom told me that she was feisty, a fighter, very vocal, and high-spirited. It was like she was describing Faith! It was undeniablya perfect match. I set out on this new adventure thinking that there were sure to be days that I wondered, "what.have.I.done?!?" But all in all, I was very excited about this sweet puppy and the fact that my days in a house filled with silence and loneliness were hopefully in the past, as I built a beautiful bond with this precious little girl.

A few weeks after bringing her home, it was evident that my world had without a doubt changed dramatically, and the change was a challenging yet very welcome one. Scarlett was an absolutely beautiful and precious little pup with lots of energy, lots of personality, and lots of love. She definitely had many qualities that reminded me of Faith—sassy, stubborn, feisty, a snuggle bunny, loving, funny, goofy, very vocal, and very smart! Something I also realized was that, as much as my world had changed, to Scarlett I basically *was* her world. She did not know anything about a pandemic, politics, bills, work, or other mundane activities and challenges of the "hooman" world. All she knew was the one who played with her, loved on her, fed her, took her outside, and taught her new things—and that was a perspective I committed to always remember and respect. I knew she deserved nothing less.

What I also realized, though, was there was nothing that would *ever* fill the hole left by Faith's passing, and nothing or no one could ever, ever replace her or take that pain away, not even time. But that was okay! First of all, I would not *want* anything or anyone to replace Faith's spot in my heart, nor would I expect that hole to ever be filled. And, secondly, Scarlett helped me discover that even with a never-ending gaping hole in my heart, God has blessed us with hearts that grow and expand to make room for new love! We can always add love to our lives without ever having to lose any love that is already there.

And Scarlett has been an absolute perfect dream! She continues to be the best puppy I could have possibly asked for. I know that she and Faith would have without a doubt been a wonderful, funny, and sweet duo, who would have been the best of friends. She is a wonderful little companion who brings a lot of joy to my life, and I cannot imagine life without her.

When Faith was eight years old, her doctor's office reached out to Make-A-Wish and put in a request to get Faith signed up for a wish. On January 14th, 2010, nine years to the day before Faith would receive her new lungs, Make-A-Wish came to the house, and she was officially registered for her wish. She waffled back and forth between wanting to go to Hawaii or Paris, but ultimately decided on Hawaii. On March 30th, a few months before her ninth birthday, I received a call from Make-A-Wish telling me that the Hawaii trip had been approved, tickets had been purchased, and we were Hawaii-bound in June of that year! We decided not to tell Faith right away but to make it a birthday surprise. So over the next couple of months, as we got all the details ironed out, we also worked on putting together a Hawaii-themed birthday party for Faith and arranged to have the Make-A-Wish representative present her with the news at the party.

The party on May 14th, 2010, one day before Faith's birthday, was a huge success, complete with a limbo competition, Hawaiian music, grass skirts for Faith and her friends, goldfish, fruit kabobs, and little hotdogs cut to be shaped like an octopus. Toward the end of the party, the Make-A-Wish representative showed up, and we hid her in another room while we gathered everyone into the living room. Once we were all there and the video camera was ready, I asked Faith to close her eyes. The Make-A-Wish representative came into the living room holding a poster board she had put together with pictures and information about the trip. When I told Faith to open her eyes, she looked at the poster board for a second, exclaimed, "I'm going to Hawaii?!?" then squealed with delight and started jumping up and down. I still have the poster board presentation to this day.

On the morning of June 19th, 2010, Faith, me, Kelsey, Jenni, and my friend, Litta (Make-A-Wish required two adults), left for Waikiki Beach in Oahu, Hawaii. Make-A-Wish had arranged to have a loaner percussion vest delivered to our hotel so we would only have to worry about packing the nebulizers and medicines.

The trip was, without a doubt, beautiful and gave our family many phenomenal memories. When we returned on June 27th, 2010, we were picked up at the airport by a stretch limo to transport us home. The only sad thing was that as Faith grew older, she remembered less and less about the trip. One of the things she could remember, however, was how clear and beautiful the water was in the ocean, and she always hoped we would get back there again. We had even talked about returning as a celebratory trip after her lung transplant recovery. So, as a final wish, she asked us to spread her ashes in those beautiful waters of Hawaii.

Shortly after Faith died, the family decided on the dates of November 8th-15th, 2020, so we could spread Faith's ashes on the one-year anniversary of her passing. The trip would include me, her sisters Kelsey and Jenni, their husbands, and Faith's nephew, Gabriel, since he and Faith had such a special bond. I began making preliminary arrangements for this bittersweet trip. But then the pandemic hit.

We were devastated with having to postpone the trip due to the pandemic. I was able to get a voucher for the airline tickets that had to be used within a year, so we hoped to be able to make the trip in 2021. As her sisters and I talked about the trip and the postponement, Jenni brought up the fact that the only problem with Faith having been cremated was that we did not have a place to go and visit. And that sparked another plan. Because we had to put the Hawaii trip off for a year anyway, we decided to split her ashes and bury half

of them locally so we would have a place for not only us to visit, but friends as well. For the one-year anniversary of her death, instead of going to Hawaii, we had a very small grave-side ceremony at a cemetery in Concord with just me, Kelsey, Jenni, their husbands, and Kelsey's children, along with a professional photographer to document the moment, and we buried half of Faith's ashes. It was a very sweet, intimate, and beautiful tribute honoring Faith. Her sisters and I each read some Bible verses, we sang a verse of "Amazing Grace," and then all seven of us dropped a red rose into the grave on top of the box containing her ashes. We were not even sure if the burial plan was going to go off without a hitch, as it had been raining all morning. But, praise the Lord, the rain stopped a couple of hours before our 1:00 pm scheduled time, and it did not rain again while we were at the cemetery.

We then followed up the ceremony with chili dogs at Sonic in honor of one of Faith's favorite meals. The Hawaii trip was then tentatively rescheduled for the week of November 6th-13th, 2021.

As things relating to the pandemic began to look better, I set about formalizing all the arrangements for the 2021 trip. I rebooked the tickets on March 30th, 2021, which I did not realize at the time was eleven years to the day that I had been informed Faith's Make-A-Wish trip to Hawaii had been approved and the tickets had been purchased.

Then things took another downward turn when the governor of Hawaii asked that all non-essential travel be delayed at least until the end of October – one week before we were supposed to leave. There were many tense days and fervent prayers concerning the trip and eventually, the Governor gave the go-ahead for travel to resume as of November 1st!

On November 6th, 2021, Faith was Hawaii-bound once again, as our family embarked on that leg of Faith's final wish—to spread her ashes (the remaining half) in the beautiful, clear waters of Hawaii! *Our* wish was that she could have been there with us in person, but we were delighted and honored to fulfill this final wish for her. The trip, from beginning to end, was an absolutely wonderful experience, and all arrangements went exactly as planned! Though bittersweet, it was a beautiful, fun-filled, relaxing week and a wonderful bonding occasion for the whole family. Faith's ashes were not being spread until Friday, so we spent the week enjoying the sights, the beach, the pools, the food, and each other's company.

We hiked up to the top of Diamond Head, like we had done with Faith in 2010, visited Pearl Harbor, went to the Bishop Museum (a museum of Hawaii's history), and of course did lots of shopping and eating. And what's a trip to Hawaii without a luau? Midway through the week, we enjoyed a beautiful sunset along with a fabulous dinner and show at Paradise Cove Luau, where we had gone eleven years earlier with Faith on her Make-A-Wish trip. It brought back so many fond memories as we created wonderful new ones.

When Friday the 12th arrived, the day was, without a doubt, very bittersweet. It was wonderful to know that we were finally fulfilling one of Faith's final wishes. It was also very sad thinking about the significance of the day and knowing that I would be returning home without her ashes that I had grown accustomed to seeing on my fireplace mantle.

Despite the emotions, the day was beautiful. The sun was out, and the temperature was neither too hot nor too chilly. We first spent some time at the beach, all wearing our purple "In Loving Memory of Faith Shaw" t-shirts, then went back to our hotel to get ready for the ceremony to spread her ashes. We had reserved a catamaran to take us out onto the ocean at 4:00 that afternoon so we could return to shore during sunset.

After a year and a half in the making—with one postponement—we were finally able to fulfill this final wish of spreading Faith's remaining ashes in the gorgeous waters of Hawaii. The weather and surroundings could not have been more perfect or more lovely for this amazing and moving send-off for Faith. Although extremely emotional, it was truly a beautiful moment that honored and celebrated Faith in a way that was very fitting, given her love for the water and Hawaii. I was so thankful to be able to share this special moment with my precious daughters, Kelsey and Jenni, their husbands, Jarrett and James, and my grandson, Gabriel.

The catamaran charter was exceptionally stunning. They took us out to a spot near Diamond Head where they anchored and lowered the swim ladder so we could spread the ashes. The captain and his crew were incredibly gracious and respectful, giving us as much time and space as we needed. They handled the entire situation with amazing compassion.

I also hired a photographer to shadow us on the catamaran and document this special occasion so we could live in and focus on the moment itself. The photographer brought along some beautiful flowers for us to drop into the water along with the ashes. Jenni, Kelsey, and I then each took a turn pouring a portion of the ashes into the beautiful waters of Hawaii three miles off the beaches of Oahu. I told Faith I loved her as I poured the last of the ashes into the water. We then sat in silence for a while as we watched the ashes and the flowers drifting, tears flowing down our cheeks. When we had taken the time we needed, we began our solemn journey back to shore with the beauty of the sun setting over the ocean's horizon. It was truly an exquisite and dazzling way to close out a fun-filled week with the family in remembrance and honor of Faith. We returned home the following day.

Several days after returning to our homes, Jenni shared her thoughts about the trip.

"Scattering Faith's ashes was beautiful, moving, and saturated with many warring emotions. Two years working towards this moment left me feeling somehow both peaceful and terribly broken when it was over, but I'm thankful for everything and everyone that came together to help us honor Faith's wishes.

"A special thank you to Royal Hawaiian Catamaran for the charter, they hosted us with incredible grace and compassion. Another huge thank you to Sunn Photography for her outstanding talent and artistry, and her willing-

ness to document something so important to us.

"While we continue to grieve, one thing our family is never without is love and support, from one another and our remarkable communities of friends and family. We are so fortunate in that way and couldn't be more grateful!"

I also received a very sweet message from the photographer, which I shared in the following post,

"FOREVER IN PARADISE — On our catamaran journey to spread Faith's ashes last Friday for the 2nd anniversary of her passing, I had a photographer join us in order to document the event so we could focus on the significance and somber beauty of the moment. In addition to the beautiful photos, our photographer also shared a beautiful and poignant message that I felt was important to pass along as a reminder that God's plans are always perfect and always have deeper meaning of some sort, even if we don't understand them with our limited knowledge and human hearts. Pertaining to the date of Faith's entrance into Glory on 11-12-19, Meredith's message read . . .

'The Lord has recently put an interest on my heart to learn more about numbers and the meaning behind them according to the Bible—I've learned our perfect God uses many ways to speak to us and one of them is numbers. Especially if we are looking! I am in the middle of a book about the meaning of numbers in the Bible right now so I scanned around and this is what I just found and it's pretty amazing . . .

11 – Number used for Heroes of Faith . . . in Hebrews ch. 11, it lists the "Faith hall of fame" those known for Victorious attributes of Faith

12 – Number used to show God is in control and has a perfect plan. Actively ruling as king. God's perfection.

19 – FAITH – again in Hebrews, there are 19 people listed who showed great faith

'. . . thought that this was so relevant! God is in control and has a perfect plan and he knew exactly when he was going to take his perfect lil daughter home who was a great example of true faith to us all . . .'

"Mahalo, Meredith with Sunn Photography for sharing not only your talent but also your heart and your prayers with our family!! You have blessed us tremendously!

"My beautiful and precious Faith, I am so thankful that we were finally able to fulfill your final wish and that your ashes now rest in the tranquil waters of Hawaii. As hard as it was to release that part of you, my heart also finds peace in the knowledge of where you truly are, and that the eternal Paradise in which you now reside is unmatched by any other!!! I love you and miss you so very much, sweet angel!"

The third final wish that Faith tasked me with was to be sure and keep her story alive. As I previously mentioned, she was not afraid to die, as she knew exactly where she was going. But she *was* afraid of her story dying with her. Keeping Faith's story alive has been equally an easy and a difficult task. There is so much to be said about Faith, her journey, and the person she was that it is very easy to talk about her . . . yet it also carries with it deep and intense grief-filled pain.

One of the ways I've worked on keeping her story alive is through social media by sharing memories as they have popped up on my personal accounts, Faith's Facebook, and on our Lungs4Faith page. One of her sisters created a Facebook page called "Keeping Faith Alive," which she hopes and plans to keep up with better once she has finished her master's degree this coming summer. This book, however, is the main avenue I am using to keep her story alive. It has been a very difficult and very therapeutic book to write, and I can only pray it honors Faith in the way she deserves and would make her proud.

The Grieving Parent Sculpture, called "Emptiness"

21

Journey of Grief: Surviving the Loss

". . . the best fruit will be what is produced by the best-pruned branch. The strongest steel will be that which went through the hottest fire and the coldest water. The deepest knowledge of God's presence will have been acquired in the deepest river or dungeon or lion's den. The greatest joy will have come forth out of the greatest sorrow."[9]
~ Elisabeth Elliot

"I will be glad and rejoice in Your love, for You saw my affliction and knew the anguish of my soul."
Psalm 31:7 (NIV)

"The Lord is close to the brokenhearted and saves those who are crushed in spirit."
Psalm 34:18 (NIV)

The journey of grief is long, hard, and lonely, no matter how many wonderful friends and family gather around you in person, in spirit, and in prayer. It is a journey that changes the trajectory of your life and who you are in profound ways that cannot be described. I never could have imagined that a heart could break this thoroughly and continue beating.

The loss of such a dear loved one does not fall into the category of "time heals all wounds" because this is a wound that can never be healed, no matter how much time has passed. The wound remains open, wide, and raw.

One only learns how to live—or at least function—around it, better on some days than others. But there are still times when you fall into that gaping hole in your heart, and the pain is no less intense than the day the loss occurred. You do not always have a warning before something triggers that fall, and sometimes it comes completely out of the blue with *no* apparent trigger. I have a picture of Eeyore on the overhead above my desk at work that states, "It's ok to not be ok. Some days are just harder than others." It serves as a reminder that it's okay to feel the pain—it's okay to continue grieving—it's okay to hurt—and it's also okay to feel okay on those days that are good.

The days immediately following Faith's death were filled with a sense of unbelief and expecting to wake up from the nightmare at any moment. The ache and emptiness in my heart and my soul were the most devastating I have ever felt in my life, and I honestly did not know how I was going to survive the loss. Sleep became a thing of the past as I found myself unable to sleep more than one to two hours a night. But my faith and trust in God was still strong. As I shared with a friend,

"It's definitely been a mix of emotions. Sheer devastation at the loss; comfort at knowing where she is and that she's dancing with the most perfect lungs ever imagined; awe at the outpouring of support and love from her school and the community; the evidence of what an impact she had on so many lives . . . it's all kind of surreal right now and the emotions change sometimes from minute to minute. I know the grief will never change . . . just our ability to live with it and manage it will become better. She was truly an amazing light in this world, and it has also been amazing to see that even though she's left us, that light is still shining just as brightly!"

I worked from home the first week, as returning to work on Monday following Faith's death just felt wrong. Even returning to work the Monday after that was devastating and felt somehow cruel. It did not feel right to return to "normal" life when my daughter had been snatched away from me. How on earth could the world continue to turn and everyone keep on living their lives? Did they not realize that one of the most beautiful souls was no longer here? When I was alone, I was in constant tears. When I was not alone, I lived on the precipice. Any time someone expressed their condolences, I could not contain the emotions and would fall completely apart. My faith and trust in God remained intact, although began to show cracks as my questions to Him began to arise.

The support, love, and encouragement from family and friends at this time were constant and sometimes actually a little overwhelming. Everyone wanted to know what they could do for me, and I honestly was not quite sure. I was still trying to figure out how to pull myself out of bed each day, let alone figure out what I needed from other people. So instead of embracing the support and the offers to help in whatever way they could, I withdrew inside myself and more or less pushed people away. I then threw myself into planning the Celebration of Life service and found it to be a good distraction from allowing myself to fully grieve. Sleep still eluded me, and I still felt in a decent place with God.

After the Celebration of Life service on December 7th, 2019, I was forced once again to face the devastating reality that Faith was gone. Without the distraction of planning the service, my thoughts were fully on her absence, and my emotional state began to take a bad turn. The questions of "why" permeated my every waking moment, of which there were many since I still could not sleep. When I did sleep, I dreamed of Faith, most of which consisted of me seeing her in the distance and not being able to reach her or catch up to her. I began to feel anger toward God that He would take my daughter from me so soon—and after having blessed her with beautiful new lungs that were supposed to have given her thirty, forty, or fifty more years. I began to drink to numb the pain.

As Christmas drew ever closer, the pain of Faith's absence loomed even larger, and my anger at God came pouring out—loudly. I found myself filled with complete rage one day and was screaming, crying, and swearing at God before I realized how loud I was actually being. If anyone had been outside, they no doubt would have heard my screaming, and I began to wonder if the cops had ever been called to respond to a domestic dispute between someone and God. And it was all sparked by coming across a small can of cheddar cheese Pringles, one of Faith's favorite snacks. It just didn't make any sense. I worked on pictures, memorial yard flags, remembrance slide shows—yet it was a can of Pringles that completely set me off.

On January 14th, 2020, in honor of what would have been Faith's one-year anniversary of getting new lungs, I chose to be "offline" for the day – no phone, no social media, etc. It was a day to cry, to reflect, to fully grieve without holding back and without interruption. The next day, I was very thankful I had unplugged because I had *multiple* text and voice messages from people offering their support given the significance of the day. I was incredibly touched and appreciative, but it would have been too overwhelming to handle on that day.

The following day, when one of Faith's friends asked me how I was doing, I replied, "I miss Faith soooo much! I've never hurt like this before. I miss her voice, her laughter, her smile, cuddling with her on the couch watching a movie or our shows. I even miss fighting with her. Just everything about her, I ache to have back. I'm struggling with believing God really cares. Struggling with caring about God. Struggling with myself for feeling this way and for some of the places my mind goes. I'm lonely and sad and angry . . . People keep telling me I'm so strong and such an inspiration, but they have no idea. No REAL idea. I'm a mess."

A couple of days later, I shared with this same friend, "I'm tired of missing her and tired of being alone. I'm tired of hurting and tired of crying. I'm tired of life always being so hard. I'm just so dang tired."

Many, many people were still trying to surround me with their love and offerings of help . . . and I continued to withdraw deeper within myself and put them off. I was never suicidal, but I began to feel that I did not really care if anything happened to me. I was exhausted, unfocused, and began to fear something was going to happen to my other daughters or my grandchildren, and was suddenly feeling convinced that God did not care for me that much.

Even through the anger and all the questions in my heart, I felt a calling to help teach the college class at church. Although Faith was not yet in college, that was technically her age group since she had started high school a year late, and my heart was not yet done ministering to that age group. Plus, since the class was filled with friends of hers and we were all hurting deeply, I believed we could perhaps minister to one another. I was also hoping that in teaching, I would be able to get past the anger and feel God's love once again.

My anger at God, however, began to grow with each passing day. I still could not sleep and the drinking continued—but now as not only a way to feel numb but also to try and help me sleep. It did neither. It only contributed to the anger and depression, now with the added emotions of shame and guilt. I was quickly spiraling.

After realizing the depression was getting the better of me and I needed some professional help, I sought out one-on-one grief counseling, which I continued for about six months. My first session on January 22nd, 2020, was by far the most difficult, as I had to tell my counselor all about Faith and dive deep into the wounds of her loss. Before long, I found myself passing the box of Kleenex to *her* as she began crying along with me. I briefly wondered if this was the right counselor for me if she was going to be reduced to tears as well. But then I realized that meant she was sympathetic and compassionate, not cold or clinical, and was *exactly* what I needed.

The evening of my first grief counseling session, the emotions and pain were raw, having been completely opened up during counseling. I found myself once again screaming at God through my sobs and asking Him why. Why on earth would He take such an amazing inspirational young lady—my beautiful daughter—someone who touched the lives of so many people with her story? How could her work on earth possibly be done? What purpose could her death serve? How could He do that to me?

In addition to my meltdown with God, I found myself experiencing an emotion that I had not previously experienced during the grief process—I found myself angry at *Faith* for leaving me. This emotion threw me for a loop and then made me angry at myself for feeling that way. When I shared my guilt over feeling this way with my other daughters, Jenni sweetly and wisely replied, ". . . try not to feel bad about feeling angry at Faith (or anything else you're feeling). Grief isn't rational, so you don't need to feel guilt over an 'irrational' emotion. The anger itself is rational of course, but it's understandable for that anger to get misdirected."

At church on January 26th, 2020, I sang "It Is Well" with the worship band and discovered that it was *not* as well with my soul as it had been the last time I had sung that song, the day after Faith's Celebration of Life service. This time I had a very difficult time making it through the song, which was then followed up by the handbells playing a song called "Breathe" and then a song called "Faith." I sent a text to Kelsey and Jenni asking, "Just what is God trying to do to me?"

Grief counseling ended up being *tremendously* helpful, and I made a great deal of progress, including being able to stop the drinking that had become an ever-increasing unhealthy product of my grief and depression.

I continued to go through the remaining items of Faith's personal belongings. When everything was distributed to those I thought would like them or could use them and I had separated the sentimental items I was keeping, on January 29th, I took the remaining items to CVAN (a store similar to Goodwill but which benefits battered wives and children). As I shared with a friend, even though they were just things, I felt like I had just dropped off the last of Faith's "life." I sat in the CVAN parking lot for quite some time unable to drive due to the onslaught of tears.

One of the things I could not bring myself to let go of for a long time was Faith's phone line. I did not feel it was right for anyone else to have her phone number. It was Faith's. But I also could not continue to pay for two phone lines indefinitely when I only needed one phone. So to protect her number, at the beginning of 2021, I had her number switched over to an iPad, which cost less than an extra phone line but could still preserve her number. Before making the switch, however, I recorded her voicemail greeting, so I could listen to her sweet voice again and again and again.

About a year after completing my one-on-one counseling, I began attending group counseling called GriefShare, which also proved to be extremely beneficial and allowed me to bond with others experiencing deep loss and grief. I have read a number of books on grief, the most impactful of which were "Shattered: Surviving the Loss of a Child" and "The Grief Guidebook" (both by Gary Roe), along with many Bible studies that have helped in healing my relationship with God.

One such Bible study was "The Chosen, 40 Days With Jesus." Two sections specifically stood out to me during my time of trying to figure out this new way of life. One was called "Reset" and the other was "Hope," both of which I shared on social media:

"RESET – John the Baptist preached in the wilderness; throngs of people followed him into the wilderness to be baptized; Noah and his family, when they stepped out of the ark, stepped into the wilderness of a new world; God told Abraham to follow Him into the wilderness to a new home; Moses led the Israelites out of slavery in Egypt into the wilderness where they would roam for 40 years before reaching the promised land—each time the wilderness served as a RESET button that says, 'Life as you know it is over, and a new thing has begun!'" [10]

My response: *"What wilderness is God calling you into so you can reset? The wilderness itself is typically not an easy place to be, but with God as your guide, the blessings on the other side can be refreshing and awe-inspiring. Be willing to follow Him into that wilderness where you can be restored, renewed, and a new thing can begin!"*

"HOPE – 'And we boast in the hope of the glory of God. Not only so, but we also glory in our sufferings, because we know that suffering produces perseverance; perseverance, character; and character, hope. And hope does not put us to shame, because God's love has been poured out into our hearts through the Holy Spirit, who has been given to us.' ~ Romans 5:2-5 (NIV)" [11]

Even many memes I saw on social media put words to what I was feeling in my heart and the emotions I was dealing with daily:

"I had no idea with grief comes fear. A terror that swoops in from nowhere. You fear the future, you fear the now. You are left feeling like an innocent child, waiting to be rescued, needing to be protected, longing to be hugged. Who knew grief like this . . . that it's not just a feeling, it's a new way of living. ~Zoe

Clark-Coates" [12]
"It takes a lot of courage to live life as a griever.
To face the world each day with a smile
When you're actually crying inside.
To engage in conversations with others
When you just wish you could be left alone.
To be made to look forward to the future
When you just wish to go back to the yesterdays.
It takes a lot of courage to reach deep down
Within yourself and tell yourself that
You will do your best to survive yet
Another day. ~Narin Grewal" [13]

"He cried—He knew Lazarus was dead before He got the news
But still, He cried.
He knew Lazarus would be alive again in moments
But still, He cried.
He knew death here is not forever.
He knew eternity and the Kingdom better than anyone else could
Yet He wept.
Because this world is full of pain and regret and loss and depression and dev-
astation
He wept because knowing the end of the story doesn't mean you can't cry at the
sad parts.
~ Stevie Swift" [14]

My response: *"Even though I know beyond a shadow of a doubt that I will see my sweet girl again, it doesn't change the fact that I miss her so deeply and so terribly right NOW on THIS side of Heaven and that I am immensely and intensely sad that she's not here! I cherish every single memory, and I wish we could've had the chance to make so many more! . . . It's ok to lean into your grief and cry at the sad parts."*

Even coming across something I had, myself, posted many years earlier struck home when it popped up in my memories —

"The God of the good times is still God in the bad . . .
The God of the mountain is still God in the valley . . .
The God of the day time is still God in the night."

Throughout the grief journey, I have learned that social media is truly a blessing and a curse. So many memories continually pop up on Facebook, TimeHop, OneDrive, and Shutterfly. I am thankful for the beautiful reminders of the wonderful times with Faith—and it aches that we won't be making any new memories. I love to see the memories of dance competitions, family gatherings, holidays, school days, transplant recovery days—the good and the bad—hospital stays, church activities—and at the same time they tear my heart in two.

There are many ways in which my family and I have tried to navigate the grief journey, one of which is not only to mourn and grieve Faith but to *celebrate* her! We gather as a family for the week of her birthday, which we have dubbed "Faith Week" (sometimes includes Mother's Day, depending on where it falls on the calendar in relation to her birthday), as well as make every effort to gather together on the anniversary of her death.

During "Faith Week," I post memories and details about Faith and her life as a way of celebrating who she was and the beautiful life she lived. The following post from May 6th, 2020, describes the first "Faith Week" . . .

"Stepping into the month of May has been a difficult journey, as it holds a very 'Faith-heavy' focus. Not only is it Cystic Fibrosis Awareness Month, but within a 5 day period, there is my first Mother's Day since losing Faith (10th), the 6-month anniversary of her passing (12th), and her 19th birthday (15th) – all of which together I've dubbed 'Faith Week.'

"My Sunday School classes and church services recently have focused a lot on joy vs. happiness, especially through difficult circumstances, and making sure our focus is on the true Source of our joy. In grief counseling, we've also talked a lot about using the word 'and' instead of 'but.' Through all of these things, I'm reminded that I can have joy AND be sad and angry; I can rejoice in the knowledge that Faith is now free of the bondage of cystic fibrosis, the lung transplant difficulties, now with perfect lungs and perfect joy in the presence of Christ AND wish with all my heart that she was still here with me; and I can be very heavy-hearted about the significance of the month as it relates to Faith AND celebrate because of the significance of the month as it relates to Faith! I pray for your indulgence as I share throughout this month things I

celebrate about her life and hope you will celebrate with me!

"One of our favorite things to experience together were her dance competitions. They were sheer chaos and very stressful—and we loved it! I loved watching her dance and we both just truly enjoyed the whole competition environment. This particular dance ("Through The Glass") has always been one of my favorites (of which I have quite a few), and I hope you enjoy it as much as I do (she's the last one to enter from the left).

"Thank you all for the continued prayers and support. And if you have any moments or memories you'd like to share in celebration of Faith, feel free to do so here, on the Keeping Faith Alive page, and/or Faith's Facebook page. God bless you always, and I pray you and your families are all safe and healthy during this unusual and challenging time! #CelebratingFaith"

On May 8th, 2020, I posted a small collection of short videos of Faith. One of Faith's deep desires was to always fight to live a life she felt was worth living. These little videos are a great representation of her sweet and pure joy for living life, and her passion for simply enjoying the moment. There's such beauty in the simplicity of these moments . . . a simplicity that speaks volumes about a part of who she was . . . someone who was definitely worth celebrating!

May 11th, 2020:

"BAE - BEST AUNT EVER – Another beautiful thing I love to remember and celebrate about Faith . . . was the love she had for her niece & nephew—and the love they have for her!! When Gabriel was really little, he couldn't pronounce 'Faith,' so it came out as 'Bae.' That endearingly stuck for the rest of her life. And continues still as they talk about their aunt Bae. A beautiful soul that is deeply missed, deeply loved, and most assuredly celebrated!"

May 12th, 2020:

"CELEBRATION OF LIFE – Six months ago today, Faith Mackenzie Shaw gained her most perfect and beautiful lungs as she fell into the loving arms of Jesus, free at last from the struggles of Cystic Fibrosis & lung transplant complications. Her life, though way too short, was a beautiful example of living life to the fullest, loving others deeply and a testimony of an unmatched strength and faith. Her trust in the Lord, especially in those final days, brings an inde-

scribable joy to my heart, even in the midst of the deepest and most painful sorrow I've ever known."

May 15th, 2020:

"HAPPY BIRTHDAY IN HEAVEN – Happy 19th birthday, Faith, my sweet angel! My world is a little darker because you are no longer here with me—AND tons brighter because of the 18 years I was blessed to have you and hold you— laugh with you and cry with you—watch movies, take walks, play games—and watch you grow into a beautiful, spirit-filled, strong and courageous young lady. You have given me a lifetime of wonderful memories that I will cherish and hold close to my heart for all time. I love you and miss you more than words will ever be able to express, and I can't wait to wrap you in my arms once again one day!"

Even beyond "Faith Week," however, I continued to celebrate, intentionally remember, and honor Faith throughout the month of May.

On May 18th, 2020, we had a "cap & gown" photo shoot at the spirit rock in front of Hickory Ridge High School, which was still painted with "Fly High Faith." Her friend, Abby, had gotten a large picture of Faith in her Homecoming dress printed for the candlelight vigil, which she gave to me following the vigil, and we displayed at her Celebration of Life service. We took this print to the spirit rock and draped her cap, gown, and some of her cords over it so she could have her cap & gown photo.

May 20th, 2020:

"EPITOME OF STRENGTH AND PERSEVERANCE — I think anyone who knew Faith . . . or simply knew OF her, would agree that she was one of the strongest people around. She's certainly the strongest person I've ever met, and probably ever will. She fought hard every day just to breathe, AND also to live

as normal a life as possible. She was such a passionate soul with a courageous perseverance that never ceased to amaze me. I'm very proud of the young lady she became and the determination she had to keep on fighting, no matter what seemed to be thrown at her.

"One of the best examples of this passion, strength, and fight is displayed in her love for dance. With only 32% lung function, she could barely breathe, yet gave it everything she had from the depths of her being. As many of you know, she would dance her heart out at competitions, leaving everything out on the stage, only to be near collapse backstage afterwards requiring oxygen to recover. Most of the time during rehearsals she would have to sit and recover following just one run-through. And more times than I can count, I also watched her walk to the side or back of the room, put on her oxygen, and continue doing as much of the dance as she could while tethered to the oxygen tank."

May 22nd, 2020:

"THE CURE – another one of my favorites of Faith's dances, ironically called 'The Cure,' is also another example of her amazing strength and determination displayed through her passion for dance. As the video opens, Faith is the one all the way to the right of the screen and will be the one lifted. As I re-watch this video, I can't help but think what a beautiful representative picture it is of Faith being lifted up into the arms of Jesus where she was blessed with the ULTIMATE cure!!"

May 27th, 2020:

"AN EYE—AND A KNACK—FOR THE ARTS – Faith's passion for dance is certainly no secret; but she also had a love for, and exceptional talent in, photography and art. In an email early last fall, one of Faith's online photography instructors told me, 'Students like Faith are why teachers teach,' and she 'could see right away that Faith was a natural with the camera.' (Personally, I think Faith was a natural with the camera, no matter what side of it she was on!).

"Her love for art would have also served her well in college, as she intended to major in Interior Design with a minor in Studio Art. I don't have any of her photography projects available, but earlier this year I came across some of her art class assignments that I found particularly impressive. There were also several of her own designs, ranging from a cute chubby bunny beloved by everyone that saw it, to pictures of the despair and loneliness she felt at being trapped in the hospital, chained to an oxygen tube. . .

"Thank you all for allowing me to share tidbits of my daughter with you as I continue dedicating May to celebrating her and her life! I have found it to be a vital part of the grieving and healing process, and I'm grateful for your patience, love, support, encouragement, and prayers! God bless you!"

On May 29th, 2020, I picked up Faith's final cord, stole, and yearbook. It proved to be a very bittersweet moment – AND one that filled me with such pride and joy that she not only made it as far as she did but excelled in the process! Even in the midst of her challenging circumstances, she worked with such a determined perseverance to reach her goals and exceed expectations. That was pretty much how she approached everything in life. It's who she was, and I will always be so very proud of her.

Looking through the yearbook was also very bittersweet. I immediately went to the pages that contained images and information about her and cried as I saw the spread from Homecoming, along with the two full-page Senior Ads—one from me and one from the staff and students of Hickory Ridge High School.

My page contained a dozen pictures from her life, along with a quote that said, "The world isn't darker because you left. The world is brighter because you were in it" (author unknown). My message read,

"My dear sweet Faith, you were taken from us way too soon and I deeply miss you every moment of every day. But even though you were here for only a short time, you enriched and influenced my life in profound ways, and I see a piece of you in every piece of me! The strength and courage you displayed was—and continues to be—an inspiration to me, your sisters and so many others who knew—or knew of—you. You fought hard to live a life worth living, and we are so very proud of you and the legacy you've left behind. Your story and your

memory live on, and we are better because of you! Until we meet again . . .

"Loving and missing you always, Mama, Kelsey, and Jenni"

This was followed by the verses we referenced on her urn and in her Celebration of Life service, 2 Timothy 4:7-8.

The next page displayed a beautiful picture of Faith from Homecoming as well as the spirit rock painted with "Fly High Faith." Their message read,

"You were an inspiration to so many of us. You showed determination and a will to keep going like nobody else. Your infectious positivity will not be forgotten. We miss you dearly.

"With all our love, the staff and students of Hickory Ridge."

May 31st, 2020:

"BREATHE – As the month of May draws to a close, and I complete my intentional dedication of the month to celebrating Faith, I'd like to share her very first solo at the age of 14. She was only in her second year of dance and really wanted to tell her story with cystic fibrosis through this medium for which she had so much passion. The dance is performed to a song called 'Breathe,' and is choreographed WITH her oxygen tank! This part of her story focuses on the struggles and frustration with the bondage of CF, as she tries so hard to 'break free' to live and breathe normally.

"At this particular competition, Faith was awarded the 'Most Inspirational' Judges' Special Award, which was a beautiful moment and one of the many I'll cherish for all time! The end of her dance demonstrates her strength as she victoriously walks away from the 'chains,' which I see again as a beautiful representative picture of her life—and death. She continually lived beyond where her 'chains' should have allowed her to go, AND she gained ultimate victory over the bondage of CF and lung transplant complications as she danced into the arms of Jesus.

"And I would have to say that Faith's love for her family and friends was surpassed only by her love for the Lord. Even when she was angry with Him and questioning His plan, she still had an underlying, steady faith that kept her pushing onward until that faith ultimately won out over the anger and doubts. Her level of such overwhelming peace was uncanny. She fought her fight to the finish and knew without a doubt when her fight was complete, and that it was time for her to go Home. Those final days she had no more fears, no more tears, no more anger, no more doubts. Only peace, comfort, calm, and a confident certainty. As painful as it was and remains to be, it was at the same time beautiful to watch this outward transformation. Definitely, in this mama's eyes, 'Most Inspirational!'"

(To view this and other of Faith's dances and special moments, you can visit my YouTube channel, @ShawManor.)

On May 9th, 2021, I went to the Charlotte Water Lantern Festival with a group of Faith's friends and family. It was a beautiful night of remembrance, where we got to design our own lanterns then place them on the water after it turned dark.

"It was a perfect night last night for the Water Lantern Festival! The weather was beautiful, the company was great, and it was a wonderful heartfelt way to pay tribute to my precious Faith!

"I pray our messages of love and remembrance reached you in your heavenly home, sweet girl! You are so deeply missed and loved!"

May 11th, 2021, I posted another one of my favorite dances Faith was in, called "Wade in the Water." If you watch it, she is the one dressed in white.

May 12th, 2021, I wrote a poem about the 18-month anniversary of Faith's death:

"18 MONTHS
18 months ago you breathed your last;
18 months ago you finally could rest.
After 18 years of an inspiring fight,
Your fight was over and you took glorious flight.
Into the arms of our Savior above,
He welcomed you Home with His mercy and love.
18 months without your smile and laugh;
18 years was not nearly enough.
18 months without you here by my side;
A part of me perished the day that you died.
I miss you, my angel, with my heart and my soul,
Yet rejoice - with the Savior you are finally whole.
And even through the vast sorrow and pain,
I know that I know I will see you again!"

May 14th, 2021, I posted another one of Faith's dances from a competition:

"BETWEEN THE LINES – As everyone has no doubt figured out, one of my favorite things to do was watch Faith dance! Her passion and grace always touched my heart and made me so proud. I'm so thankful for the beautiful memories and getting to watch these over and over again! In this dance, called "Between the Lines." Faith starts off all the way on the right hand side. #Celebrating Faith

May 28th, 2021:

"THE BEGINNING – I recently came across Faith's very first dance from when she started in the spring of 2014 at age 12—when she was finally able to do what she'd always wanted to but I hadn't previously been able to afford. The following fall, she made the competition team at a new studio and never looked back, even when her lungs were permanently damaged later that year from the ravages of CF and she ended up with 32% lung function!! She may have started later in life, and under incredible challenges, but she put a full lifetime of passion and heart into it and came such a long way in her short 5 years of dance. Her technique wasn't necessarily always up to the same level as others her age who had started at 3 or 4, but she definitely had a beauty in her movements and

a raw, natural talent that poured out of her every time she danced. I so miss watching her dance. #CelebratingFaith

"With the perfection of your glorified body, sweet girl, I can only imagine the beauty and joy with which you now dance in Christ's awesome presence! I long for the day when I can witness you #DancingWithJesus!"

Lungs4Faith

1.5K likes · **1.5K** followers

Dedicated to the memory of Faith Shaw, her fight against Cystic Fibrosis and her journey on the road

Add to story

Promote   See dashboard   ···

22

Journey of Grief: Journaling Through Social Media

Beyond the month of May, social media also became my journal of sorts, as I posted many thoughts and feelings while sharing many of the memories that popped up. I think one of the best ways I can share this journey of grief is by continuing to share some of those social media posts since they adequately capture the thoughts and emotions I was experiencing at that particular moment in time.

November 22nd, 2019, upon hearing a song called "Why God:"

"I continually ask, 'Why God,' the answer for which I will probably not get until I stand face to face with Jesus myself. But as this song says, even when I don't understand the reason for all the pain, grief, and shattered hearts, I understand 'Why God I need you / It's why God I run to Your arms / Over and over again / It's why God I cling to Your love / And hold on for dear life / And find You are right by my side.'" [15]

On November 24th, 2019, Faith and I had tickets to see *for KING & COUNTRY* in Greenville, SC. This was supposed to make up for the concert she had missed the previous year due to being in the hospital. As difficult as it was, being only twelve days since Faith died, our family still went to the concert in her honor. We were blessed with the opportunity to chat with Joel before the concert, as well as hug both Joel and Luke following the concert. Every detail of the concert was incredible, from the vocals to the lighting and set design. We laughed, cried, and sang our hearts out for Faith. Throughout the night, the band once again demonstrated their servant's hearts and love for Faith. After having dedicated "God Only Knows" to her at their concert one year earlier, they dedicated another song to her at this concert, "The Proof of Your Love." The chorus says: 'Let my life be the proof, the proof of Your love. Let my love look like You and what You're made of. How You lived, how You died, love is sacrifice. So let my life be the proof, the proof of Your love.' [16] Faith's passion, fight, and life were without a doubt proof of God's love, and our prayer was that this legacy of hers would continue to shine and impact many.

After the concert, while on our way home, I texted Chico, the stage manager of *for KING & COUNTRY*, a thank you message for all they had done not only for Faith, but for our entire family. He replied, "It really was so good to see you. Your family has been on our hearts and a big part of the narrative of this tour for us. Whatever impact J&L had on Faith—she made a much bigger impact on us all. Praying for continued peace over your family. Please let me know anytime we are close to you guys in the future."

November 30th, 2019, when the memory of Faith's visit from Joel & Luke popped up:

"One year ago today, Faith began this special journey and friendship with for KING & COUNTRY. None of us knew at that moment what the next year was about to bring—we didn't yet know Faith was going to rapidly decline in the days that followed and so quickly enter the realm of needing a double lung transplant—we didn't yet know that in less than 3 weeks from this day, Faith would be transferred to Chapel Hill for transplant evaluation—we didn't yet know that Chapel Hill would become our home for the next 8 months—and we didn't yet know that the Thanksgiving we had celebrated the week prior would be our last Thanksgiving with Faith this side of Heaven.

"But we also didn't yet know what amazing experiences and joys Faith would be able to experience—and that we would get to share with her—because of the

new lungs she was about to receive, even if only for a short time, breathing free and easy without feeling like she was breathing through a straw—riding a bike and jogging, which she hadn't been able to do for years—dancing without the need for oxygen, something else she hadn't been able to do for years—developing a very special connection and beautiful friendship with Joel and Luke from for KING & COUNTRY—and the number of lives she would touch and inspire through her story and the strength and courage she exemplified.

"And now one week from today, we'll gather together as family, friends, and community to celebrate this beautiful life and the light & love that Faith left indelibly etched in our hearts for all time."

The days leading up to the Celebration of Life service scheduled for December 7th, 2019, were a whirlwind of activity that, at times, distracted me from allowing the reality to truly sink in. There were things to delegate, meetings with the pastoral staff for planning the order of service, food to arrange for the reception, music to decide upon, bulletins to design and have printed, a slideshow to put together, speeches to prepare, flowers, guest book, memorabilia to pull together for the reception, and of course getting the word out as to the date and time of the service. The day of the service, itself, was no less a flurry of activity and distraction. I would later reflect on that day and be grateful for the distractions, as they kept me from completely falling apart and enabled me to hold it together as I spoke. I would also later reflect on the fact that, even in the depths of my grief, I was actually in a very good place spiritually. My trust and faith in God were strong, and I knew that Faith was happy, healed, and whole. But over time, as the reality of Faith's absence loomed larger and my grief intensified, my anger at God also began to slowly intensify, as did that of her sisters. But we continued to press on as best we could.

December 10th, 2019, post by Jenni:

"As we approach one month since Faith's passing and have her service behind us, my heart continues to feel heavier and more broken each day. Reality is setting in, along with the overwhelming grief, anger, hopelessness, and other array of emotions I can't identify. Even so, through it all, I am grateful and blessed. Faith's service was beautiful; there were a multitude of people who attended, helped with logistics, and shared their music or spoken tributes, and I hope all of you know how moved our family was by your outpouring of love.

It was a perfect honoring of Faith, her memory, and legacy.

"This was the last picture we took as a family, the last moments we had to say goodbye and hold each other tight. One thing I said at Faith's service is that amidst the pain, I am so thankful for those days, because not everyone gets them, not everyone gets to spend intentional time with their loved one and hold them while they peacefully meet Jesus. So I thank God for that privilege, and also for the blessing of getting to love Faith and be her sister. Right now we are broken, but Faith is whole, and I know she and our Father will carry us through."

On December 12th, 2019, the first month anniversary of Faith's death, it was becoming increasingly difficult to navigate through each day, especially through the long, sleepless nights:

"As I open my eyes after a relatively sleepless night, my broken heart aches as I think on one month ago today when I also opened my eyes from a relatively sleepless night, knowing it was to be my last day with my sweet baby girl. I spent my final night with Faith cuddled up next to her in her hospital bed, watching her sleep, not wanting to take my eyes off of her. I recall how peacefully she slept for most of the night, realizing she must have been so at ease knowing her long fight and struggle was finally about to be over, and how she was looking forward to falling into the arms of Jesus.

"In the early morning hours long before the sun would make an appearance, she opened her eyes, looked at me, and gave me the sweetest, most beautiful little smile. She mouthed 'I love you,' and snuggled closer. After a few minutes, she mouthed 'Netflix?' as we always loved watching movies together. We dozed off and on, snuggled up together while 'Ratatouille' played quietly in the background. This final night is forever etched in my heart and will always be one of my most cherished memories.

"In some respects, it seems like it was just yesterday. And in other respects, I

find myself wondering how on earth this past month feels so much longer than the preceding 18 years. . . .

"I miss you so much, Faith – more and more every day! I mourn your loss and grieve at not having you here with me anymore. But I'm grateful and feel so blessed for the time I had. My life has been, and will forever be, deeply enriched by your presence in it, and you are always close to me in my heart. . . ."

On December 15th, 2019, I shared with a friend how incredibly thankful I was for the presence of Kelsey, Jenni, and my grandchildren in my life because without them to keep me tethered, I would not want to remain here myself.

On December 24th, 2019, after hearing the Mark Schultz song, "A Different Kind of Christmas," I created a slide show of Christmases past set to the song, as a tribute to Faith and the blessings of our Christmas memories together, as we now tried to learn how to navigate a 'Different Kind of Christmas.'

December 25th, 2019, – I knew how difficult that first Christmas without Faith was going to be, just as the first Thanksgiving had been. Christmas, however, having always been Faith's favorite holiday, was likely to be more difficult. So I chose to spend Christmas Eve with Kelsey and her family because I wanted to wake up and see the joy of Christmas morning through my grandchildren's eyes. It was a wonderful and bittersweet day:

"JOY SO BITTERSWEET — Christmas 2019 has been filled with a varying mix of emotions all rolled into one that my heart has never before experienced and no words can adequately describe. I deeply miss Faith every minute of every day, and the holidays have magnified that loss. Even through the joy of being together with family, the hole in our midst loomed large, remaining painful and intense.

"But as I told a dear friend, I also kept envisioning Faith laughing and having a great time celebrating with Jesus and all those who went before her. And when I picture that beautiful smile and my heart hears her sweet laughter, it fills me with a sad joy that can't be explained.

"I miss her terribly, but am also very thankful for the beautiful years we had, and makes me cherish, all the more, these precious times with family. Precious times such as Christmas day with my oldest daughters, their husbands, and my beautiful grandbabies. Getting to experience the joy of Christmas through the little ones' eyes was a blessing and much-needed distraction. The day was rich with good family, good food—and even what I like to think was a Christmas message from Faith painted in the skies as we prepared to eat.

"Thank you to all who have kept us lifted in prayer and shown us such amazing love and support throughout this whole journey, and especially for this first holiday season without her. Please continue to remember us in your prayers as we face this coming year of 'firsts.'"

With my birthday quickly approaching, Jenni wanted to make sure I did not spend my birthday alone, so she invited me to spend the weekend with her in Raleigh. Since I was going to be so close to Chapel Hill, I decided to pay a visit to Faith's medical team. So, on Friday, January 27th, 2020, the day before my birthday, I made my first visit to Chapel Hill since Faith had died.

"[It] was an odd mix of emotions. It simultaneously felt strange being there and yet somehow so natural and familiar—Knowing, however, I wasn't there to visit Faith—and why—brought on a hatred for the place and a feeling of missing it all at the same time. I was overwhelmed by the deep longing to walk into one of the rooms and see her quietly sleeping or her smiling face. Visiting with several of her care team from over the years was a pleasant distraction. It was nice to catch up, share memories and stories of Faith, laugh together, share some hugs and even some tears together . . .

"Then visiting Southern Village, where Faith and I lived for [eight] months, was also very bittersweet, but brought a flood of wonderful memories of the time we shared there and the beautiful bond we developed. And of course, no visit to Southern Village would be complete without a trip to Al's Burger Shack, which was one of our favorites—and most frequented—places to eat. Best burgers ever. And I finally got my Al's shirt, which I had talked about getting for about 8 months.

"Please continue to keep our family lifted in prayer for strength and peace as we struggle with our new 'normal.' . . ."

I received a small reprieve from my grief when my friend, Janet, and I took a long weekend in early February to Gatlinburg, Tennessee. It was a precious time with a precious friend and was sorely needed. I can't remember the last time I laughed so hard or slept so well. It was the first time since even before Faith died that I felt like I was *living* and not just surviving or existing! We hoped to make it an annual event (unfortunately, as with so many other things, this goal would be disrupted by Covid and lockdowns). I was a little nervous about returning to reality but hoping the weekend would give me a boost forward rather than reality bringing me back down.

But returning home threw me fully back into reality. As the world continued to spin and people continued to live their lives, my grief intensified, and each day seemed to grow harder and harder to get through. When February 12th, 2020, came around, it felt so much longer than only three months since Faith had died. As my anger also continued to grow, I tried very hard to remain positive and think about those things for which I was grateful . . .

"3 MONTHS IN HEAVEN -- Hard to believe that it's been only 3 months since Faith fell into the arms of Jesus and gained her most beautiful and perfect lungs. To my shattered heart, it feels more like 3 years.

"Shortly after Faith's passing, for KING & COUNTRY sent a very sweet & touching video message expressing their love and condolences for me and the family. For Faith's Celebration of Life service, I put their video message together with a slide show in remembrance of Faith's journey with fK&C as well as her beautiful life. . . .

"Words will never be able to adequately express how much I miss you, Faith. You were not only my baby girl, but also my sweet friend who filled my life with love and laughter! And although life no longer makes sense right now, and my heart aches for the day when I can see you again, I do rejoice for you and the wonders you have no doubt beheld these past 3 months!!! So for now, I cling to the many wonderful memories we created and the life we shared. I love you and miss you deeply."

February 14th, 2020, upon seeing the memory from Valentine's Day the year before:

"Last year's Valentine's day spent in the hospital with severe migraines and

seizures due to her brain swelling vs. this year's Valentine's day spent in the presence of Love, Himself with no pain and no suffering! '[Dear friends], let us love one another, [for] love comes from God. [Everyone who loves has been born of God and knows God.] Whoever does not love does not know God, because God is love.'
~1 John 4:7-8 (NIV)"

March 12th, 2020:

"FOUR MONTHS WITHOUT YOU – As we face another month's 'anniversary' of Faith gaining her perfect eternal lungs, [a] memory came up, [showing] another beautiful example of how she never let her circumstances define her or keep her from doing what she so loved. [The memory was a picture of her at a dance competition in 2017 called 'Inspire,' in her dance costume with her oxygen on, smiling brightly]. Her strength, courage, determination, and perseverance were unmatched by anyone I have ever known—and probably ever will know. How appropriate that this particular competition was called 'Inspire.' Faith was, without a doubt, a true inspiration to so many people near and far.

Throughout these days of mourning Faith, it was also becoming increasingly difficult to remain in the rental house we had shared for the past four years. The memories were raw and painful with every step I took throughout the house. I avoided the side of the house where her bedroom was, and I knew a dramatic change was necessary to hopefully keep me from falling deeper and deeper into depression. After looking at several houses, I found the one I knew was meant for me and moved in on March 20th, 2020. Although most of the household items were moved by a moving company, there were still many trips I made back and forth to retrieve the remaining boxes and clean the rental house. On March 31st, 2020, I left the rental house for the final time:

"ONE CHAPTER ENDS AS ANOTHER BEGINS – Saying goodbye to this house for the last time. And although Faith and I had desperately wanted to move, I find myself very emotional as I prepare to drive away. A whole lot of memories—good and bad—are tied up in this house. Lots of fun times, lots of hardships, a whole lot of adventure, exciting times, devastating news, joyful moments, lots of tears, tons of laughter, but above all, a tremendous amount of love shared!—sweet and beautiful memories with my precious family that I will cherish for a lifetime! This little house definitely served its purpose for the

time we needed it. It got Faith to the school district she wanted to be in, and what a fabulous school, staff, and student body it was, too!! Thank you to all at Hickory Ridge High School for providing Faith with such an amazing home and for the unwavering love and support you all showed her—and our whole family for that matter! As I journey into this next chapter I know that Faith, tho not physically by my side, is with me every step of the way and always close by in my heart and mind. And I know she will still be a part of the new memories made in the new house. Love and miss you so very much, sweet Faith!!"

The five-month anniversary of Faith's passing, April 12th, 2020, arrived soon after moving into my new home and also happened to be Easter Sunday:

"As I reflect on this 5-month 'anniversary' of Faith's passing, the significance of today is not at all lost on me. And tho the grief and pain of losing Faith remains just as strong and intense today as it was 5 months ago, I find joy in celebrating the resurrection of Christ Jesus, and peace in the knowledge that because of His sacrifice, Faith rose to new life, eternally in His presence. AND because of His sacrifice, we too can rise to this new life by trusting Him with our lives here on earth. Faith's complete trust in Him was evidenced by the profound peace she had in her final days, and her joy in knowing without a doubt where she was going. I look forward to celebrating a happy reunion with her one day, along with those who will have gone before.

"Happy Easter to all of you! I pray each one of you also knows this peace and joy through life in Christ! #HeIsRisen #AliveInChrist #HappyEaster

"Faith, Happy Easter in Heaven in the presence of the risen Savior!! I love you and miss you dearly!!"

As high school graduation was quickly approaching, the Cabarrus County's "Adopt-A-Senior" initiative also began. With this iniative, parents would post information about their senior on Facebook and anyone could "adopt" them, presenting them with a basket of gifts such as items for college, notes of encouragement, etc. to commemorate the occasion. Seeing all the posts of graduates and their "adoptions" was heart-wrenching, as it only brought to mind how very close Faith had been to graduating and pursuing her college plans and dreams. Feeling that she should also be recognized and somehow included in the initiative, on April 29th, 2020, I made the following post:

"In light of the Adopt-A-Senior initiative during this unusual time in our world, I wanted to say a few words about my beautiful senior. This isn't, however, your typical ADOPT-A-SENIOR post. I guess it's more like Adopt-A-Senior's-Family?

"Faith Shaw, a senior at Hickory Ridge High School, had a passion for life unmatched by anyone I know. She loved the Lord, her family, and her friends deeply. She also had a deep love of the arts—dance, music, art, photography— and poured her heart & soul into everything she did. What she is most known for, tho, is her fight—her strength, courage, determination, and perseverance. Having been born with cystic fibrosis (a genetic, life-shortening lung disease), Faith fought every day of her life to just breathe and to live a normal life. Most specifically in her teen-age years.

"At 13, she got a lung infection so bad, it caused permanent lung damage, and she lived with her new norm of 32% lung function for the next 5 years. She continued to beat the odds she was given by her doctors, continuing to dance competitively and fight for a life she felt was worth living.

"2019 became both the most beautiful and most difficult year of her way too short life, following her double-lung transplant in mid-January. She experienced being able to fully breathe for the first time in her life and was able to do things she couldn't before or hadn't been able to in many years. But the year was also not without many complications, which ultimately led to her passing on 11/12/19.

"Through it all, she continued with her schooling remotely from Chapel Hill. And even while her junior year was spent in and out of the hospital and dealing with multiple doctor appointments, procedures, etc., she managed to finish that year completely online from Chapel Hill, ending the year with a 4.1 GPA! Her plan was to major in Interior Design at either Belmont University in Tennessee, High Point University, or Meredith College. She was an amazing young lady who deserves to not be forgotten as we celebrate our seniors!!

"If you would like to 'adopt' her family (her sisters and me) and send some notes of encouragement and support during this very bittersweet time, please PM me. Thank you very much, and CONGRATULATIONS to the entire 2020 Senior Class!!!"

I received many sweet messages of encouragement and support.

Graduation was held on June 12th, 2020, the seven-month anniversary of Faith's death. Leading up to the graduation ceremony, Faith's sister, Jenni, posted the following tribute:

"Graduating from high school was one of Faith's dreams. Some might think this silly, but it was a big deal to Faith because everything she wanted in life was a big deal to her. She understood from early on that each moment of her life was a gift, and she didn't take any milestone or achievement for granted. Even when going through the worst pain and experience of her life with PRES a month after transplant, she fought just to sit up in bed and do homework.

"Tonight, our family will be accepting her diploma on her behalf! We are lucky to be in Cabarrus County, which because of the proximity to the Charlotte Motor Speedway, gets to hold a unique, socially-distanced 'drive thru' graduation. I'm incredibly thankful we still get to have this experience in the midst of COVID-19.

"I'm also angry, sad, and a whole other host of emotions that she didn't get to make it to her hard earned graduation day and accept her diploma herself. But through it all, I'm still so proud of her, and forever glad she doesn't have to fight so hard anymore.

"Congratulations, Faith! You did it!"

My post on June 12th, 2020, following the Hickory Ridge High School graduation ceremony in which I got to accept Faith's diploma on her behalf:

"CROSSING THE FINISH LINE — The bible verses engraved on Faith's urn, as well as referenced in the bulletin for her Celebration of Life service, include 2 Timothy 4:7, which states, 'I have fought the good fight, I have finished the race, I have kept the faith.' How fitting, then, that graduation would be held at the Charlotte Motor Speedway. Through several instances of tears combined with a mama's heart full of pride and admiration for her daughter, it was truly an emotionally-charged moment as I had the privilege of crossing the finish line in Faith's honor to accept her diploma. It was a beautiful moment on a beautiful

day for a beautiful and deeply loved young lady; AND my heart aches beyond description that she was unable to accept her diploma for herself . . .

"Thank you, Hickory Ridge administration, staff, students, and families for your wonderful love and support and for allowing us the opportunity to share in this moment with the rest of the graduating class. Thank you, also, to the Speedway for making this venue available. And congratulations to all of the Class of 2020!"

As Faith's name was read over the loudspeaker, all the students in their cars began honking their horns in honor of Faith while I accepted her diploma. In addition to her diploma, I was also presented with a lovely bouquet of flowers and a Hickory Ridge Raging Bulls football helmet with a sticker on the back showing the spirit rock that said, "Fly High Faith." It was a deeply touching moment during a beautiful ceremony (can be found on YouTube by searching for "2020 Hickory Ridge High School Graduation").

On July 2nd, 2019, I posted a *for KING & COUNTRY* video I had spliced with a slide show (with *for KING & COUNTRY'S* permission), about when Faith was able to see them at Carowinds on June 1, 2019.

"In all the ups and downs, victories and disappointments, of battling Cystic Fibrosis and the post-transplant recovery process, there are those special moments that stand out and shine brightly, even in the darkest times – the ones you can cling to, reminding you to CHOOSE JOY, when the fight is the hardest. The impact for KING & COUNTRY has had throughout Faith's double lung transplant journey is one of those moments, and we can't thank Joel, Luke, Josh, and the whole FK&C team enough for their kindness, love and friendship, and for sharing God's message through their music!

A year later on July 2nd, 2020, when this memory popped up, it brought tears of both joy and sorrow to my eyes:

"MEMORIES – Memories have a way of side-swiping you when you least expect it. This is one of those memories that is both a treasured moment in time that I'll forever cling to—AND very painful to have come up.

"When we saw for KING & COUNTRY at Carowinds June 1, 2019, Faith was at a high point in the recovery from her double-lung transplant. I am so very thankful that she got to have this special moment during one of her best periods physically. But boy does it drive the point home that so much can drastically change in such a short period of time. Little did we know that this high point would be short-lived, and Faith would be taken from us less than 6 months later.

"One week after posting this a year ago, everything started to go terribly wrong and the transplant team discovered that her body was rejecting her new lungs. The next [four] months were spent trying to stop the rejection and get her ready for a second transplant. God obviously had a different plan that I will undoubtedly never understand until the day I stand face to face with Him myself. But I am forever thankful for the 18 years I was blessed with this beautiful girl, and I'm so very thankful for the many beautiful memories, even through the pain they bring!"

July 12th, 2020:

"8 MONTHS IN HEAVEN – One month ago today, we celebrated receiving Faith's diploma on her behalf. Today marks 8 months since she danced her way onto the streets of gold, and fell into the sweet, precious arms of Jesus—the ultimate graduation—the ultimate, complete healing. And I miss her terribly— more and more every day. . . ."

August 12th, 2020:

"9 MONTHS OF ETERNITY – Time is such an interesting thing. How can something completely constant feel so fluid and flexible? Time, of course, does not change, yet our perspective—even when thinking of the exact same time period—can fluctuate so much. When I think of Faith and the many beautiful memories we made, 9 months feels like only a few weeks ago. When I think of living WITHOUT Faith, 9 months feels like an eternity. And when I think about the future days ahead without Faith, any amount of time feels unbearable. Thankfully, I'm blessed with a phenomenal family, friends, and puppy! I still have many unanswered questions, the anger still comes and goes, AND I know God is providing for my needs. Thank you all for continued prayers. The road is long, most of the time very lonely and sometimes quite bumpy."

August 29th, 2020, upon seeing Faith's first day of high school post from 2016:

"FIRSTS – My heart breaks at not being able to ever experience firsts like this again – no first day of college, no first one-on-one date, no first day on a new job following college, no watching her take that first step walking down the aisle, along with the many other firsts that life brings – my heart aches that the only firsts I now experience are the firsts associated with being in the midst of the first year since her passing – my heart rejoices at all the firsts I got to share with her during her too-short 18 years – and my heart celebrates for her when I envision what she must have felt at her first glimpse of Heaven, taking that first step on the streets of gold, and the sheer joy she must have had at her first face-to-face encounter with our Lord and Savior, Jesus Christ! I can't say that I don't still struggle with feelings of anger and betrayal that He would take her Home so soon. The roller-coaster of emotions remains very raw, and no doubt will for a very, very long time. I also know, however, without a doubt that she is perfectly healed and happy. I was reminded by someone recently that, as much as she loves us, she wouldn't want to leave the perfection of eternity and return to this broken and fallen world. And, as she told me before she passed, she wants us to be happy for her! Thank you for your continued prayers, love, and support for me, my family, and Faith's friends during this time!!"

September 12th, 2020:

"10 MONTHS – The amount of time that Faith has been gone has now reached the same amount of time with which we were blessed to have her following her double lung transplant. And true to the oddity of time vs perspective, this last 10 months has creeped along with an agonizingly slow speed, compared to the previous 10 months which feel like they flew by! My heart continues to ache with wishing that time could have been longer. AND, as I remind myself daily, it also continues to rejoice at the memories of the 18 beautiful years of her life!

"I know these past 10 months for you, Faith, have been phenomenal and I'm so happy for you, as much as I miss you terribly. Until I see you again—#holdingontoyourname

On September 27th, 2020, a year after Faith had made the final decision to proceed with pursuing a second transplant, the memory of her post about her decision popped up on Facebook, where her final line read, "I've decided I want to fight, I want to live. #continue," and I realized what a rollercoaster ride grief was as well.

"My heart breaks when I read Faith's words from a year ago. They are so filled with pain, fear, frustration, and discouragement. Then my heart rejoices knowing she's no longer dealing with ANY of that pain & discouragement but is experiencing the ultimate healing and joy of the glories of Heaven!

"Still my heart breaks at her words of hope for a future this side of heaven that was never to be, and how close we were before it fell completely apart (the same day insurance approved her for the second transplant was also the day her doctors told us she had grown too sick for the surgery). My broken heart aches at reading the last line of her post AND bursts with love and pride at her strength, courage, and fighting spirit up to the very end.

"I long for her to be here with me, to be able to wrap my arms around her, to laugh with her, cry with her, and just sit quietly by her side as we relax on the couch watching a movie or one of our shows. And then I look again at her final words of this post and think about what a beautiful, wonderful, glorious life she is now living in the eternal presence of our Lord Jesus Christ with no longer any need to fight! And selfishly I still want her here.

"A part of me died along with her, and I know I will never be whole until the day I stand face to face with her once again, together in the arms of God! And through all the grief, pain, and brokenness, my heart is also full and blessed with an amazing family, friends, and prayer warriors the world over!! Please continue to pray for me and my family as we limp down this road of grief. It is the hardest journey we've ever had to face, and it is far, far, far from over."

October 12th, 2020:

"LIVING LARGE – With a zest for life and unmatched love for family and friends, Faith always lived large knowing she was living on borrowed time and that each day was a precious gift. It seems surreal that 11 months has passed since she gently fell into the arms of Jesus. It has been the longest – yet simultaneously quickest – 11 months of my life, and the world somehow now seems

wrong without her in it! I would give almost anything to be able to wrap her up in my arms once again and laugh with her at her quirky sense of humor. She was a bright light in so many lives and one that will never grow dim because of the beautiful memories and legacy she left behind.

"I know you are shining brightly in heaven, sweet Faith, and living even larger than ever in the presence of our Lord and Savior!"

October 17th, 2020:

"Always so proud of you, my sweet Faith, and how you handled everything in your difficult, challenging life – not the least of which how you handled the END of your life, which was handled with an uncanny maturity, strength, and certainty in the knowledge of where you were going! Cystic fibrosis may have robbed you of many things in your too-short 18 years, but it definitely didn't rob you of your amazing and inspiring spirit!!! I miss you and love you with all my heart."

October 26th, 2020, upon seeing a memory from 2018 when she was in the hospital struggling after her gallbladder removal:

"And so, unbeknownst to us at the time, the rapid spiral down the path to transplant began . . .

"My sweet Faith, the anguish, grief, and suffering you faced, especially these last few years, were so much more than any young lady should've ever had to endure. And although you didn't see it in yourself, the strength and grace you displayed throughout it all was uncanny and far beyond your years! Your love for and trust in Christ, even in the midst of anger and doubt, was an amazing thing to watch and an inspiration I'll forever cling to and only hope I can emulate! Loving and missing you always, precious angel."

November 4th, 2020, after seeing the post describing her decision to continue fighting—to keep on living:

"You fought hard and courageously, my precious #CFWarrior! Harder than

anyone I've ever known or witnessed! Seeing the words of this post from a year ago reminds me of the grace and maturity with which you faced decisions no one should ever have to make, especially one of such a tender age – and it breaks my already fragile heart. The life you were dealt was unfair and I can't WAIT to see how God uses it and is glorified through your pain and suffering and legacy you've left behind. I know you've been richly blessed with an abundant, beautiful life in the presence of Christ and are completely healed with your #PerfectEternalLungs! As always, darling Faith, I rejoice in the knowledge that you ultimately won your amazing fight; AND I miss you with every piece of my heart and soul."

November 10th, 2020:

"On this day last year, Faith had already arrived at the realization her long, hard fight had reached its completion, and she was in a state of uncanny, phenomenal and unmatched peace. Her niece and nephew were brought in so she could see them one last time and I was tasked with making the most difficult phone calls I've ever had to make. She wanted to keep things as simple as possible, so the following two days would be spent with small groups of friends then family coming to spend their last moments with her; then her sisters and I would hold her as she gently and peacefully drifted into the arms of Jesus. Judging by the aching in my heart, one would not think a whole year had passed, as the pain is just as intense now as it was then.

"I miss you deeply, my sweet Faith, and as much as I know you are now pain free, breathing in the sweet aroma of Heaven with your #PerfectEternalLungs, I selfishly wish you were still here with us!"

November 11th, 2020:

"UNTIL WE MEET AGAIN . . . One year ago today, small groups of some of Faith's friends came to Chapel Hill to spend some final moments with her, laugh with her, pray with her and say their 'see ya' laters,' having chosen not to say goodbye. It was beautiful and devastating, heartwarming and heartbreaking all in one. I will never forget how her friends and the community rallied around her, and have continued to rally around our family since then! God bless you all! I love you!!

"You deeply touched so many lives, sweet Faith, and have left a beautiful and lasting legacy!!"

November 12th, 2020:

". . . OUR LOVE WILL NEVER END – November 12, 2019, The family and the pastoral staff, along with a few others from our phenomenal church, came in to spend their own final moments with Faith. Her insurmountable peace was—and is still—an amazing inspiration and could only be attributed to her knowledge that she was soon to be free from the struggling and the pain, and was bound for the glorious gift of heaven, safe and whole in the welcoming arms of Jesus!

"After everyone had shared their final goodbyes, her sisters and I stayed by her side as the medical team made her comfortable. When it was just the four of us, we turned off the lights, played gentle music from for KING & COUNTRY and Michael O'Brien, and held her close as she drifted off to sleep. At one point, she looked like she was trying to grasp a straw with her mouth. She opened her eyes, looked at each of us with a cute, sweet smile, and mouthed, "I thought I was drinking lemonade." Those were the last words she would 'speak' this side of heaven.

"Her passing was peaceful and gentle, and she approached it the same way she approached life—with grace, maturity, strength, and courage.

"Beautiful Faith, you are deeply, deeply loved and missed beyond what words can describe.

On November 20th, 2020, Faith's sister, Jenni, and I got our tattoos in memory and honor of Faith. Jenni's tattoo is a small bouquet of three flowers, representing each of the three sisters, one with a dotted line around it signifying Faith's ascension into Heaven, and hidden in the stems are the words "With Faith." My tattoo is an infinity symbol made up of green leaves, her birth and death dates on one side, and her full name, Faith Mackenzie Shaw, making up the other side, with a purple rose in the center of one of the infinity symbol loops.

November 30th, 2020, upon seeing the memory of f*or KING & COUN-TRY's* visit to Faith in the hospital in 2018:

"START OF A BEAUTIFUL FRIENDSHIP – On this day two years ago, for KING & COUNTRY made a surprise entrance into Faith's journey, and it would be the beginning of a beautiful friendship that continues to this day! Forever thankful to Joel, Luke, Josh, Chico, Ashley, and the entire for KING & COUNTRY team for your sweet, humble, and spirit-filled kindness, love and support these last couple of years. God bless you all and many prayers for a beautiful season of celebrating our Lord and Savior!"

December 8th, 2020, upon seeing a memory from Faith's hospital struggles in 2014 that would result in the month-long stay:

"Faith fought battle after battle her entire life yet remained a ray of sunshine and amazing inspiration to so many, including this mom!! When I see memories like this come up (12/8/14), it amazes me all the more that she continued to have such a positive outlook on and zest for life! She truly was the strongest, most courageous person I've ever known, and someone who did not allow her circumstances to define her! Not only did she fight so many battles that were beyond her control, but also fought so hard to live life to the fullest and make every moment count!!!"

December 20th, 2020:

"From her very first Christmas in 2001, when she was diagnosed, to her final Christmas this side of heaven in 2018, when she was waiting for new lungs, Faith seemed to have had a lot of Christmases in the hospital. And now she has the ultimate blessing of spending all her Christmases and all her days with the Savior Himself, free from pain and free from the struggles of compromised lungs!! I would give almost anything to spend Christmas with her once again, and yet I rejoice greatly at the glory she now beholds and the #perfecteternal-lungs with which she now gets to celebrate each and every day!"

January 14th, 2021, when the memory of having new lungs available for Faith appeared:

"This was such a terrifying and exciting day, and one that I will cherish for the rest of my life!!! Even though Faith's earthly journey ended way too soon, having gained her #PerfectEternalLungs, and even though I'd MUCH rather be celebrating her two-year Lungaversary with her beside us, I still rejoice for the additional 10 months of her life we were privileged and blessed to share because of this day! I still also think of and pray for the family whose loved one donated the beautiful lungs that gave us more time with Faith, and gave her those special months of breathing easy for the first time in her life."

On January 31st, 2021, my grief and anger were compounded by receiving the horrific news that my dear friend Litta's daughter, Payton, a long-time friend of Faith's, had passed away suddenly and unexpectedly. I simply could not believe that God would take yet another beautiful life way too soon, and I started screaming at Him for some answers. It just didn't make any sense.

As I watched Payton's funeral service on February 4th, 2021, so many thoughts, memories, and feelings flooded my soul:

"Today I watched a funeral service for the 20-year-old daughter of a very dear, long-time friend. It was a beautiful service for yet another beautiful soul taken from us way too soon. During the message, one of the Bible verses referenced was James 4:14 (NIV), which says, '. . . you do not even know what will happen tomorrow. What is your life? You are a mist that appears for a little while and then vanishes.'

"With having recently lost my own daughter at the tender age of 18 and thinking about several other young lives taken from us over the last few months and couple years, that verse hit me hard. Tomorrow is not promised to any of us. Are you ready? Do you know where you will spend eternity if your tomorrow doesn't come? What legacy will you leave behind? Death is not 'reserved' only for those who have lived a 'long, full life.' It can come to anyone at any time and it's so important to have not only your earthly affairs in order, but more so your eternal affairs. Life is but a vapor, but God is eternal. And the only way to spend eternity in His loving embrace is through a saving knowledge of and relationship with Jesus Christ. Because of this relationship, I know that I will see my daughter again! I know that my friend will see her daughter again! Please don't waste another day without knowing for sure your eternal destination.

"Come just as you are to Jesus, and He will welcome you with open arms!"

The anger began to deepen as I began to seriously question God. February 18th, 2021, upon seeing the memory of Faith's two seizures, that questioning spirit began to seep through my post:

"What Faith had to endure in her fight against CF and her lung transplant recovery seems senseless and unfair. Even with the knowledge of where she is now and that she's no longer struggling in the least bit, revisiting this post still breaks my heart into a million little pieces and transports me back to one of the most difficult times I've faced as a mom. I know there must be a phenomenal reason for it all because I know God's ways are perfect, and I look forward to one day standing with my Lord and Savior and having it all make sense! For now, I trust and rejoice even as I cry and question why. #godisgoodallthetime"

On February 24th, 2021, my heart smiled even through the tears when the memory popped up about Faith doing better and even getting a "hall pass" off the floor and going to Starbucks at the other end of the hospital:

"Faith sure did love her Starbucks! I even learned how—and got quite good at — making her favorite, 'caramel iced coffee with cream,' so I wouldn't go broke buying it for her each day! I'm sure it doesn't even begin to compare, however, to the glorious feast she's experiencing in heaven! No doubt the absolute BEST 'caramel iced coffee with cream' she's ever had!"

The questioning spirit, however, would continue to plague my soul, and I began to realize that my anger at God was not diminishing. I also realized that I was just "going through the motions at church" and in the worship band, and I needed to get some things sorted out before that anger took up permanent residence in my soul as bitterness. In addition, I was finding it very difficult at church sitting next to an empty chair formerly occupied by Faith. So I decided to take a step back and regroup—address the anger and grief. I felt it would be good for me to go to a church where nobody knew me or my story, where I had no obligations and expectations (mine or other's), so I could focus fully on my relationship with God and face my grief and anger head-on. In early April, I took what Pastor Mike was calling a spiritual sabbatical and temporarily stepped away from West Concord Baptist Church. After much research and viewing several sermons online, I began attending a large church in the Charlotte area where I knew I could get "lost in the crowd" and make it about just me and God. I also began a couple of new Bible studies in an effort to restore my relationship with Him.

On April 10th, 2021, I walked outside and saw my dogwood tree, which I call my "Faith Tree," beautifully in bloom:

". . . When my middle daughter, Jenni, was a senior in high school, she was the lead in their spring musical, 'Next to Normal.' Her 'husband' in the play sang a song that had the line, 'out back the dogwoods bloom . . .' I sang this one little line in my head EVERY time I pulled into the parking garage at the hospital in Chapel Hill—so in other words I sang it a LOT—because it was called the Dogwood Parking Deck.

"November 12th, 2020, on the first anniversary of Faith's passing, my brother, Tim, sent me a dogwood tree to plant in her honor. Today I walked out to the backyard and again started to sing 'out back the dogwoods bloom . . .' This beautiful little tree has no idea how many emotions it sparks in me for multiple reasons and for the multiple cherished memories it brings to mind—yes, even the number of times I had to enter the Dogwood Parking Deck because it takes me back to a time when Faith was still with me this side of Heaven. I look forward to watching this beautiful little tree grow in remembrance of my beautiful Faith, and holding tight to all the memories it brings, as my life without Faith continues to be merely 'next to normal.'

"I know you have bloomed more beautifully than this little tree, sweet Faith, in the glorious presence of the Lord Almighty!"

On April 13th, 2021, the memories of Faith's prom from 2019 came up on social media, sparking some more smiles combined with tears:

"A NIGHT TO REMEMBER – SUCH an amazing night for Faith two years

ago!! Just a few short months prior, being in respiratory failure on 30+ liters of high-flow oxygen, we didn't even know if she was going to survive. So what a joyous occasion it was when, after receiving a pair of beautiful new lungs, she was able to return home from Chapel Hill for a weekend to enjoy her junior prom! You can see the sheer joy in her eyes and in her smile. I'm so thankful we were able to share in this exciting event with her. She and her wonderful friends looked so incredibly beautiful!

"Can't wait to see the beauty that shines from you now from the light of the Son in the glory of heaven."

On May 2nd, 2021, even with faithfully doing my Bible studies, I was still feeling very distant from God, and the anger did not seem to be subsiding. I shared with a friend the realization that I was probably going about things the wrong way. I was attempting to draw closer to God when I still had not dealt with my anger at Him and the loss of Faith. I began a couple of new books on dealing with grief and finding God's purpose in suffering, as well as one dealing with loneliness after loss. I was just so tired of being a shell of who I once was and needed to face it all head-on.

And the fact that it was now the month of May only exacerbated the already fragile emotions.

On May 4th, I was reminded of the time two years earlier when Faith and I went to see the movie, "Breakthrough," based on a true story, at Silver-spot Cinema in Chapel Hill. Hopefully not to spoil anything for anyone, but I often think of the movie and wonder why my prayers and cries out to the Lord didn't work in healing my daughter as they did for the parent in this movie. It hurts.

On May 6th, 2021, the memory of Faith winning the "True Inspiration" Judges' special award at one of her dance competitions came up:

"A true inspiration in dance, in her life and even in her death with her over-whelming peace and assurance of where she was going! I miss Faith with all

my heart AND I know I'll see her again – and what a glorious day that will be!!"

May continued to be a difficult month as I continued struggling with an overwhelming array of emotions and challenges. I kept working on my Bible studies, which more than likely contributed to the struggling emotions since they were so focused on grief, loss, and loneliness.

As Faith Week arrived, we gathered together as a family for the week and continued celebrating Faith. We brought balloons to her grave site, and I created a slide show in commemoration of what would have been her twentieth birthday.

As I continued my quest to address my anger at God, I could feel a shift in my emotions and the beginnings of a restored and renewed relationship with Him. On June 11th, 2021, I had a realization, of which I made a note on my phone . . . "I think there was a part of me that was afraid to no longer be angry at God for fear it would mean I no longer hurt about Faith being gone or that I was somehow ok with it all. But I realized that was not the case. I can trust, love, and submit to God AND still hurt. It's ok to both hurt and be ok with God. They are not mutually exclusive. I will never ever stop hurting or stop grieving. And that's ok. God knows and understands. After all, He's been there." I did not want to be angry at God anymore, but also realized that I had been angry for so long, I was not sure how *not* to be. The following day, I made another note on my phone stating that I had wasted so much energy on being angry at God that I had not allowed myself the "freedom" to simply and purely grieve. I wrote that I did not want to waste any more time or energy on being angry at or blaming God and cried out to Jesus for help in that endeavor.

After making these notes to myself, I came across a post Pastor Mike shared on Facebook containing a quote from Lewis B. Smedes that said, "To forgive is to set a prisoner free and discover that the prisoner was you." My comment to that post stated, "Especially when you realize the One you must forgive, as it turns out, is God Himself." I then made a note that freedom from the chains of anger, bitterness, and blame are free indeed!

On June 19th, 2021, I posted:
"My circumstances are difficult and painful, but my God is good—ALL the time and in ALL things! Even when I don't understand the 'why,' I know I can trust in the Who—the One who loves and cares for me unconditionally at all times, even when I am unlovable—the One who understands my grief like no other –

the One who comforts me and brings me peace in the middle of the storm – the One who gives me life everlasting through His amazing grace and the gift of His Son, Jesus Christ! Thank You, Lord Almighty, for never giving up on me and never leaving my side!"

In mid-July 2021, West Concord Baptist Church held its annual Vacation Bible School (VBS). Kelsey brought her kids to Concord for the week so they could attend. I went with Kelsey to drop the kids off at the church, and when I stepped back onto the campus for the first time since temporarily leaving, I immediately felt I was home. I knew that I had made a lot of progress over the past several months in my journey with God and would be returning to WCBC very soon. I returned in August feeling much lighter and freer than when I had left. I did not, however, return to the worship band right away. I still wanted to make sure that when I returned, I was returning for the right reasons and with the right heart.

September 28th, 2021, brought up a memory of the post I had titled "Rollercoaster Ride of Grief" in which Faith shared Claire Wineland's post along with her own thoughts. It was a good reminder that, even though the rollercoaster continued, Faith was healed and at peace.

"Although my heart still grieves deeply over the loss of my sweet Faith and continues to be a rollercoaster of emotions, I also continue to rejoice that she no longer has to deal with the pain and discouragement that plagued her basically her whole life, especially her final few months. Knowing she is whole and fully healed in the presence of Christ our Lord brings me a comfort and peace only He can provide, even in the darkest depths of my grief and broken heart. #throughitallwehavefaith #wisebeyondheryears #ComfortinChrist #untilwemeetagain"

October 4th, 2021, upon seeing the memory of Homecoming 2019:

"FOREVER CHERISHED – The memories of Homecoming on this day two years ago are so bittersweet. It was an absolutely amazing and beautiful night for Faith and all who loved her. My heart fills to the brim when I think of the awesome, exciting, and magical time she had, and the overwhelming love she was shown by the staff, students, and families of Hickory Ridge High School!! She was deeply touched and walked on cloud nine that night and the several weeks that followed. Then my heart aches anew at how none of us knew on this cherished night that we were just shy of six weeks away from losing her, how desperately I miss her, her beautiful smile, sweet voice, and precious laughter. October 4th is one of those dates that's forever etched on my heart with feelings of joy and sorrow combined. #beautifulqueen #homecoming2019 #magical-night #anighttoremember #HRHSBulls #bullsnation #hornsup

"As much as I miss you deeply and intensely, I rejoice that you now walk, not on cloud nine, but on streets of gold in the presence of the Almighty King!"

    As a way of celebrating Faith's family and friends and thank them for all their support, I worked with *for KING & COUNTRY* one last time and acquired some free tickets to their concert scheduled in Greensboro, NC. After being rescheduled multiple times due to Covid, the concert finally took place on October 28th, 2021. Many of us wore our purple "In Loving Memory of Faith Shaw" t-shirts in honor of Faith.

"Had such an amazing time at the for KING & COUNTRY concert last night!! The show was incredible, the seats they got us were fantastic, and—although sadly missing a few of our group due to school, work, and illness—the company was awesome!! It was a magical night of music, worship, and fellowship as we also remembered and celebrated Faith, who had such a beautiful friendship and connection with this band. I will forever be grateful for the part they played in her journey and for the love and compassion they showed her . . . and us! #forkingandcountry #relatetour2021

"Precious girl, I know you were in our midst as we all rocked out to some of your favorite songs. In my heart, I could definitely hear you singing along and

see you dancing with a huge smile on your face, and that brought a smile to mine! I love you and miss you with all my heart."

November 4th, 2021, the post about Faith deciding to "Fight to Live Another Day" came up again in my Facebook memories.

"Although one of the most difficult days and decisions in Faith's life that rocked us all to our core, it is also one of the most beautiful pictures of the phenomenal, unmatched strength and maturity she had in the face of life and death. She was truly an amazing and inspiring young lady and I'm forever thankful for the gift of her in my life for 18 hard fought yet beautiful years!

"My precious angel, in the midst of my pain and grief that still plagues me every moment of every day, it is a joy knowing you are now and forever living a life more full and free than any of us could ever imagine!! My broken heart rejoices at the knowledge you are completely healed and whole!!"

December 12th, 2021:

"Thankful that because of my Lord and Savior, Jesus Christ, the pain and broken heart that still plagues me daily will one day come to an end and be replaced by the joy of a glorious reunion. Thankful for the beautiful life of this beautiful girl named Faith and the cherished memories created – even the tough ones."

January 9th, 2022, after placing new flowers at Faith's grave where the first half of her ashes are buried:

"Happy New Year, sweet baby girl! As those of us this side of heaven think about the new year and all we hope it holds for us, I reflect on the joy of the newness you have been blessed to experience these last couple years – new perfect lungs that breathe in the beautiful aroma of heaven with no restrictions or limitations; new glorified body with no more scars or pain; new wondrous home in the presence of our Lord and Savior, Jesus Christ, with no more sorrow or tears! I miss you, Faith, more than words will ever be able to adequately express, and the selfish side of me wishes you were still here. My heart aches in unimaginable ways thinking of going through another year without you. And

yet I also rejoice for you and the amazing eternal life you now have and the beauty you get to behold! I love you so much and look forward to the day I get to hold you in my arms once again. Until then, even as I lament your absence, I will celebrate your newness of life in glory!"

January 14th, 2022, again seeing the post about having new lungs for Faith:

"Hard to believe it has been three years since this amazing day—it was without a doubt one of the scariest and most exciting days for Faith and the whole family—and one filled with so much hope and promise. I wish it would have given us more than just 10 short additional months with Faith, but I am so very thankful for those 10 months!!!

"Unfortunately, not all 10 months were good months for her, being saddled with many challenges, infections, and setbacks. But within that time she did experience some of the best months of her life, in which she was able to breathe freely and deeply in a way she had never been able to do her entire life. In her final days, she expressed how much she cherished those few good months and that they made it all worth it. I'm grateful she was given the opportunity for that experience. And I miss her immensely . . ."

February 8th, 2022, with the memory of Faith's migraines and beginning struggles with PRES:

"What this sweet, brave young lady had to endure on her journey—and the grace and strength with which she endured it – will never cease to amaze me. I'm so thankful she is now fully healed, safe, and whole in the arms of Jesus, never having to go through anything like this again, but man do I miss this girl!!! Love you so very much, Faith, and look forward to seeing you again one day."

February 12th, 2022:

"Time marches on and the world continues to spin, but my heart aches for you as much as it did back then. —I love you and miss you so much, Faith!"

February 14th, 2022:

"Forever in my heart—forever in my thoughts—forever loved—forever missed —forever healed and whole in Glory! Forever my sweet Faith."

February 22nd, 2022, upon seeing the memory of Faith, though still in the hospital in the Medical Progressive Care Unit, having gotten through the worst of her PRES symptoms and feeling much better:

"A great reminder that even in the darkest of times, God is always there, always on the throne, and always in control . . .

"Missing you every moment of every day, Faith! Until I see you again . . ."

April 17th, 2022, after placing Easter flowers at Faith's grave:

"Happy Easter, my love! I know you are enjoying this glorious day with the risen Savior, Himself! And because of Resurrection Sunday—because He is ALIVE—and because of your trust and faith in Him, I can rest in the knowledge that you are alive, too, and that we will see each other again! #HappyEaster #resurrectionSunday #HeIsRisen #HeIsAlive #missingfaith #cfwarrior #untilwemeetagain"

The struggle with grief continues daily, even though the good days are more frequent, and I have been able to experience moments of happiness and joy again. When the bad days occur, they are still very bad, but thankfully they are growing fewer and farther apart. I still struggle in my relationship with God from time to time and continue to question 'why.' But I *am* experiencing more peace, comfort, and trust in His plans. I visit Faith's grave regularly, although I have progressed from going every Sunday after church to the first Sunday of every month. I change out the flowers each season to keep her plot looking fresh and cared for. There is not a moment that goes by that I do not think of her and miss her, but I am thankful that the many memories now bring me smiles more often than tears.

23

Legacy of Faith

Throughout her life and her journey, Faith touched and inspired a multitude of people from all walks of life and all around the world. The impact she had on those around her reached not only family and friends, but also groups and organizations such as Snowbird Wilderness Outfitters, HISRadio, and the Christian rock band *for KING & COUNTRY*. Through our Lungs4Faith Facebook and Instagram pages, Faith had people following her story from all over the United States, the United Kingdom, the Netherlands, Japan, and more. From social media comments to letters and emails we received following her death, to the speeches given at her candlelight vigil and Celebration of Life Service, Faith's impact was profound.

Shortly before Faith died, an acquaintance of hers from school posted a blog about her and her impactful life:

"In my freshman year, I met Faith. I only introduced myself to make small talk and she has since transformed my life.

"Faith has Cystic Fibrosis. Last year, I witnessed her leave school with a stomachache, then have her health rapidly decline, leaving her hospitalized with a double lung transplant. Now, she continues fighting as she painfully battles organ rejection.

"As someone who has every right to be angry, every right to blame God, and every right to want to give up, she does not do any of these things. In some of her toughest moments, she still goes out of her way to ask others how their day is. She makes sure others are okay before there is even an opportunity to talk about her daily trials. She has shown me what it means to persevere and

to hold others higher than yourself. Her overwhelming positive attitude, and much larger outlook on life has changed the way I see mundane annoyances.

"Before I met Faith, I lived a fairly typical teenage life. My surroundings often determined my reaction, and in that way, my choices were merely consequences. However, despite her circumstances, Faith chooses her actions and doesn't live reactively. Now, I too, choose my attitude; to see what 'will be' and not 'what is.' Because of Faith, I am able to look past disagreements and teenage drama and instead focus on solutions, compromise, and the betterment of relationships. I see value before I see flaws."

Following her death, one of Faith's dear friends from high school also chose to write about Faith in a college scholarship essay. The prompt was, "Describe a situation or event that has shaped or influenced your understanding of yourself and/or others." The essay read as follows:

"Faith Shaw, a close friend of mine, and a closer friend of my sister, passed away this past November. She was the kind of person who naturally drew others to her. She was extremely friendly and kind, and immensely strong. She fought Cystic Fibrosis all throughout her life against all odds of the doctors' predictions. They didn't know she had God on her side every step of the way.

"In the months prior to November, her new lungs she had received in January of that year had undergone a tumultuous decline. We visited her as often as we could (now, I'd say not enough). Her breathing labored and needed a machine's help. The week before her passing, after a terrifying and teary visit, Mama Shaw (Faith's mother, and now partly ours too) told our group that things are looking up. The doctors had received positive results and Faith might recover over the next few months.

"The following Monday we rushed to her in Chapel Hill knowing this was goodbye. Her family would visit the next day, and after that her breathing machine would be shut off. We spent two hours with her and Mama Shaw, part of which we spent deciphering Faith's nearly illegible handwriting to figure out she was trying to say "spill the tea." All of our weeks had been hectic before coming up to visit Faith, but right then few topics came to mind.

"During our final goodbyes each of us went up to her bed and hugged her. I had been trying to come up with anything to say for the whole four hours we spent

driving up and spending with her. I was at a loss of words but I managed to get out 'I love you, and I'll see you again.'

"That was that. The last I'll see of her in person before my own time has come. That Tuesday, God finally ended her pain and welcomed her with open arms at the front gate.

"It's cruel how words come to you not when you need them but after. I spent the next weeks daydreaming in class, at home, and before bed what I'd say to her now. Since November, and even up to now, I still talk to her, and ask God to send my messages to her.

"Through this, I have observed the strength of a mother, the attempt of a dying friend to comfort others, and have glimpsed the depths grieving friends and family may sink. I've seen the darkness in myself expand in response to November 12th, and after hearing Mama Shaw tell us her progress toward healing, I know that same darkness hides in all of us and that no matter how angry we can be at God, He still loves us, and wants to help us heal and see the joy He places in our lives every day. I thank God for putting her in my life, and I thank her for giving me a stronger faith in God."

The day that Faith died, another dear friend, Lance, wrote a rap song in honor and memory of her, called "Good One." . . .

"I'm just lucky to call you a friend
Loved, all the good times we had
I wish that they never had to end
But the times always went too fast
All the movies and the parties and the car rides
We'd talk for hours and all through the night
All the laughs and the smiles that you brought to my heart
Sad to say that we grew apart
And now your time has come
And you're going over soon
So I'm sitting here writing, up inside my room
Losing a friend, I hate the feeling inside of my brain
But I'm glad that you no longer have to feel the pain
I'm sitting here missing you as the time goes on
I hope you listen and hear all of the song

Journey of Faith

Cause life moves so fast,
Wishing I could go back to the past,
Hope the times we had, now are gonna be a blast,

God, you got yourself a good one,
Oh lord said God, make sure that she has fun,
And I'm not trying to write a sad song,
Just trying to tell you how I feel,
Just know my love for you is crazy,
And I hope you know it's real
God, you got yourself a good one,
Oh lord said God, make sure that she has fun,
I'm so lucky to call you a friend,
And your heart is what you would mend,
Oh, you got yourself a good one

God needs you back cuz you're the best of us all,
But I'm gonna miss the trips walking around the mall,
Where we go out for dinner or just chill at home,
You made me feel good and I was never alone,
All the memories of you always give me a smile,
Wish I could talk to you just for a little while
Sit down and talk, just like we used to,
You mean so much, and you always will do too,
The thought of losing you just breaks my heart I'm feeling pain,
You're forever in my heart can't wait to meet again,
God has a plan and it's always meant to be,
Even if it's hard to see, trust the process and believe,
You always wore a smile, I could take that for while,
Watching you be strong and conquer anything and going miles,
Now I'll think back on the better times,
When we hung out, and everything was fine.

God, you got yourself a good one,
Oh lord said God, make sure that she has fun,
And I'm not trying to write a sad song,
Just telling you how I feel,
Just know my love for you is crazy,
And I hope you know it's real

God, you got yourself a good one,
Oh lord said God, make sure that she has fun,
I'm so lucky to call you a friend,
And my heart is what you would mend,
Oh, you got yourself a good one.

A few days after Faith died, I texted Elliott, her Durham dance instructor, the sad news. He replied, "I am so, so sorry for your loss . . . I can honestly tell you that I have never met a young lady who I admired more. I was lucky to have her in my life for the short time I did. I still have the picture of her in her prom dress on the staircase. Do you know . . . I still talk about her to other girls who are not willing to work for what they want. I will miss the idea that she is out there dancing up a storm and thank you for letting me know of her passing . . . I am having trouble understanding it."

Lowes Foods put together a large poster board with pictures and information about Faith which they displayed in the store for quite a while. It read,

"Faith fought cystic fibrosis her whole life with courage and grace. Last year Faith was hospitalized due to failing lung functions and infections which ended her up on the transplant list for a set of new ones. On January 14, 2019, she was given the amazing gift of life [with] a double lung transplant. This young lady lived life like she was an ordinary kid, but we all know she shined brighter than the rest! She didn't want any special treatment even when she was having a bad breathing day. Faith's love of dance and her love for God is what got her thru the most difficult times. The fact that she was always positive and hopeful is a true testament of how she tried to live her life. Faith was recently voted Homecoming Queen at HRHS. She was a treasure to us all and will be dearly missed. Fly high and breathe well sweet angel. ~YOUR LOWES FOOD FAMILY HARRISBURG STORE 210."

They provided food and drinks for her Celebration of Life service. As of the writing of this book, they still have a framed copy of her Celebration of Life bulletin displayed at Guest Services in remembrance of her.

On November 18th, I received a message from Faith's friend, Mia. "I wanted to tell you that for our basketball game tomorrow coach bought us all 'Faith is Bigger than Fear' shirts that we're running out and warming up in to honor your Faith (also the boys' team too). I personally am so thankful for her and this is super special to me so I thought you might want to know."

Ten days after Faith died, Hickory Ridge High School had what they called a "purple out" at their football team's second playoff game, in which everyone was encouraged to wear purple in Faith's honor. There was a sea of purple in the student section, scattered throughout the stadium, as well as on the players' and cheerleaders' uniforms. They were selling the purple "Faith is Big-

ger Than Fear" t-shirts in memory of Faith donated by a local screen printing company. Another high school in the area whose school colors include purple, donated purple paint to Faith's high school, so they could paint their logo on the field in purple for the night. The football team, rather than racing out at the beginning of the game like they normally do, walked out slowly carrying a huge banner that read, "Through It All We Have FAITH." The entire stadium erupted in cheers.

On December 3rd, I received a very sweet email from Doctor D.

"I hope this note finds you well, or at least in a moment of peace. I thought about you and Faith a lot over the Thanksgiving holiday and was glad to see on her Facebook page that you were surrounded by family, celebrating, grieving, and loving together.

"As you approach her service, I can only imagine all the feelings you must be having. Your words, to 'celebrate a beautiful life,' honor her so perfectly. She brought a lot of joy and beauty and humor and strength to everything. . . .

"I wanted to share with you a poem I stumbled upon as I sat in a Rosh Hasha-nah service with my family a few months ago. I'm not Jewish, but my husband is and our older daughter asked to explore her Jewish heritage and has been attending services. This service, celebrating the new year, includes a pause for 'mourner's kaddish,' or prayer sequence, to honor those who've died in the past year and to support those who've lost loved ones. There was a poem in the prayer book preceding the mourner's kaddish, . . . and I wanted to share it with you because I found it to be beautiful and giving, and it made me think of Faith, and of you and your courage and selflessness.

'When I die give what's left of me away to children and old men that wait to die.
And if you need to cry, cry for your brother walking the street beside you.
And when you need me, put your arms around anyone and give to them what
you need to give to me.
I want to leave you something, something better than words or sounds.
Look for me in the people I've known or loved, and if you cannot give me away,
at least let me live in your eyes and not in your mind.
You can love me most by letting hands touch hands, by letting bodies touch
bodies and by letting go of children that need to be free.
Love doesn't die, people do. So, when all that's left of me is love,
Give me away." ~Merrit Malloy'"

For Faith's Celebration of Life service, Miss Donna's School of Dancing (where Faith was on the competition team) closed their studio for the day to allow instructors, students, and students' families to attend the service.

On December 15th, 2019, at the sixth annual Jingle Bull 5K Run sponsored by the Hickory Ridge High School Athletics Boosters, they presented the first annual "Faith Mackenzie Shaw Award" in memory of Faith's life, courage, and strength. This award would be presented to the overall winner of each year's Jingle Bull Run and hangs inside Hickory Ridge High School.

"FAITH MACKENZIE SHAW AWARD – ~ Courage, Determination, Perseverance ~
Braving the cold and the remnants of the previous day's rain, it was a great turnout for the 6th annual HRHS Jingle Bull 5K Run yesterday, hosted by the HRHS Athletic Boosters, complete with Santa, the Hickory Ridge Raging Bull —and even a Christmas tree!

"It was such an honor to be a part of presenting the 1st Annual "Faith Mackenzie Shaw Award" in memory of Faith's unwavering and awe-inspiring Courage, Determination, and Perseverance! Congratulations to Bryce Anderson (HRHS 2021) for being the first recipient of this award. And thanks to Bryce's little bro for accepting the award on Bryce's behalf, who had a basketball game to get to.

"As I've said before, Faith's sisters and I continue to be deeply moved by the support and love from the school, community, church, friends, and family near and far. Please continue to keep our family in prayer, as the grief appears to intensify with each passing day and the approaching Christmas holiday seems so incomplete. As the reality of our loss settles in and looms large in our broken

hearts, please join us in praying that we're able to cling to what truly makes Christmas complete, as well as rejoice and find comfort in the knowledge that Faith is enjoying the ultimate Christmas celebration in His presence."

On that same day, as I waited for the 5K to begin, I was interviewed by reporter, Adam Thompson, with the Independent Tribune who had heard about Faith and wanted to share her story. The article was entitled "Having Faith: The inspiring story of Faith Shaw and the disease that could not define her."

HARRISBURG — Faith Shaw loved to dance. She loved art. She had a strong faith and was active and involved in the church.

She wanted to be an interior design[er] after she graduated from college.

Shaw had big dreams but had an even bigger fight in her. She was persistent, sassy, and hard-headed, according to her mother.

For 18 years, Shaw battled with cystic fibrosis, a chronic disease that causes persistent lung infections and limits the ability to breathe over time.

Statistics show that more than 30,000 people in the United States are diagnosed with cystic fibrosis.

Shaw was diagnosed when she was just 7 months old.

The teenager, who was born into a close-knit family and was a senior at Hickory Ridge High School, died due to complications from cystic fibrosis and a double-lung transplant Nov. 12 in Chapel Hill.

While Shaw's battle ended in that hospital bed, her inspiration, memory, and story continue to live on.

Faith's mother, Susan Shaw, said her daughter was sassy, stubborn, and "hard-headed," and they both knew she was going to battle cystic fibrosis until the very end.

That's what she did.

"That grew into that incredible strength that she had, and that fight that she

had," Susan Shaw said. "She fought for living a life she thought was worth-while."

Shaw kept fighting for her family, especially her niece and nephew. She wanted to dance freely, go to college, become an interior designer, and one day get married.

"She never gave up," Susan Shaw said. "She made sure to tell us, 'I'm not quitting. I'm not giving up. I just know my time to fight is done.' She fought the fight she was supposed to fight for as long as she was supposed to fight it."

In her final weeks, Shaw was voted Homecoming Queen at Hickory Ridge High School.

The community showed its unwavering support with candlelight vigils, painting the school's spirit rock, honoring her before the final football game, and honoring her at events.

The school also is using her name in an annual award given to a student who displays "courage, determination and perseverance."

"That was amazing," Susan Shaw said. "It just, again, was proof of how wonderful the student body here is and how supportive they were and how much they loved her and how many lives she touched."

'She would not let cystic fibrosis define who she was'
Faith Shaw was born in May 2001. She was the youngest of three children.

In that initial year, she had pneumonia a couple of times, to the point of doctors testing her for cystic fibrosis.

Shaw was in and out of the hospital, seeking treatment for her lungs.

"She would not let cystic fibrosis define who she was," Susan Shaw said. "It was something that she had. That little spitfire attitude that she had, that personality that she had, she wouldn't let it control her. She did everything she could to live life to the fullest in spite of it."

In December, five years ago, Shaw got a lung infection, one that was so bad that it caused permanent lung damage.

Still, she wouldn't let that prevent her from dance, even with 32 percent lung function at the time.

When Shaw left the hospital, she was on oxygen full time. Doctors told her she wouldn't be up to competitive level for dance.

She didn't accept that, so she worked hard with a physical therapist, with specific goals in mind, and she was cleared to dance one week before her first performance.

"She was still on oxygen full time, so she went backstage with her oxygen on, ready to go," Susan Shaw said. "As soon as she was ready to [go onstage], she took her oxygen off and she literally flew across that stage. You could just see the joy on her face. She danced competitively on 32 percent lung function for the next four . . . years."

Faith receives her first lung transplant
In December 2018, Faith Shaw was in urgent need of a lung transplant.

Her condition continued to worsen and she was going into respiratory failure, so she was placed very high on a transplant list.

On Jan. 14, Shaw received a lung transplant and was out of the hospital relatively quickly.

However, not long after, complications arose. She was dealing with massive migraine headaches.

Susan Shaw said reactions from one of the anti-rejection medicines she was taking caused her brain to swell.

She was back in the hospital. She lost her vision for a few days and suffered seizures.
Doctors had to stop that medication and try to find one Faith could tolerate.

It took a while, but during that time, they found the right medication.
In the meantime, her body had already recognized the new lungs as foreign and

had slowly begun attacking them, undetected by the medical team until it was too late.

But for a short time last spring and summer, the medication was working, and she was feeling better.

"She was dancing again," Susan Shaw said. "When she got out of the hospital, we found a local studio that allowed her to come in and do some dancing. She didn't need oxygen at all. She had some really great months."

In mid-July, Shaw was having trouble breathing.

That's when doctors discovered the rejection that had been taking place and had gone undetected.

"They tried several different procedures to stop the process," Susan Shaw said. "They basically killed off all her white blood cells and her immune system. That stopped them from attacking her lungs, but too much damage had been done by that time."

'She had so much peace those last few days'
Faith Shaw was sent back to Chapel Hill.

She was put back on a transplant list, and the day the family got insurance approval for the second transplant, the doctor said she was too sick to proceed.

Shaw was put on a trach tube for breathing and a feeding tube to eat. She used a board to communicate.

When Shaw knew it was her time, she let her family know.

She spent her final night watching the movie "Ratatouille" at the hospital with her mother, the breathing tube was removed and she died Nov. 12 with family, her mother and sisters Kelsey Biggers and Jennifer Wilson, by her side.

"There was such a neat moment when she made a decision that it's time to call in the family," Susan Shaw said. "The nurse she had that day came in to tell her how proud she was of her for making that decision and being so mature and asked if she could pray with her.

"After a really moving and beautiful prayer, there was this amazing look of awe on Faith's face. She grabbed her board and wrote, 'She must have been an angel. I felt God.' She had so much peace those last few days."

'Don't give up. Keep pushing through it'

Like any child being tested, Faith Shaw complained and asked why this was happening to her.

She felt like giving up. She was angry and felt betrayed by God, momentarily.

Susan Shaw said her daughter kept a positive outlook through pain and hopelessness.

"She also knew where she was going," Susan Shaw said. "Her faith was very real and very important in her life."

Susan Shaw said her daughter kept telling people, "Be happy for me. I'm excited."

"She went through more than any adult would ever go through in a lifetime," Susan Shaw said. "She always had so much maturity and grace going through it."

According to the Cystic Fibrosis Foundation, 1,000 new cases of cystic fibrosis are diagnosed each year, and more than 75 percent of people with cystic fibrosis are diagnosed by the time they are 2 years old.

Susan Shaw said the biggest message Faith Shaw would give to those dealing with the same issues is to keep fighting.

"Don't give up. Keep pushing through it," Susan Shaw said. "Some of it is the most painful, most difficult stuff you will go through, but you just have to keep pushing."

Faith Shaw said she wants her ashes spread in Hawaii, where the family went for her Make-A-Wish trip when she was 9 years old.

"She always wanted to go back because she didn't remember it very well," Susan Shaw said. "It was one of the celebratory trips we talked about doing once

she recovered from the transplant. But one of the things she did remember was how clear and beautiful the water was, so that's where she asked us to spread her ashes."

Not too long after Faith died, I went to the Department of Social Services (DSS) to have her child support discontinued. The lady I worked with that day at the DSS suddenly made the connection between my daughter and someone her son had talked about. Her son, who went to another high school in Cabarrus County, came home from school one day and said that Faith Shaw from Hickory Ridge High School had passed away. When his mom asked how he knew Faith since they went to different high schools, her son replied, "Oh, mom . . . *everybody* knows Faith."

On March 20th, 2020, I received what I called a "Message from Faith:"

"Sitting in the closing attorney's waiting room with my realtor, the sellers and the listing agent talking about the craziness of the times right now and all the things that have been canceled and postponed, and how thankful we all were feeling that we were still able to close today! I turned to my realtor and expressed my deep hope that Hickory Ridge's graduation wouldn't end up being canceled because of how special it was going to be with my accepting Faith's diploma on her behalf. One of the sellers then said, 'Do you know Faith??' I sat there and just stared at her for a few seconds in my mind asking, 'Is she really talking about MY Faith??' She then asked, 'Wait, are you Faith's mom?' To which I replied, 'Do YOU know Faith? Faith Shaw? How do YOU know Faith?' She said she didn't know Faith personally but that she followed her story on Lungs4faith!! How crazy is that?!! (I guess, given how many lives Faith touched, perhaps it's not really that crazy after all.) It made us all feel like it was confirmation that this house was meant to be and that Faith had been a part of the process all along! Even in the midst of how bittersweet this has been, I definitely know Faith is with me through it all!!"

On March 31st, 2020, my mom received a very sweet reply from for KING & COUNTRY to a message she had sent them –

"Shirley, Yes, we got your message, thank you so much! We were truly blessed to meet Faith! She impacted our lives in far more profound ways than we probably ever could have done for her! Her faith was inspiring and challenging to all of us! To see the grace she exhibited in the midst of her journey was truly

remarkable! We continue to pray God's blessings on you, Tim, Susan and your whole family! May God's love continue to strengthen you all and give you hope as you walk in Him! Bless you! – Joel, Luke and the for KING & COUNTRY team."

On June 9th, 2020, the HRHS Seniors account on Instagram posted,

"We have received a kind donation of purple ribbons to the Hickory Ridge class of 2020 in honor of Faith Shaw! As we all know Faith was such a big part of our school community and she made such a big impact in so many lives we want to make sure we celebrate her life. This Friday at our graduation fare-well, these ribbons will be available for us!!! We will wear these ribbons on our gowns during our ceremony and pictures! Thank you for the kind gesture."

It was such a sweet sight to see all the purple ribbons worn that day in her honor.

On November 9th, 2020, the Hickory Ridge High School Student Council and the Bulls family put together another purple-out scheduled for Thursday the 12th, to mark the one-year anniversary of Faith's passing. They told the student body, "to honor her, wear purple this Thursday, November 12th. Faith was a bright student who led with kindness and will always hold a special place in our hearts." There was a comment to this post on Instagram from a Northwest Cabarrus High School student, who replied that this purple-out didn't have to be just for HRHS students, and he also planned to wear purple in honor and memory of Faith.

On the first anniversary of Faith's death, a friend of her sisters', also named Faith, posted the following beautiful tribute:

"Words cannot even begin to describe the feelings I'm feeling. I can't believe it's been a whole freaking year. This beautiful young warrior soul took her final breath with failing lungs, surrounded by family, and at the same time her first breath with perfect ones in front of the Creator.

"I knew her through her sisters, and from the jump, she inspired me. Our conversations, though few and far between, will stay with me. Even when I myself was struggling with my own issues, she encouraged and inspired me both with words and the way she handled her own health. She didn't let it define her, and she didn't let it stop her. (She danced while she was on oxygen!)

"I will forever be grateful to Faith Shaw for her strength, tenacity, encouragement, steadfast faith, and her willingness to be open and honest about her position. I will forever be grateful to Mama Shaw and Jenni and Kelsey for sharing their loved one with us. For being open and honest themselves during the entire process of starting the transplant all the way through the grieving process. For keeping us informed every step of the way and allowing us to share in the highs and even in the lows; for allowing us to both rejoice and grieve with them. I know my sadness is only a fraction of what they experience, and my heart, love, thoughts, and prayers are with them always.

"Rest In Blissful Peace to Faith Shaw the young warrior who danced her way into our hearts."

Also, on the first anniversary of her death, a friend of Faith's from elementary school, Grace, wrote a poem in remembrance and honor of Faith:

Dancing With Jesus
I look into His eyes,
The eyes I have always seen,
The eyes that have always been the real prize
The eyes so calm and serene
I feel His hand on my shoulder
The hand that was nailed
The hand that was my molder
The hand that led me through my final exhale
He smiles down at me
And the angels start to sing
My heart fills with glee
As I dance with the King
We've done this again and again
He says the dance doesn't have to end
And if I want it to, to tell Him when
But how could I ever stop dancing with my friend?
We spin and twirl
He lifts me and catches me
We swing and whirl
He tells me there's no place He'd rather be
I dance above the world weightless
My lungs are open and filled with life

I have felt Love's unending caress
And I know no strife
My life was a short glance
But here, I am free to dance

That same day, I received a very touching letter from one of Faith's dear high school friends. It was just another testament to the impact Faith had on the lives of those around her. The letter read,

". . . It was such a pleasure to know and love Faith. She was such a bright spirit no matter her circumstance. I do wish that we all got to see her continue her journey, but I have so much comfort knowing that she is continuing her journey with Jesus. After saying 'see you later' to her I decided I wanted to truly follow Jesus. While that didn't fully happen till quarantine she is the reason I got baptized in September and the reason I opened up to God. . . ." She then shared the Bible verse Matthew 19:14 (ESV)—*"But Jesus said, 'Let the little children come to Me and do not hinder them, for to such belongs the kingdom of Heaven.'"*

Another message I received around that same time from an acquaintance of Faith's, read,

". . . I did not know Faith too personally, mostly just passing by in the hallways during high school. But my mother [was] the school nurse . . . at Rocky River Elementary, at the time we were in elementary school. Whenever she comes up in conversation (which she does on occasion) my mom just praises the person she was at such a young age! I wish I had known her more. I wish I would've gotten to witness her light on a more personal level, I just felt the need tonight to reach out because her story still affects me and my family, more than a year later . . . I just wanted you to know that Hickory Ridge [High School] will always support you, and have the deepest love for Faith, for whatever future there is to come. Whether we knew her well or not, she has our love."

In January of 2021, a little over a year after Faith died, I received an email from a teacher at Hickory Ridge High School. She told me her students had watched a movie based on a true story that had many cultural connections to their course content as well as several life lessons. At the end of the unit, she had her students respond to some reflection questions, one of which was, "If one day a movie is made about HRHS, what do you think the movie will be about? Think about a POSITIVE story that has happened in the past or is happening now. This could be academic, athletic, or something else." She went on to tell me, "I had several students write about your amazing daughter, Faith. She has touched the lives of so many at HRHS and in the community." She then attached some of the responses, which filled my heart in indescribable ways! Even in her passing, she had such a positive and inspirational impact on so many lives!

Student Responses:

1. "The first story that comes to mind of someone that positively impacted the lives at HRHS is about Faith Shaw. I knew her very briefly though I was close with her best friends. Not everyone knew her, but everyone was aware of the strength she exhibited throughout her life, especially in the last year of her life. Her life impacted so many people in the school and changed many of us for the better. I wish I would have gotten to truly know her as she seemed like one of the kindest and most genuine people there has ever been. Watching the school come together in the way they did around the time of her death was unlike anything I had ever witnessed before. Though the student body coming together was because of a very sad event, the fact that it came together the way it did is incredibly uplifting and positive. I would hope that if there were ever a movie about HRHS it would be centered around the life of Faith

2. "If a movie was made about HRHS, I think the movie would be about Faith Shaw, who passed away from Cystic Fibrosis last year. Even though it was a sad and terrible event, Faith was an extremely kindhearted person and was friendly to everyone she met. A movie about HRHS and Faith Shaw would highlight this aspect of her personality and how she carried positivity and kindness with her everywhere."

3. "At HRHS, many positive things have happened, but I think that one that I would make a movie about is the coming together of our community to pick Faith Shaw as our homecoming queen and our togetherness when she passed. A lot of schools hold homecoming as a competition; however, at our school we use it as a way to show our appreciation for all that someone has put into our school and community. To me that's something that is movie worthy."

4. "While I have been at Hickory Ridge a lot of eventful things have hap-

pened both good and bad. With that being said if a movie was made about our school it would be made about Faith Shaw's story and how our school and community supported her through it. While Faith's story did not end positively, her journey and the way our community supported her is an inspiring and uplifting story that could help many people."

On March 29th, 2021, having been postponed due to Covid, Hickory Ridge High School held its Homecoming for the 2020/2021 year. The HRHS Student Council/Leadership asked if I would stand in Faith's stead as the previous year's Homecoming Queen, and I was honored and privileged to crown the new Homecoming Queen. It was a beautiful gesture and touched my heart deeply. In remembrance of Faith, I carried with me her dress, sash, and crown from her Homecoming the previous year.

My brother, David, wrote a suspense novel titled "As Fate Would Have It" (by David M. Brooks). On May 7th, 2021, I received a signed copy from him with the following dedication in the front of the book –

"Dedicated to Faith Mackenzie Shaw (2001-2019) and all those who are born to a fate not of their choosing yet proudly create their own destiny."

Sitting in the Zaxby's drive-through in early October 2021, a young girl approached my car and motioned for me to roll down the window. She asked me if I was Faith Shaw's mom. She said her name was Khalia, and she had gone to elementary school with Faith. She went on to say that, when she moved to Concord in the 2nd grade, Faith had been the first one who spoke to her. She talked about having so many wonderful memories of Faith and with Faith. She also said that she visits Faith's grave site whenever she's in town.

On more than one occasion, when I have gone to visit Faith's grave site, someone has placed flowers on her grave marker, which always warms my heart to see.

On the second anniversary of Faith's death, her friend, Mia, posted a tribute in her honor on social media:

"As year two passes by since we said goodbye, not one day passes that you don't cross my mind. Faith Shaw, you were a light in my life and so many others. It is always my favorite when I get to tell new people about you and the legacy you left here on earth. I hope to never stop telling of who you were. You were so special and I remind myself daily of how lucky I was to get to experience

your love.

"I cannot wait for the day I get to hug you again. I cannot wait for you to show me around when I get there but for now I'll be waiting on this side of heaven. Miss you so much & love you so much more!"

And, of course, there are the many text messages and social media comments I have read over the past several years—before and after her death —including from people who never even met Faith. They, too, are a wonderful testament to the legacy she leaves behind.

Emma W. "I never knew Faith Shaw. I had never heard of her story until after she passed. I'm a freshman in high school and hearing about the light Faith was and continues to be in the lives of others inspires me to live like every day is my last. Mama Shaw, I'm so sorry for your loss. I can't wait to meet Faith in Heaven someday. I'm actually going to the [for KING & COUNTRY] concert this coming Sunday. RIP Faith Mackenzie Shaw. You touched the hearts of many, including mine."

Jen E. "I never knew it was possible to miss someone I've never even met. I wish I could've been friends with Faith or experienced her contagious smile just once in person. Her life and story still touch me so deeply, and I very much wish all of her friends, relatives, and team members an amazing day in honor of her. Happy Birthday, Faith! Enjoy your eternal celebration in Heaven."

Erin N. "I didn't know Faith and I don't know your family, but her story/your story has touched me so deeply. My son is a current senior at HRHS. You remain in my thoughts and prayers. What a remarkable young woman!"

Abby "Thank you so much for allowing us to come see her yesterday. She truly is a once in a lifetime soul that I'm so blessed to have known. You raised the most outstanding and God-loving young woman. Thank you for sharing her with us."

Mrs. Tucker (her NCVPS math teacher) " . . . She was one of my hardest working students despite all her medical complications. There were so many times that her strength and perseverance reminded me of the blessings I have. She was one amazing lady. I'm very sorry for your loss."

Rachel K. "thank you for sharing—her beautiful life. Faith and you touched

many lives and kept many of person's faith strong! Thank you"
Jodi M. "Oh sweet Faith. She was a light in this world."

Terry F. "She sure was a true inspiration to me. Her strength and courage was just amazing as she cherished everyday as we all should. My prayers are always with you."

Sheree B. "Will always be blessed to have known her sweet spirit and determination. She is dancing in heaven today."

Frances C. "I never had the pleasure of really knowing Faith. I only met her once a long time ago when she came to visit her grandmother . . . in Florida. But I followed her journey through your postings and cannot tell you how inspired I was by her strength! Hugs and prayers to you and your family."

Malinda V (after watching Faith's dance solo about her life with CF). "How could anybody watch this and NOT believe in God. Life is not fair but God knows the whole picture. We are each an individual tool that was only placed here for a temporary number of days. I see God in Faith. Thank you for sharing. I cried like a baby . . . "

Erin N. " . . . Thank you for sharing pieces of your daughter with us. I didn't know her and don't know you or your family, but I hold you all close to my heart in prayer."

Jodi A. "What passion & dedication. Every time you post about Faith, I know it will be inspiring."

Andrea H. "I just have to share this: I went to pick up masks from a friend this morning and based on her address I got chills. I thought it sounded familiar with me. As I was driving up the road to this house I prayed about old memories on this street (our first house, where our children grew up, and met this wonderful family) low and behold she lives in the house where Faith grew up and we first met her. Then as I went up to the porch my goodies were in a bag with a note. [Let your] FAITH [be] bigger than [your] fear. Faith Shaw you sent me a message this morning. My FAITH is bigger than fears. I will wear this mask today in honor of you today."

Sharon C. "Thank you Faith for touching so many lives in your 18 years. Your faith in the Lord has brought so many to prayers. Your sweet Spirit has been an amazing inspiration for people all over the Country. We will miss you so much. You will always remain in our hearts. We will join you in Heaven. Thank you for being part of all our lives."

Jodi A. "Faith – how beautiful. I wonder if you knew what a perfect name it would be for her when you named her? We don't know you, or ever met Faith, but became aware of your Faith b/c we are fans of For King & Country. I'm so sorry for the loss of your beautiful daughter & literally can't even imagine how much your heart aches. I keep your family in my prayers. Finally, & this may be a little weird—your hashtags are so descriptive. They really evoke emotions in me. #TheFightIsWon #JustAHeavenAway"

Jimmy G. "Absent from the body, present with Christ. Go fly high Faith, the Lord has much for you to do. And you have already done much for us down here on earth . . . "

Premier Festivals/Rock the Park. "We join the for KING & COUNTRY family in mourning the loss of a dear friend named Faith, who attended Rock the Park as a special guest. The band posted this on their Facebook page recently: 'The news of Faith's passing has deeply saddened our hearts . . . Faith's journey was quite the roller coaster, and we cannot help but be wildly inspired by her constant hope through it all. The few times we had the pleasure of meeting her, she radiated with a joy that could only come from trust in a greater purpose than her current pain. Our hearts are heavy, but we know she is inhaling the peace of Heaven that she left this earth a brighter place than when she entered it.'"

Susan S. "She and her mother are such an example of faith and courage."

Aaron T. "Faith, it's more than just her name—it's also what she clings to in her fight with cystic fibrosis. Watching her battle has been so humbling. But more than that, seeing her grow in her relationship with the Lord over the years has been awesome. She's wise beyond her years . . . "

Judy L. "Prayers and love coming to you from Washington State. May you feel the nearness of the Lord as you adjust to life without your beautiful daughter. We are so sorry. Faith has been such an inspiration to me. Her courage and hope was contagious, and this is a gift that will continue to bless many in the days ahead. Breathing in Heaven's air . . . just imagine! It has been an honor to pray for her (and for you) every day over the last months."

Bridgette. "What an amazing woman. I am honored that I was able to take care of her. Faith touched my life beyond words."

Snowbird Wilderness Outfitters. " . . . We are thankful for the life Faith lived and for her love of Christ!"

Cat. "She was the biggest inspiration to so many people. Miss her every day."

Janelle G. "There's not a day that goes by that I don't think about her and you. I am making a better version of myself in honor of her."

Tina. "Faith is a warrior in my heart."

Kate D. "Faith made a lasting impression and I will never forget her!"

Lexi. "even though I didn't know her seeing her walk through life with positivity filled my heart with joy . . . "

Cystic Fibrosis Daily. "Faith, your story will be remembered and your story will carry on with the CF community."

Hannah. "Heaven has gained an amazing, beautiful girl. Faith, you were such a happy and an amazing follower of Christ. Rest easy gorgeous."

Loren. ". . . I'm so blessed to have known such a beautiful soul and a huge inspiration to many!"

Mickey B. "Faith you were truly the most kind and positive person I've ever met. Every time I saw you there was always a smile on your face. You have taught me so much about life and I will cherish our little lunch group forever."

Snowbird Wilderness Outfitters. "We are so thankful for the legacy and the love of Jesus that Faith displayed throughout her battle. Praising the Lord for her healing and praying for those closest to her that are hurting!"

Danielle C. "The kindest person I have ever known. Faith, you are the biggest inspiration. I will cherish our friendship forever. You are so so so loved and admired. I know God is wrapping you in His arms."

Jordan C. "She was such a beautiful girl inside and out . . . Faith's strength and love for others was so inspiring . . ."

Cathy H. "She will be so missed but what an example of how we should all live our lives while we have them!!! She was such an inspiration and has left a beautiful legacy of faith in the One that created this beautiful soul!!! Susan, you knew what you were doing when you named her!!! Though my heart breaks for this loss and for her family, I will try to live by her example in Christ!!! . . . "

Melissa H. " . . . I only knew Faith through Instagram. I loved her positivity and optimism!!"

Emma B. " . . . Faith touched my life in a way I could have never touched hers she truly was an inspiration . . . "

Rachael. "Prayers for everyone. I didn't even know her personally but I followed her through her journey and I am so sad."

Alycea. " . . . I never talked to her personally but she inspired me and so many others!"

Kayla F. "I am blessed to have known such a strong and incredible young woman. Her fight inspires all of us . . . "

Anna C. "Faith you were the most inspiring girl I knew hands down. I love you, and am praying for peace and comfort."

Reagan G. " . . . She inspired so many and was so strong."

Karly. " . . . so blessed by her courage and faith and her story!"

Allie S. "I didn't know Faith personally but I know for a fact we've been in the same room quite a few times just by both of us being fans of for KING & COUNTRY, it's crazy to think how we are all connected in so many ways by God and by the music He brings into our lives, I didn't know her personally like I said, but from her Insta she seemed like such a bright and brave soul, I'm sending all my prayers to her family in this very hard time of loss. May she rest in peace with Jesus."

Lilikoi. "God works in so many ways. Faith showed us all how to worship and stay strong through hard times. She really was a gift and touched people that didn't even know her personally . . . "

Leah. "Sending prayers to your family. She had such a great impact on her school and community, her legacy will live on."

Anna Claire E. (before Faith passed away) "Faith's story is truly amazing I love how hard she works and it is a true honor to know and dance with her. She really is a great dancer and I know that she will do great things in her life. Anytime I see, think of, or hear about Faith it makes me realize how lucky I am that I actually have the ability to dance without limits. And I take it for granted. So I want you to do something anytime that you think or feel like you can't move on or can't do it or just plain don't wanna think about Faith and how she wants to be able to be pushed to those limits!"

Lauren E. (note to Faith Dec. 9, 2014) "Faith, You are such a beautiful example of strength & grace. Your determination is such an inspiration & your smile that lights up a room is such a witness of God's love. I am so blessed that God put you in my life! Stay strong & continue to fight hard. Remember what beautiful plans God has for you & through you! Love & prayers, Ms. Lauren"

Paloma "Here in Brazil you have a fan and someone that prays for you. I was very happy and inspired by your story. I have a family member that needs a double lung transplant and your story filled my heart with hope and faith. You are a beautiful young lady. God has amazing plans for your life."

Cara S (upon my sharing Faith's Valentine's Day Vlog entry) "Oh sweet Faith —you were sent here to save *US*. What a powerful testimony shared. Susan, thank you for sharing that with us—you have allowed Faith's story to bring an awakening in many lost souls searching for that hope that only can be found in Jesus and this life is just a small spot compared to the eternity He has planned for us!"

Eve P (12/8/19 post) "It still doesn't even feel real—yesterday we laid to rest such a beautiful soul and celebrated the life of the most precious angel to walk this earth. Our hearts are going to hurt and that's ok, but my heart is at peace knowing you're holding the hands of the Lord himself. You dance those streets of gold and sing with the angels. We promise to continue your legacy and keep your story going forever my sweet angel . . . I miss you more and more every day and love you with every ounce of my heart. Thank you for allowing everyone to view life as something so beautiful and something to not take for granted. God please (hold her) today, tonight and forever—This is for sure not goodbye, it's until we meet again one day."

Litta F "Oh what fun we've had through the years . . . beach, Hawaii, Awana, birthdays, Halloween, church events, and the list goes on. Faith was one of a kind and I'm better because I knew and loved her. She's one of the reasons I decided to become a nurse. Enjoy heaven sweet girl!! I bet you danced right through those pearly gates!!"

Madell P (regarding the candlelight vigil) "What a precious tribute to a young life who lived for God to the fullest!!!"

Kathleen H. "My heart is so heavy. It's been so many years since I have seen Faith and her family, but they were all such an important part of my life during middle school to early high school. So many movie nights and church trips with Jenni, Kelsey, Faith, and of course Mama Shaw. It's so strange to lose someone you haven't seen in so long and lost some of that connection with. But that time apart, and those threads of connection that faded away don't change the impact they had on your life nor the memories you have with that person. She fought longer than most would have. Certainly more than I would have been able to. I'll always be inspired by her strength, as will so many others."

Mia B. "my sweet Faith, I'm not sure what to say as I didn't yesterday so I'm not gonna say much but . . . thank you. Thank you for teaching me how to love and live like you. Thank you for teaching me how to be so selfless, as you always were. Thank you for teaching me how to face fear head on, as you always did. Thank you for teaching me how to always stay positive, as you did so well. Most importantly thank you for teaching me how to always believe in Jesus and have faith, you were the true representation of your name. I am truly a better person for knowing you. I refuse to say goodbye so see you soon my sweet Faith, see you soon."

Jenna T. "Some people have influential lives, and Faith certainly did. But what impacted me most is the way she died. Hearing her comfort *us* the day she went home to Glory, because she knew that God would keep His promise of a new body on a new earth . . . *that* was the most beautiful and powerful death I've ever witnessed."

Elisabeth D. "I have such fond memories of conversations with Faith in the clinic and at the bedside when she was hospitalized. There was a predictable progression from lighthearted chit chat and catching up on life events to a deep dive into her concerns about health to a process of negotiating a plan that addressed challenges in ways that she found acceptable and meaningful. And we would end with talks of hopes and dreams and future plans. Beneath Faith's delicate, fragile appearance was a fierce, loving, goal-driven, gregarious young woman. She lived with grace and intention and died this way as well. She taught me so much, and I will never forget her."

David B. "Faith Mackenzie Shaw was a rare individual that touched and positively influenced more lives in her short time on earth than most of us could in 100 years. She was a warrior, a role model, and an inspiration. She lived her life fearlessly the way she wanted to live. No matter how hard her disease pushed her, she pushed back even harder, and she did it with the passion and grace of a star – a Superstar. She was my beautiful, sweet niece. But even more than that, for me, she will always be my Hero."

Cherish each and every moment with those you love! Love deeply, laugh often, and live life to the fullest and best that you can—just some of the many things I loved and admired about Faith Mackenzie Shaw!

Faith Mackenzie Shaw

05/15/2001 – 11/12/2019

The Fight Is Won!

Appendix: YouTube Video Links

Faith rolling the first pitch at the "Fight CF with Jordan Gross" Kick-Ball Tournament https://youtu.be/mb-OnYhnjeQ

Piano Tiles Fundraiser information video with Faith and her Uncle David https://youtu.be/6cRV91xv_P8

My interview with HisRadio December 21, 2018
https://youtu.be/UDA5Kdk4t60

"Rescue," by Lauren Daigle
https://youtu.be/3U4Q2R7ZZAE

Surprise video for Faith arranged by the Leadership class at her high school
https://youtu.be/ZeOiSmW1IOQ

"Faith," by Faith's friend, Sara
https://youtu.be/PvB-N2npZ3k

Spectrum News interview following the candlelight vigil, 11/15/19 https://youtu.be/hMLYpmCByLI

Faith's Celebration of Life service, 12/7/19
https://youtu.be/6tC8YCzL2ww

for KING & COUNTRY message of condolence and slide show played at the Celebration of Life https://youtu.be/TDW5xqu2Blc

Faith dance, "Through the Glass"
https://youtu.be/TKehstWWYHM

Collection of small videos showing Faith's pure joy for simply living https://youtu.be/DNBmLedjQSQ

Faith continuing to dance while tethered to her oxygen tank https://www.youtube.com/shorts/b1rSoF9arL0

Faith dance, "The Cure"
https://youtu.be/NLAyMk-iVtw

Faith dance with her oxygen tank, "Breathe"
https://youtu.be/JX5SSH13gyg

ShawManor YouTube channel, https://www.youtube.com/channel/UCBobK-tELsN4Dqb5r0Crrx6w

Faith dance, "Wade in the Water"
https://youtu.be/fnnrn449AVk

Faith dance, "Between the Lines"
https://youtu.be/lyVt0-2YTgI

Slide show of past Christmases set to "A Different Kind of Christmas"
https://youtu.be/UDWk691oiEI

Video footage of Faith meeting with for KING & COUNTRY at Carowinds, 06/01/19 https://youtu.be/Aq8XMMlUgP4

Faith 20th birthday slide show
https://youtu.be/I-8aB0q0ynM

"Good One" by Faith's friend, Lance
https://youtu.be/7k88yLm3k9Q

Notes

1. Cystic Fibrosis Foundation. "65 Roses Story."
https://www.cff.org/about-us/65-roses-story

2. Cystic Fibrosis Foundation. "About Cystic Fibrosis: What is Cystic Fibrosis?"
https://www.cff.org/intro-cf/about-cystic-fibrosis

3. Elliot, Elisabeth. *A Path Through Suffering: Discovering the Relationship Between God's Mercy and Our Pain.* Ventura: Regal Books. 2003.

4. Jenkins, Amanda. Hendricks, Kristen. Jenkins, Jerry. *The Chosen: 40 Days With Jesus.* Savage: Broadstreet Publishing Group, LLC. 2019.

5. Mayo Clinic Staff. Mayo Clinic. "Extracorporeal Membrane Oxygenation (ECMO): Overview."
https://www.mayoclinic.org/tests-procedures/ecmo/about/pac-20484615

6. National Cancer Institute. "aspirate"
https://www.cancer.gov/publications/dictionaries/cancer-terms/def/aspirate

7. National Cancer Institute. "port-a-cath."
http://www.cancer.gov/publications/dictionaries/cancer-terms/def/port-a-cath

8. Thompson, Adam. "Having Faith: The inspiring story of Faith Shaw and the disease that could not define her." Independent Tribune. December 18, 2019.

Acknowledgments

First and foremost, I would like to extend a very special thank you to my daughters, Kelsey Biggers and Jenni Wilson. Not only did they *live* this journey with me and Faith, but I also never could have made it through the book-writing process without their emotional support and their being my constant cheerleading section—especially when I was, at times, feeling very discouraged. I also thank Kelsey for her many words of wisdom after reviewing some early drafts, as well as Jenni for lending words to my emotions on a few of the Lungs4Faith social media posts when I was mentally too exhausted to do so myself.

Another group I wholeheartedly would like to thank is my amazing family for their phenomenal support through this whole process (and, frankly, throughout Faith's entire journey!). Thank you to my mom, Shirley Tobin, stepdad, Donald (Toby) Tobin, and my brother, David Brooks, for offering great feedback and recommendations after reviewing early drafts. To David, who sat with my mom, reading the draft copy to her once she reached the point she could no longer read it on her own. To my dad, Michael Brooks, who provided me with an extremely helpful, full-blown, personal "book review," and agreed to write the *Foreword* when I asked. I also thank my brother, Tim Brooks, for his assistance with building my website, journeyoffaithbook.com, for being physically present so many times throughout Faith's final journey, and for offering such amazing support to me, Faith, Kelsey, and Jenni (and for treating me to a UNC Tar Heels basketball game one evening while visiting us in Chapel Hill).

Many, many thanks also go out to my dear friend, Janet Rackley, who gave me great feedback after reviewing one of the earliest drafts, and who let me talk her ear off about the book, the book, and the book—especially when I was bemoaning the editing process—during our many walks in the park.

To my author coach, Keagan Hayden, from United House Publishing (UHP), sincere thanks for allowing me the space to be vulnerable and transparent as I traversed through the process, as well as offering great encouragement, support, and prayers. And many thanks to Caitlyn Spencer and the entire Editing and Revision Team with UHP, for taking my heart and helping turn its words into something so much better by pulling out of me the very best of Faith's story—and for being compassionate and patient with me as I sometimes questioned the editing and revision recommendations. Through it all, they allowed me to still be me, the narration to still be my voice, and Faith's story to still be told in a way that truly honors her and her journey.

I would be remiss if I didn't also give a shout-out of thanks to Joel & Luke Smallbone with *for KING & COUNTRY*, along with the entire fK&C team, for the way they rallied around Faith and our whole family throughout Faith's final year and following her death. They were an incredible source of encouragement and inspiration for us all, and they will forever have my heartfelt gratitude.

Many special thanks to the thousands of people the world over who followed Faith's remarkable journey. Our hearts were—and continue to be—truly blessed by your love, support, encouragement, and prayers.

Above all, I thank my Lord and Savior, Jesus Christ, for never ever leaving my side—even when I sometimes left His—throughout Faith's entire journey, the grief journey, and the book-writing process. I thank Him for helping me realize I needed to loosen my grip on the book a little during the editing stage and not cling so tightly to what I thought was "the way it had to be"—for helping me trust Him and trust the process. And my undying gratitude for His never giving up on me, never being finished with me, and for loving me unconditionally no matter what!

About the Author

Susan Shaw was born in Durham, North Carolina, in 1965. As she grew up, she spent many years in the Midwest followed by Arizona before returning in 1999 to the Carolinas, where her heart had always remained. She now lives in Concord, North Carolina, with her sweet dog, Scarlett, whom she thoroughly loves to spoil. The youngest of three children, Susan grew up in a close-knit family and considers her family and her faith to be the most important priorities in her life. She enjoys spending quality time with her daughters, their husbands, and her precious grandchildren, who also all live in North Carolina. She sings in the worship band with her church of more than fifteen years and works for an environmental company that she has been with for nearly twenty-four years. In her spare time, she enjoys playing guitar, playing competitive pool, and 'power walking' in the park with her best friend. She is an avid reader, however *Journey of Faith* is her first venture into writing a book of her own.

Printed in the USA
CPSIA information can be obtained
at www.ICGtesting.com
JSHW010753110524
62945JS00009B/72